Tales from the Steep

John Long's Favorite
Climbing Literature

To Mariana, mi todera e mi amor.

Tales From the Steep: John Long's favorite climbing Literature
Copyright © 1993 by John Long
10 9 8 7 6 5 4 3 2 1

Printed in U.S.A.
1st printing 9 / 93, 2nd printing 3 / 95

Published by:
ICS Books, Inc.
1370 E. 86th Place
Merrillville, IN 46410
800-541-7323

Library of Congress Cataloging-in-Publication Data
Long, John, 1954–
    Tales from the steep : John Long's favorite climbing literature / by John Long.
        p.   cm.
    Includes index.
    ISBN 0-934802-92-0 : $9.99
    1. Mountaineering—Literary collections.   I. Title.
PN6071.M738L66 1993   92-45869
808.3'9355—dc20   CIP

Acknowledgements

Thanks to the many writers who contributed to this anthology; to the various publishers who were kind enough to grant us re-print rights; to Michael Kennedy of *Climbing Magazine*, John Harlin of *Summit*, Steve Roper, Esq., Steve Goldfarb of *Tri-Quarterly*, George Meyers of Chockstone Press, Michael Chessler of Chessler Books, Nancy Prichard of *Rock & Ice*, Sylvia Horn of *The Paris Review*, Richard Ballantine, Brendan Healey, Paul Edwards and all the others whose opinions helped me determine the stories in *Tales*; to fellow editor Tracy Salcedo whose assistance was, as usual, invaluable; and to Tom Todd and all those at ICS Books, Inc. who handled much of the actual work.

Table of Contents

Fiction

Introduction

Not so long ago I'd do about anything to go climbing. "Just a phase," Dad promised, and he was right. It only lasted about twenty years. I rarely questioned myself about any of it. Lashed 2,500 feet up El Capitan, peering over the edge of my hammock and wondering how I was ever made to be alive—who could ever sort out the *why* of it all? Of course, the whole business was never just about climbing at all. It was about freedom and pure experience. So, I'd return time and again to grapple and curse and encounter myself in a way impossible anywhere else. On the high crag, I was truly alive.

Trying to capture the flavor of this on paper is like trying to describe aquamarine or God or fear. Yet occasionally, and in various fashions, a story can hurl a reader straight onto the high crag or the mountain of ice, where they can taste something of the sweat and exhilaration and naked vulnerability that lured climbers there in the first place—and made them return over and over. When a story can accomplish this, it's a classic. A classic endures because it continues speaking to us no matter the time or the era. A story can achieve this only when it is undeniably true and guileless, and you know it the second you read it. Most of all, the classic always has the feel that it *had* to be written—not for an exacting editor, or a cast of wannabe outdoorsmen, or even for aficionados, but as a sort of catharsis for the writer himself. *Tales from the Steep* is a collection of such stories.

Because this collection is geared for the non-climber as well as the expert, I'd originally planned to footnote the more technical terminology. However, since the same twenty or so terms kept popping up in many of the stories, I've tucked in a little glossary of key terms at the end of the text.

John Long
Valencia, Venezuela

Touching the Void

Joe Simpson

When Joe Simpson and Simon Yates set out in 1985 to climb a new route on the west face of Siula Grande—at 20,866 feet the second-highest point of Peru's Cordillera Huayhuash—they were happy-go-lucky British lads out for high adventure. But the adventure turned into something much bigger, as an accident near the summit led to a series of fateful decisions.

Their story, while it took place in recent history, can be called an "instant classic" without fear of contradiction. It is a simple story, a tale of one man's fight to survive. It is the stuff normally found in fiction, yet it really happened.

Although Simpson wrote a best-selling book about his adventure— Touching the Void—we take our story from an edited version of the diary he wrote while recuperating in a Lima hospital. Our narrative begins as Simpson and Yates, tired but thrilled by their successful new route completed the previous day, awake on June 8 at their bivouac at twenty-thousand feet.

Saturday   Just as we finished the last handful of fruit our stove ran out of gas. That was it, then, for the food and hot drinks. Since we expected to be back at base camp by nightfall, we seemed to have judged our rations perfectly. It had been our fourth bivy since leaving base, and we were right on schedule. We had moved faster on the west face than expected but slower on the descent ridge. It had balanced out well.

I moved up to the ridge line just above the bivy and was disappointed to find that the hardest section was still to come. We had expected a relatively straightforward crest all the way, but this one had the kind of tortured beauty I prefer to admire from a safe distance. The snow conditions forced us too close to the crest, and following some of the cornices seemed very much a matter of hope. We cautiously moved along together, making good if somewhat nervous progress.

By midmorning the worst seemed behind us; large, stable-looking cornices undulated away from us. A thought that it would now be easy evaporated as I fell into five consecutive crevasses cutting through the first huge cornice. Filled with powder, they were exhausting to get out of, even though I never went in more than shoulder deep.

As I contoured around the last significant cornice, I was startled to find an ice cliff on its northern side. This descent was becoming a little exasperating! The cliff, forty feet high where I was, thinned out to about fifteen feet near the crest of the ridge. It looked hard to descend there, and abseiling off this snow was out of the question. So I began to contour along the edge of the cliff, looking for a possible weakness, a crevasse or a ramp-line perhaps, which would allow an easy descent.

Suddenly the edge broke away beneath me and I was falling. I dropped twenty feet, slamming onto the only hard ice for miles. My right leg took the brunt of the fall; I felt an instant flame of excruciating pain as I flipped forward and slid on my back, head down, another thirty feet. I stopped with a painful jerk, hanging upside down with my good leg tangled in the rope.

It took an awful struggle to release it and right myself, and then I knew with a shock of fear that my right leg was broken. My first thought was how unlikely it would be for me to get down. I dug a hole and made a powerful effort to control the panic and despair and think things through. We would have to take everything in stages, never looking beyond the stage just ahead.

Simon joined me, sized up the situation, and set off for the ridge. I decided that I had to try to help myself, so I started to traverse slowly right along Simon's tracks. I was unroped but didn't think much of my chances anyway, so it didn't seem to matter. There would have been no good belay for Simon in any case.

Despite the tracks, the slope proved difficult to cross with my super-sensitive leg. If I had fainted or lost my balance, I could not have prevented myself from falling down the entire east face, which plunged steeply below me in a chaos of powder flutings and twisting snow gullies.

I began to chop a narrow trench in front of me. Simon soon joined me and went ahead, cutting a good trench for me to follow. When we got back to the ridge, we set about digging a huge bucket seat for Simon to sit in. The plan was for Simon to lower me in stages down the entire west face. In fact, we had no other choice. But since the snow was deep and unconsolidated, sound belays were impossible. We had no snow stakes left, but even they would have been useless.

I was resigned to a bad end by then, but Simon was quite capable of descending alone. He could have left me at this point—and would have been justified in doing so. I half expected matters to come to that, but I was too scared to voice my thoughts. Simon acted as if the idea had never crossed his mind as he mounted a phenomenal one-man rescue effort. No doubt, he was risking his life to save mine.

He chose to sit in a loose snow hole and lower me three hundred feet at a time on the two tied-together ropes. When one hundred fifty feet of rope was out, I would struggle upright and take my weight off the rope so that he could change the knot over to the other side of his Sticht plate.

Down we went. Simon lowered me straight down to a point roughly level with where we had intended to descend the west side of the ridge that led down to the glacier. I had to make another painful traverse leftward about one hundred feet until at last I could look down the face to the glacier, two thousand feet below.

My mind had by now entered into a survival mode. It was only mid-afternoon, so perhaps with luck we could get down to the glacier this night and dig ourselves a snow hole. Spindrift continuously swept our descent line. This complicated things, especially communication, but again there were no other choices. Down I went, sliding on my good side, vainly attempting to make a slightly rightward descent. Gravity said otherwise and I dropped like a plumb line. This would cause disaster later, but there was nothing we could do about it. Three tugs on the rope and I would dig a hole, hop into it, and wait as Simon changed the knot over the Sticht. Then, off again, until further tugs meant the end of the rope, and I would set about digging Simon a vast bucket seat for his next lower as he downclimbed steadily toward me.

After about thirteen hundred feet, we came to some steep ice-covered rock bands. Placing an ice screw, Simon abseiled first and I followed, bumping painfully over the cliffs. This one-hundred-fifty-foot abseil took us back onto the unconsolidated, belayless snow slope. Conditions worsened. Either the spindrift was especially bad, or it had started to snow. In addition, the temperature had dropped. It was nearly dark.

We started the penultimate lower, fully expecting to be down on the glacier in a few hours. But after descending only one hundred feet I felt myself drop suddenly. I had plunged over the edge of a large, overhanging serac. We had no idea it was there, since our intended descent would have taken us diago-nally down the face. I swung in space about fifteen feet under the lip. Simon knew from the dead weight that I had dropped over something—what it was and how big he had no idea. He couldn't haul me up, obviously, so I managed to fix one prusik knot onto the rope; frozen-fingered and fumbling, I dropped the second one. My hands were nearly useless. I clipped into the prusik to hold me upright, then swung back and forth on the rope, spinning gently.

Simon, hoping I would reach level ground, soon continued to lower me. I looked down to see a large crevasse directly beneath, roofed over where I was, but yawning open at its southern end, fifteen or one hundred feet below me, I couldn't really tell. A jerk, and the lowering stopped abruptly.

The knot had reached the Sticht and had jammed fast.

I vainly tried to swing toward the ice wall, hoping to get some purchase, enough to take my weight off the rope: I got nowhere near it. I was hanging about fifty feet above the roof of the crevasse, maybe fifteen feet out from the cliff wall, spinning helplessly, and freezing slowly. Simon was no better off, struggling with two frostbitten hands, taking the full force of the spindrift, and incapable of doing anything but hanging on.

After an hour I was in a bad way. I wouldn't have lasted the night. Suddenly the rope slipped a few inches, then a bit more. I briefly thought Simon had managed to change the knot over, but guessed the truth: my weight was dragging him off. If he came off he would have no chance.

Simon didn't think of the knife in his pack until it was almost too late. The rope parted like cotton as soon as the blade touched it. Simon, shocked and numb, hoped I might be lucky and hit a slope and slide down onto the glacier. It would have been my only chance.

I fell free for fifty feet, smashed through the soft crevasse roof and fell another fifty feet into the crevasse, landing upon a snow bridge. It cushioned much of the force of my fall, but I was winded and had landed awkwardly on my bad leg. Ten feet to my left, an awful slot dropped away forever. To my right, a steep slope swept down some eighty feet to a black hole, presumably another bottomless pit. I had our last remaining ice screw on my harness, and after I recovered, I thumped it into the icy wall and tied myself off. I'd had enough falling for one day.

I doubted I could get out alone and felt sure Simon would think me dead. He would be able to see only the bottomless end of the crevasse. In the eerie silence, I felt overwhelmingly lonely and forgotten. But at least I was out of the cold and the continual snowfall. I wondered whether Simon was all right. After about an hour of scrambled thoughts, I secured the cut end of the rope to my one and only ice screw, slipped a prusik onto the line as a self-belay, and tried to climb out. A mass of jumbled snow blocks rose above me. I fell off four times, never getting higher than ten feet. I gave up.

It was close to midnight. I was cold, exhausted, in pain and frightened. Mentally, I was ebbing away. All my fight had gone. I quit shouting Simon's name, couldn't be bothered with it any more. I felt extremely bitter after the long struggle with the ridge and the long way down the face, and now this, only one more lower from the glacier. It seemed easier to die now. I could have slipped into my sleeping bag and bivy bag but didn't. Why prolong the agony? But by two in the morning, I was no nearer to death than before. My gear was too bloody good! I felt angry, cheated. What was I playing at? Fight it, take it in stages, see what the morning brings.

Sunday   Light filtered through my entry hole in the roof. I looked up at the jumbled snow blocks I had tried to climb earlier and almost laughed. Preposterous! I could never have climbed it with both legs, let alone with a smashed knee. I shouted at regular intervals. It was still early, and I hoped I might attract Simon as he came down to check on me.

Simon, meanwhile, had traversed horizontally above the cliff on steep and treacherous ground and eventually arranged an abseil. As he came down he had a clear view into the slot but could see nothing except the vast drop. He got as close to the edge as the lip would allow but heard no response to his calls. Anyone seeing the crevasse and the distance I had fallen could never have believed I had a chance. He started toward base camp, arriving at midday.

Now certain this was the case, and not believing I would ever get any help, I was forced to help myself. My only option was to drop further into the crevasse and hope for a passage out to the north, out of my view. I cringed at the thought of going deeper. What if there was no exit? What if the floor was just unstable powder? I pulled in the rope and ruefully examined the frayed end. That in a way decided it, confirming that I really was alone. No one had ever been here or would ever come again.

With the other end of the rope still tied off to the ice screw, I weighted the frayed end with some carabiners and flung it out and into the void. I couldn't see or hear if it touched bottom, but I really hoped it did. Yet what difference would it make if I died where I stood or one hundred fifty feet lower?

I slid sideways off the snow bridge and gingerly lowered onto the floor. It was solid. Above me, a fifty-degree slope swept up to the roof. At the roof was an exit passage, only a couple of feet wide, but through it a column of golden sun angled in, making the ice walls gleam blue-green. That sun was like gold. It was only about one hundred fifty feet to the surface of the glacier. Five and a half hours later I crawled into the sunlight and saw before me all the world.

Below, a two-hundred-fifty-foot snowfield fell steeply to the glacier. Directly below me I could see the top of a rock band. I would have to traverse about seventy feet to get to a point where the slope ran uninterrupted down to the glacier.

I hauled out the remaining rope that I had kept tied to my waist. With it stretched diagonally up toward me from the snow bridge below, I had just about seventy spare feet. I clipped into my Sticht plate and leaned onto the rope, starting a slow and difficult sideways-crawling pendulum. My main worry was that I might lose my grip and swing all the way back; but all went well and by the end of the rope I had skirted the steep rock band and was able to stand on one foot above the snow slope that ran out uninterrupted to the glacier below.

Above and off to the side, I saw a rope hanging down a sheer section of rock and ice. So Simon was gone. He wouldn't be coming back. I began to make a series of controlled hops and slides down the slope, always with my axes well planted. I managed about one hundred feet before coming to hard ice, where I took the inevitable fall. I plunged sideways at first, then head down, reaching incredible speed. My bad leg took a pounding, and when I finally slid to a halt I was again in great agony. I lay still and absorbed the pain, waiting for it to pass.

Looking up, I was happy to see Simon's tracks close by. Now it was early afternoon; I had a good six hours of light left for crawling. Ahead, a long way off, I could just make out tracks climbing a slope between two prominent circular crevasses. To get past these was my next stage. I would try not to stop until I was above them, and then see how things looked from there. Crawling on my side, dragging my leg, or shuffling backward on my bum, was slow, exhausting, and tortuous duty. I felt dangerously dehydrated, having had no fluid or food in the last thirty hours. My hands quickly froze; I had to stop frequently to warm them.

I made much slower progress than I thought I would, which depressed me. At five o'clock a strong wind blew in, with snowfall and quite a drop in temperature. Spindrift swirled across the glacier and Simon's tracks began to disappear. I kept going as long as possible, fearful that the tracks would be gone in the morning, when I would most need them on the intricate crevassed section near the moraines.

Darkness and the increasingly severe weather eventually stopped me. I was exhausted. At a point where the tracks dropped steeply down a short slope, I managed to dig a snow hole. This took several hours of awkward and tiring work; my leg always seemed to get in the way. I struggled into my hole sopping wet. My feet stuck out the entrance but drifting snow soon covered them and sealed the exit. I wasn't warm, but not extremely cold either. Pain woke me frequently and my nagging fears didn't help, but it was better than the crevasse. I got a few hours of sleep.

Monday   I awoke totally snowed into the cave and had some difficulty extracting myself. Outside, only a few of Simon's tracks were visible—sometimes I found nothing for hundreds of feet—but I remembered enough of the route to follow the correct line through the crevassed glacier. My first stage was to reach the cairn I had built at the start of the moraine—a hard task, and risky toward the end, with narrow and steep passages leading through a maze of slots. I reached my pile of rocks by noon. Glad to have gotten off the snow, I decided to rest for a whole hour. I tried to melt snow in our shallow brew pan but the sunlight produced only a dribble. I made a crude splint, cutting up my sleeping pad and binding it on with tape and straps from my crampons.

I felt better for the long rest. Knowing I couldn't get to the camp that night, I still hoped to get within striking distance. But I wasn't too optimistic about my chances. I started the painful process of perfecting a hobble. Axe in my right hand, leaning on it heavily, I would lift my bad leg forward with my left hand, then execute a fast hop with my good leg. The axe was short, and I was doubled over like a geriatric.

I fell many times, and the pain was really awful. The flares of agony rarely diminished, but I stopped screaming when I found it made no difference. I was moving ever so slowly, half the speed of crawling. Sometimes I belly-crawled over the larger boulders. I was losing height gradually. I hoped to reach an area we had named "Bomb Alley" on the way up. There, granite slabs with copious streams offered a good resting place. But, confused by fatigue, I had miscalculated how far away these were, and by nightfall I was disappointed still to be a long way from this place. Thinking I would reach them made me push on much further, staggering and falling over in the dark until forced by exhaustion to stop at ten o'clock.

I was still chronically short of water, having found only trickles from which I could spoon mouthfuls. I needed quarts, not mouthfuls, and I felt the thirst more than the lack of food. Three days and nights had passed without food and water. I would definitely find plenty of water the following day and hoped

I could do without food for another day. I *had* to reach camp tomorrow. At least I had passed the most difficult section of the descent that day, steep, overhung seracs where the glacier pinched off against the moraine and the granite side walls.

I fervently hoped that Simon hadn't struck base camp, but knew that Spinosa, the mule man, would be around with supplies we had ordered. He might stay on tomorrow but would definitely be gone the next day. After all, there was nothing but bad memories to keep him there. I doubted I would have the strength for two more days, so tomorrow would be crunch-time. I felt I could do it with luck, but didn't think about it, choosing instead to stick to my stages. First, get to "Bomb Alley" in the morning; then reach the top lake; then cross the moraines; then traverse the bottom lake and the final moraine, then drop down to the riverbed and campsite. Six stages. It would be my hardest day.

That night was warm and dry, though my niche was wet. Exhausted, I managed to get some disjointed sleep. My leg ached abominably all night.

Tuesday   Despite my sleep I awoke in very poor shape. The previous numbing of the pain was gone, and my leg felt hypersensitive to any movement. I was quite scared by how weak I felt and my sense of lethargy. The lack of food was having its effect. I dreaded not getting to camp that night. My first few attempts at hobbling confirmed how I felt. I thought I couldn't do it; it was even slower than last night in the dark—and despairingly painful. I reached "Bomb Alley" at 11:00, having set out at 6:30.

By then I had recovered or gotten through whatever wall had been in my way. I was back to plodding on with a fixed mind, gradually getting there, but I was going so slowly now. By early afternoon I reached the small lake and here again, I began to feel I had a chance. I crossed the big moraine dividing the two lakes and took a half-hour rest on the shore of the large lower lake. I had gorged on water at "Bomb Alley" and at every opportunity since. Perhaps this was why I felt better. I now hoped to be atop the moraine at the end of the lake by 6:30. From there, base camp would be in sight, a mere fifteen-minute walk away. I was nervous at the prospect, wondering what I would do if I saw it had been abandoned. I traversed the lakeside and struggled up the steep, hard mud slopes on the moraine.

Sadly, it was darkening when I got there, and the weather had closed in again. I couldn't see the campsite in the gloom and cloud. It began to snow wetly. It was all downhill now, a steady descent down cactus-covered slopes to the campsite. Normally this would have taken fifteen minutes; it took me more than six hours. I was moving slowly, headtorch dead, bum-sliding down the dark outline of the mud path, muttering, singing, gibbering to myself like a Bedlam lunatic. Occasionally I shouted Simon's name, but it was lost in the storm. Simon later said he heard an indistinct cry at about 7:30 but thought nothing of it.

Shortly after midnight I sat swaying on a boulder in the riverbed, moaning and desperately trying to make out shapes. Camp must be there. *Must* be. I knew I was close, but I felt almost too weak to call out. I wouldn't last the night like this. I shouted Simon's name and stared intently into the darkness. Suddenly, a light flashed and there was the dome tent glowing like a spaceship, one hundred feet away, floating in the darkness, with shadows moving inside it, and muffled voices.

The feeling of relief was indescribable. I saw headtorches bobbing toward me and kept repeating, "Help me, help me."

They dragged me to the tent and filled me with tea, painkillers, antibiotics, chocolate, tea porridge, cheese, more tea, sleeping pills. I was home. It felt good to talk with Simon and confirm that nothing more could have been done, and that I completely agreed with his actions. With every gesture, every look, Simon and I shared an intimacy we would never have shared earlier.

When Simon took the splint off my leg, we saw that it was clearly broken, displaced, enormously swollen and bruised. Stern orders were issued about me going down on the mule the next morning despite my protests; all I wanted was rest, sleep, and food. But infection was a serious worry.

Wednesday and Thursday   I awoke totally shattered and terribly weak, unable to eat more than a bit of porridge. I dreaded the days to come, but I knew Simon was right to hurry, and anyway I wasn't strong enough to argue. Passing out at regular intervals was my forte now.

Two days aboard a mule gave me an almost pathological hatred of the beast. It always walked to the right, repeatedly crushing my leg against walls and boulders, totally ignoring Simon's efforts at dissuasion. Things improved at Cajatambo with a good supply of cigarettes and beer. The next evening, following a wild ride in the back of a pickup, I was in a Lima hospital. I would lay there for two indescribable days without food, painkillers or antibiotics until my insurance was confirmed by telex.

X rays revealed a complex and serious fracture: my tibia had been driven up through the knee joint. I had also lost forty-two pounds! I spent eight days in the hospital enduring drips and injections, and operations with pins. Then came my release and a beery week before I flew back home. The future? Who knows. But I'm still here.

The View from Deadhorse Point

Chuck Pratt

Embedded in the red earth of an austere and isolated section of America's Southwest is a metal plaque marking the single point in this country common to four states. The Four Corners Monument, where it is possible to stand in Utah, Arizona, New Mexico and Colorado simultaneously, is the geometric center of an area that has been frequented for more than twenty years by a cult of desert-loving rock climbers obsessed with the alien beauty and legend-filled history of the area. Why the desert should exert such a fascination on this handful of climbers is a mystery to those who are not attracted to it, for the climbs in Four Corners, with a few remarkable exceptions, have little to recommend them. They are generally short, often requiring less time to climb than to approach. At best, the rock is brittle and rotten; at worst, it is the consistency of wet sugar. Perhaps it is significant that desert climbing presents objective dangers not usually encountered by climbers used to more solid rock. Although the dangers inherent in sandstone climbing are infinitesimal compared to those faced by the mountaineer, it is just these small-scale threats that are more suited to a rock climber's temperament. Among the traits shared by virtually every climber who is active in the desert is the conscientiousness with which they avoid the expedition game.

The quality of the climbing, be it safe or dangerous, cannot by itself fully explain the desert's appeal. There have been too many California Desert Expeditions that have returned home without achieving a single climb, yet judged the trip a complete success. A desert environment is maintained by an irresistible force whose nature cannot be penetrated by superficial efforts. To gain any lasting worth from what the desert has to offer, we had to learn to put our pitons and ropes away and to go exploring in silence, keeping our eyes very open. It wasn't easy. We wasted a lot of time climbing until we got the knack.

Easter 1960 We are walking down the blood-red Canyon de Chelly toward the place where it intersects its twin canyon. Everything around us is a shade of red: the walls, looming above us for a thousand feet; the sand beneath our shoes; the river, sluggish with its cargo of silt; even the dog that explodes from a nearby hogan to warn the canyon of our presence. His bark, echoing between the canyon walls and amplified by a dozen tributary canyons, becomes deafening and we hurry through his territory to escape the sensation of having climbed over a neighbor's fence into his backyard.

We pass an occasional oasis of color wherever a natural amphitheater in the canyon wall protects a grove of luxuriant cottonwoods, the bright green of their leaves made almost luminous by the red walls surrounding them like a fortress. Turning a final corner into Monument Canyon, we see Spider Rock for the first time. We already know that it is eight hundred feet high but it is the proportion that excites us. Slender and majestic, it rises from its talus cone like a crimson arrow aimed at the sky. On its summit dwells the Spider Lady, nourishing herself on the flesh of disobedient Navajo children, leaving their bones to bleach in the noonday sun. The Indian legend is a convenient explanation for the pile of white rubble seen on the summit of Spider Rock, and the Spider Lady, the Navajo equivalent of the bogeyman, is an equally convenient device for maintaining discipline among rebellious children.

Slowly we circle the spire to see it from every possible angle. We go mad looking at Spider Rock and so we climb it. I have memories of flared chimneys; bolt ladders whose bolts fall out under the rope's weight; Kamps stuck in a mantel position on a piton trying to pull his pant leg from under his foot; and the summit pitch, a lieback over a flake that looks loose enough to come off in somebody's arms. For a while we stand on the summit, taking it all in, and then start down, the first two rappels producing more adrenaline than the ascent. Retracing our steps out of the canyon we feel the temporary depression which accompanies an exhilarating experience that belongs to the past.

Returning to the cosmopolitan atmosphere of Chinle, we disguise our- selves as tourists and edge discreetly toward the ranger headquarters to find out how much of a stir we have caused, for we know intuitively that since we feel so happy, we must have done something illegal. "Are you the boys who climbed Spider Rock?" We can't tell if the ranger is merely curious or if he is trying to trap two criminals. After a pause, Bob finally admits to the crime and the ranger invites us into his office for a friendly chat. He informs us that the Indians are furious. It seems a conclave of the most powerful medicine men in Navajodom have just completed a three-year ritual to remove the curse from Canyon de Chelly that was placed there by the first ascent of Spider Rock. Now they have to start all over again, so the best thing for us to do would be to leave on the next stagecoach or something.

On our way out of town we stop at the local trading post and I go in for an ice-cream bar. The place is filled with Navajos, and within half a second the conversation disappears to the point where I could have heard a feather falling. A shadow stirs in a corner and an Indian built like a buffalo looms above me as I lean for the door. "Did you climb Spider Rock?" he asks. "Why yes," I answer, reaching for the doorknob. "Now that you mention it, I did. But there's another guy outside who climbed it too." Spread the guilt and the punishment might be less severe—the logic of Nuremberg. "What did you find on top?" Every eye in the trading post is upon me, every ear straining for my reply. It's bad enough to place a curse on the land by climbing Spider Rock, but to contradict the cherished myths of the Spider Lady would be go- ing too far. "We found a pile of bleached bones on the top." Now it's so quiet I can hear molecules colliding in midair. Slowly I start turning the doorknob, but the buffalo takes one step toward me and, demonstrating a remarkable intimacy with the nuances of a native tongue not his own, asks, "What do you take me for—a fool?" and the room erupts into hysterical laughter. I gather my ego up off the floor and carry it out the door in my hands.

Not bad for a first desert trip. I get up one climb—the finest in the Southwest—and I learn a couple of things about Indians. Best of all, I want to come back.

Autumn 1961   Dave Pullin and I are wandering through a graduate course in quicksand trying to find Cleopatra's Needle. We offer our kingdoms for a canoe at the stream crossings, but we're stuck with an automobile and have to nurse it cross-country. About noon we find the spire and start up, with lucky me getting the second lead. It is grim: The pins go in easily by hand and come out just as easily under a load about five pounds less than I weigh. How to lighten myself by five pounds? Strip? There is a cruel east wind rising and the sky is growing dark with clouds. I send the hardware down and haul up one pin at a time. I stand on one and count until it pops out. Fifteen seconds. The higher I get the less time I have to place the piton and get off the thing before it grinds out. Halfway up I reach a bolt and retreat, leaving fifteen pitons shivering in a crack. We'll finish it tomorrow.

Christmas City. The snow is everywhere—just crept in during the night and decided to stay. Through the howling wind I can hear an occasional metallic thud, as though someone were gently beating Cleo with a hardware loop. I look out of the car window toward the spire, barely able to see it through the snow flurries. I see my rope, slowly swaying from the bolt, and at the bottom of the rope is a ten-pound mobile of assorted pitons and carabiners. "Shit, Pullin," I say, "every goddamned piton I put in got blown out by the wind." We retrieve the gear, toss it in a corner of the trunk and drive to the nearest bar.

We are learning that the rocks of the desert are organic. The climbs in Four Corners have a quality of aliveness not usually associated with the inanimate world and for me that quality is becoming a source of increasing attraction. It is fascinating to view erosion as a process rather than an end result, for the wind can visibly alter a spire even as we climb it and a good rainstorm will dissolve the softer sand into mud, so that no two parties ever visit the same summit.

Dave and I are disappointed about Cleo and we would like to stay in the bar and get drunk, but we leave when an Indian tells Dave, whose beard is rather gnarled and intermittent, that he looks like a pale-face werewolf.

Autumn 1963   Shiprock, fabled monument, rises before us in splendor and silence, a tableau from the genesis of the Southwest, historical remnant of a unique volcanic violence which has created a collage of mountainous fluted columns, jagged aretes and sheer orange walls that intimidate us into silence. Once on the summit, Roper and I can see for a hundred miles in every direction, though there is nothing to see but a vast plain of sand and sagebrush and a dozen miniature Shiprocks dotting the horizon. Then we hear the tom-toms. Or rather we feel them, a dull sympathetic response in the pit of the stomach, which we eventually interpret as a drumbeat. Is this the prelude to a thousand shrieking savages circling Shiprock, launching flaming arrows at us? Are they waiting for us on the ground with their fires and sharpened stakes? We can see nothing stirring on the plain below, yet the drumbeat continues, insistent and sinister. We descend cautiously to be greeted only by silence and an empty desert. The drums are silent now and we joke about it, attributing the whole thing to fancy. Even so, we nearly break an axle driving back to the main road.

Moab is a small community in southeastern Utah, founded by Mormon pioneers and nurtured in modern times by uranium and potash. North of the town is the Colorado River, on whose shore Steve Roper and I decide to camp while climbing Castleton Tower and The Priest. I am just out of the army and Roper is just going in, so this trip will be our only meeting in four years. Each of us has two years of information and gossip to exchange, so we babble until the moon goes down. We are lulled to sleep by the night sounds—wind murmuring through the willows, the fluttering of a thousand leaves in the cottonwood above our heads, the ringing call of crickets competing with the frogs down by the river, where the deep currents of the Colorado flow westward to become cataracts.

We are going to try Cleopatra's Needle. Roper has already climbed it, so there is little question as to who gets to lead the aid pitch—me. Again. I am reminded of the last time I was here, when my pitons fell out from under me, dislodged by the simple action of pulling up five feet of slack. The sandstone, disintegrating with each hammer blow, rains down into my face, so that I have to climb most of the pitch with my eyes closed. When the rain stops, I open my eyes standing on the summit, red from head to toe.

Roper prusiks up, cleaning the pitons with his hands. Not bothering to step onto the summit, he jumps into rappel and vanishes. I hardly give him time to get off the rope before I take off too, and within seconds we are both on the ground shouting and jumping up and down as though we have just gotten away with the crime of the century.

A new day arrives and we drive around a corner to try Venus' Needle. We fail, and instead of recognizing our failure as a sign that our trip is over, we become stubborn and drive vehemently to Canyon de Chelly. The snow catches us on the second pitch of Spider Rock and we can no longer ig-nore the message. There is a time on every desert expedition when the end of the trip is signified by subtle changes either in our own temperament or in the environment. One morning the sky is somehow different, or the sunset will be of such surpassing splendor that no climb can match it. Now that our two failures have brought us to a halt, we pay attention to the wind and migrate west with the clouds.

Spring 1964   T. M. Herbert doesn't want any part of Cleopatra's Needle. He's heard stories about pitons being blown out by the wind, so we try Venus's Needle instead. It's the same height as Cleo and the rock is just as soft, but T. M. hasn't heard any stories about it so that makes it okay. The last time we were here the weather was so cold we couldn't even touch the rock; the closest we could come to a desert experience was sitting in a theater in Gallup, New Mexico, watching *Lawrence of Arabia*. T. M. attacks the first pitch vengefully and I can hear his ribs cracking as he tries to force himself through a narrow slot fifty feet up. There is a tumultuous mechanical clatter behind me, and a pickup arrives with two Indians aboard. I am paranoid about Indians ever since the incident in the trading post and now here I am, lashed to an immovable desert spire while some gadget-festooned freak grunts and thrashes above me. One of the Indians gets out of the pickup and strolls nonchalantly over. I untie from my anchor and brace myself for running. "We're looking for arrowheads," I volunteer. His laughter is profuse. "Well, you won't find any up there. I thought you were just climbing it." Then he gets back in his truck, says something to his companion in Athabascan and drives off, both of them laughing hysterically as they bounce away across the dunes. When I climb up to T. M. he wants to know what the Indians thought was so funny. "Oh, they thought we were looking for arrowheads." And T. M. laughs.

Spider Rock again. It's been three years since the last ascent, so the Indians will have to bring the medicine men back for another ceremony. Rock climbers have their religion too, but I doubt that we could explain it to them. We manage it in one day this time, but have to rappel in the dark. Two rappels from the ground my mind cracks when an aid sling jams behind a block and I'm left suspended under an overhang trying to cope with a pack, two extra ropes and a camera strap that is strangling me. T. M. shouts up fatherly advice and I finally struggle back onto a ledge and start over.

This time no one seems aware of the ascent. No council of war from the Indians, no friendly chats in the ranger's office. We remain in the campground for two days and the only visitors we receive are a blind, arthritic donkey and the chief ranger's daughter, who is selling Girl Scout cookies. We stock up with enough to last us for the journey home and drive off. If it's this easy to get away with it, I think I'll climb it again.

Spring 1966   We have come directly from Berkeley to Zion, a mistake, for the monstrous walls of Zion Canyon, more intimidating than those of Yosemite, have reduced us to tourists. We abandon all thoughts of climbing and turn instead to the trails until we once again dare study the walls for routes. But it is useless; we are too small and the lines we have drawn to define the limits of the possible have not been drawn far enough to include Zion. The place oppresses us and we leave, thinking that someday when we are younger and suction cups are in vogue, we will come back and climb the Sentinel.

We enter the role of tourist with a passion. Southern Utah contains landscapes so alien to anything in our experience that we feel that we are traveling on the moon. Cedar Breaks, Bryce Canyon, Kodachrome Flat—areas where ancient varieties of sandstone have congealed like damp soot into formations so grotesque and fragile that climbing is out of the question. Much of this country is for the eye only—great reefs of crimson rock, scalloped and capped with foam, stretch across vast areas of the desert plain like waves frozen in time at the instant before breaking. And there is the San Rafael Swell, an oceanic expanse of crumbling sandstone columns, sinuous and baroque, standing in clusters around Gothic arches, the whole merging into a larger pattern of plateaus and mesas that again merge into the timeless design of the desert's evolution. The horizons beyond Four Corners strain the limits of vision and of imagination. The desert can be comprehended only in its detail, for we are dealing with the sea.

Spring 1967   This trip is going to be a strange one. For the first time we are taking a woman along on a desert expedition and I feel that ancient superstition of sea captains. "But this is a bird of a different hue," Roper assures me, and I take his word for it as we arrive in Zion from Death Valley. The walls seem less intimidating this time, perhaps because we have no climbing plans until we get to Arizona. Still, we don't feel big enough for Zion—maybe next year, since we seem to be growing.

One last try at Spider. It will be Roper's first time and my third. We are wary of the Indians and the rangers both, so we use a bit of stealth finding the Bat Trail into the canyon. At the start of the path we find a sign that states, quite unequivocally, "No Climbing." "Balderdash," I say, and "Bullshit," says Roper and we turn the sign around so its blank side shows and proceed into the canyon. We will sleep in the canyon tonight, try to get up the climb tomorrow and back up to the rim and the highway without getting caught.

The early morning chill is destroying our resolve and we just about rationalize our way out of the climb when Janet contributes her opinion. "You guys are not only cowardly, you're soft. It really isn't all that cold and now that you're here you should do the climb." "Roper, will you please discipline your woman." He makes a fist, but cannot look her in the eye. We glance at each other, then at the rock, and silently begin to climb. We reach the summit when the sun is close to the horizon, casting Spider's shadow down the canyon into infinity.

Spring and Fall, 1969   On the rim of an immense plateau high above the town of Moab is a newly constructed visitor center at Deadhorse Point State Park. Like most visitor centers, it was built on the assumption that a modern building, with picture windows and flush toilets, will somehow attract people to an area of scenic beauty that did not attract them before. Certainly the center was not built in response to the pressure of an ever-growing population, for very few visitors to the area ever see Deadhorse Point. Not the hunters who each season swarm into Moab to display their trophies and trade deer hearts for elk livers; not the tourists whose schedules allow only for a trip through the uranium plant; and not the climbers either, for there is nothing there to climb.

The visitor center houses drawings, graphs, charts and working models all neatly and logically arrayed to explain the view from Deadhorse Point. Some of the tourists who do find their way to the point wander through the building and then leave, without bothering to look at the reality itself, just as tourists in Yosemite, content to remain in the security of the lodge, will watch movies of Yosemite Falls rather than walk the quarter mile to experience directly the spray from the second highest waterfall on earth. Such is the level of their curiosity.

Approaching the edge of the world, we separate to experience the view in solitude. On the far horizon, the ramparts of a snow-shrouded range of peaks rise above the dark red expanse of Canyonlands National Park. Across the entire plateau all sounds are hushed, and the desert colors, so bright and varied during the day, are subdued by twilight. Directly before us nothing is visible, for the earth drops abruptly into an emptiness vast as the sky. Slowly the view expands as we reach the edge, where a sandstone cliff plunges below us to a sloping plain. We are standing on the summit of an incomprehensible series of steps, separated by sheer sandstone cliffs. Far below, so distant that we cannot see its motion, is the silver curve of the Colorado River, performing its endless task without regard to night or day, the river and the land living in a unity that will last as long as time will flow.

Journey to
the Stone Age

Geoff Tabin

from Summit Magazine, Fall 1990, Text © 1990 by
Geoff Tabin Introduction © 1990 by Summit Magazine

To the Indonesians who rule Irian Jaya (the northwestern portion of New Guinea, the world's second largest island after Greenland), the mountain is Puncak Jaya or "Victory Peak." To the Western world, it's Carstensz Pyramid, named for the Dutch Explorer Jan Carstensz who described it from his ship in 1623 during a rare break in the fog. Naming the peak was easy. Getting there took more than three hundred years. In 1914, a British expedition of 262 people spent fifteen months inching just thirty miles into the jungle. Following the expedition, A. F. R. Wollaston reported to Britain's Alpine Club: "Even if we spent twice the time in the country, I doubt if we should have come as far as the foot of the highest range."

Indeed, the first foreigners to climb 16,023-foot Carstensz were Heinrich Harrer and team in 1962. They made first ascents of the three highest summits in the area while getting to know the Dani people of the surrounding jungle. In his book *I Come from the Stone Age*, Harrer evocatively describes the climbs and the year he spent among the people he described as "gentle cannibals." Gentle from his own interactions. Cannibals by reputation.

While cannibalism on the island of New Guinea is a fact, the local evidence is unclear. In the late 1960s a Harvard-Peabody anthropology expedition lived with the Dani near Wamena, two hundred miles from Carstensz Pyramid. They discovered piles of bones that seemed to imply occasional cannibalism; and the Dani, when pressed, would admit that perhaps such deeds happened. Mostly, though, the team described constant ritual warfare, with men of rival villages gathering on a hillside to fight with sharpened sticks. The fight ends as soon as someone is mortally wounded, with the losers fleeing to their home territory. Before long, however, both groups begin preparing for the next battle—deaths must be avenged to appease the spirits. Such battles have since been stopped by missionaries and government soldiers.

In 1962, the Dutch turned over control of Irian Jaya to Indonesia. For reasons still unclear, the new proprietors closed access to the entire Carstensz Pyramid area. Perhaps the Indonesians didn't want visitors to think their country primitive. More likely there was too much truth to rumors of fighting between natives and Indonesian troops.

In any case, the effect was to limit the Dani's contact with the outside world to a few missionaries. Until the late 1970s, those Dani inhabiting remote areas close to the mountain had had almost no western contact at all. In 1979, Britishers Peter Boardman and Hillary Collins arranged for a missionary pilot to land them illegally near the mountain. They returned with wild stories about the natives—and an alluring photo of an unclimbed two-thousand-foot rock wall leading directly to the summit of Carstensz Pyramid. When I saw their slide show, I had to go.

July, 1980:   Bob Shapiro, Sam Moses, and I bounce down a grass runway at missionary/pilot Leroy Kelm's home outside Jayapura, the capital of Irian Jaya. Our Aerocommander lifts off, bound for Ilaga, the closest Dani village to Carstensz Pyramid. We drone inland over an endless sweep of jungle-green hills furrowed with jagged, twisting canyons. The peaks grow larger, more dramatic as we near the Carstensz Massif; flat land is nowhere to be seen.

We wing over a few clusters of round brown huts and terraced fields clinging to steep green walls. "There's no landing strip," Leroy drawls. "I'll try to put her down in the sweet potato patch," pointing to an ominously tiny clearing on a hillside above a group of huts. He noses the plane into a sickening dive, muttering the Lord's Prayer under his breath. My terror mounts as we swoop to the slopping, muddy field.

We touch down softly enough, but Leroy's wide-eyed look says something is seriously wrong. The plane doesn't slow down, instead it skids on the mud as if it were ice. The end of the clearing looms closer at an alarming rate. We slide diagonally until one tire sticks in the mud, and spin violently to a halt with the left wing tip five feet from the drop off to an oblivion of jungle.

As Leroy chops the engine and silence washes over us, my heart races with giddy relief. But when I look around, new sights and sounds electrify me with a jolt of adrenaline. From all sides, men and boys come at us screaming a guttural "Oooh-whah, Oooh-whah," with their voices cracking to a falsetto on the "whah." Each carries a spear or a stone. All are naked save for a *koteka*, or penis gourd, which they pound with their palms, drumming a resonant counterpoint to their shrieks. They surround the plane, pounding and screeching.

Leroy steps out, a big grin splitting his silver muttonchop sideburns. He makes eye contact with a couple of Dani in the front of the group. They return bright, toothy smiles. Sam tapes their chanting on a small cassette recorder, and when he plays it back for them the sounds break the ice completely. Dani boys close around us, yelling and singing, curiosity filling their eyes.

Below us stretch terraced sweet potato fields, some only fifteen feet wide, linked by footpaths down to a central group of dwellings. Scattered on the surrounding slopes are a smattering of round huts and other fields carved out of the foliage. Further below and all around, tangled rain forest hems the inhabited land. Here in the high foothills, warm tropical air sweeps up to meet cool mountain breezes, creating a zone of near-constant mist and precipitation.

Leroy's inventive pantomime organizes a group of Dani men to wrestle his plane out of the mud. We unload our packs and he hops aboard, revs the engines, and takes off, leaving the three of us to find our way to the mountain. We have a two-hundred-word Dani vocabulary list from Harvard anthropologists and ten loads of gear. We hope to enlist ten Dani men as porters to haul it all to the base of Carstensz Pyramid—or Dugundugu, as we understand in the Dani tongue. For payment we've brought ten steel axe heads, ten bags of salt, ten bags of sugar and ten Boy Scout knives.

We embark on our own wild game of charades trying to explain what we want. Only three of our Dani words seem familiar to these Ilaga villagers, two hundred miles from the tribesmen that the anthropologists studied. We draw pictures and show photographs of the mountain. One older man, Seppanous, becomes very excited and demands my pen. I hand it to him. He immediately removes the *am whyak*, or boar's tusk, from his nose and proudly inserts the pen.

We sit on the ground amid a cluster of thatched huts negotiating, gesticulating, laughing. The women go bare-breasted, wearing only beads and loose grass skirts. Naked infants and children play in the mud around us. Pigs, the only domesticated animals, roam freely. Women carrying stone hoes walk past on their way to and from the fields. A few steel axes are the only visible sign that we aren't in the Stone Age.

We are at eight thousand feet, and despite our proximity to the equator, when it clouds over and rains, I feel chilled. The naked Dani seem perfectly comfortable and a bit amused as I search for my rain top.

Eventually we think we've struck an agreement: ten men will carry our loads and escort us through the jungle to Dugundugu. After a night of singing we hand out ten equally weighted packs. To our horror, the Dani rip the bags open and spread gear all over the ground. Villagers come by, picking from our things. Bob, Sam, and I stare at each other in disbelief, amazed at how quickly our climb is over. As we watch helplessly, dozens of men, women and children gather up our belongings and file out into the forest, chanting a song.

We're left with no choice. We get up and follow the merry expedition past the farthest cultivated fields and into the cool, dark jungle. We wander under a canopy of dense foliage, sometimes in thick mud, sometimes on rotting logs suspended high above the ground, always on trails that I could never follow on my own. At first, the compass says we are traveling north; a few minutes later it reads south. Before long, we put the maps away and just walk along, hoping we are hiking toward Dugundugu.

After five hours we stop in a small clearing. The Dani spread out, shouting and laughing, each taking on a task. Some gather firewood while others chop at large trees with stone axes. Yoni, a graceful athletic young man, takes dry moss out of his *koteka*, strikes two flints together, catches the spark in the moss, blows gently, puts the glowing pile on the ground, covers it with wet wood, and fans it into roaring flame.

Women take pandanus fronds, break the tips and pull single strands from the fibrous palm leaf to make instant organic needles with thread. Then they sew the fronds together to make a waterproof covering for their shelter. When a giant oak is about to topple, great debate ensues about where it will fall. As it comes down, much "oooh-whah-ing" and pounding on the *kotekas* accompanies the descent. By the time we set up our tent, the Dani have built a wooden hut covered with a waterproof layer of Pandanus leaves.

Minutes later, Martinus, one of the older men, sees me struggling to boil water on my pack stove. He returns with a pot of boiling water. I thank him with a piece of chocolate and watch, amazed, as he takes only a tiny nibble and then brings it around so everyone can have a taste. At night they build a huge fire in their shelter with the flames licking at the wooden roof. Songs and laughter radiate from the smoky hut well into the night.

As I observe the Dani, they observe me. They are fascinated by miracles (like zippers) that I take for granted. But I see no sign of jealousy, either toward us or among themselves. Not a single item of ours will disappear. When the stronger Dani men drop their loads at the top of hills, they go back to help the older, slower members.

Their emotions ride close to the surface. Displeasure shows quickly, often evoking tears. But moments later, the same two people embrace and laugh. They are constantly amused by my struggles to adapt to the changing environment and care for myself with all my bulky possessions.

Every day I grow more amazed by our companions. We mountaineers are immediately dependent on them for our directions. By the second night they bring us water, fire, and other necessities—treating us like children who have not yet learned to care for themselves. When I try to kindle the sopping wet wood using a lighter and finally fuel from my stove—all without success—Yoni watches knowingly from a distance. Just as my frustration peaks, he walks over, plucks a clump of moss from his *koteka*, strikes two pieces of flint, blows, piles on soaked wood, blows some more, and stands back, smiling at the blaze.

I come to see that the Dani live in perfect agreement with the rugged, hilly rain forest. The forest meets their needs as surely as the malls provide ours at home. Most of their diet consists of fire-roasted *mbee*, or sweet potatoes, which they carry in *yums*, orchid-decorated woven reed bags that hang from their foreheads down their backs. They also gather roots, grubs and insects to eat as we walk.

On our third day in the jungle, Wanimbo, a tall athletic Dani in his mid-twenties, presents me with a live bat he's holding by the feet. He smiles gently; I flinch away. With a shrug he takes an arrow, pushes it into the bat's anus and sticks it into the fire. A few minutes later he carefully divides the meat among everyone.

Twenty-four Dani stay with us for the full ten days it takes to reach Dugundugu. In the last days, we climb steep, muddy hills to finally emerge from the forest onto the expansive Ngorilong Plateau, a flat, moss-covered bog. At twelve thousand feet, our naked escorts stay warm with frequent fires and Pandanus-leaf ponchos made on the spot. We cross a snow-covered, sharp-cobbled limestone pass at nearly fifteen thousand feet; they all pad along barefoot.

No one seems surprised to see snow; they have clearly come this way before. I wonder why naked people would climb to a snowy mountain. Perhaps the easier trade route involves climbing through the high mountain passes rather than fighting thick jungle. Unfortunately, we are still communicating through gestures and I cannot ask such a complex question.

In the end, we succeed in making our planned first ascent on Carstensz and a few other fine climbs besides. And while I came for these routes, the real experience was the privilege of spending time with the Dani. To their mountains we have brought the latest Gore-Tex rainwear, freeze-dried foods, high-tech everything. Still, we are humbled by our Stone Age companions. With one stitch of a palm leaf needle, one strike of a flint against *koteka*-dry moss, I learn how much we have sacrificed in our modern world.

The Only Blasphemy

John Long

from "Gorilla Monsoon," chapter 3 Published by Chockstone
Press in 1991 Reprinted with permission from John Long

At speeds beyond eighty miles an hour the California cops jail you, so I kept it right around seventy-nine. Tobin used to drive one hundred, till his Datsun exploded in flames on the freeway out by Running Springs. Tobin was a supreme artist, alive in a way the rest of us were not; but we could see from day one he was going to die, and soon. He never drew the line, never knew there was such a thing. Time seemed too short for Tobin, who always lived and climbed like he had only months or days or perhaps only minutes left. It came as no surprise when he perished attempting to solo the north face of Mount Alberta—in winter.

I charged on toward Joshua Tree National Monument, where, two weeks prior, another pal had "decked" while soloing. I later inspected the base of the route, wincing at the grisly blood stains, the tufts of matted hair. Soloing is unforgiving, but okay, I thought. You just have to be realistic, not some fool abetted by peer pressure or ego. At eighty-five miles an hour, Joshua Tree came quickly, but the stark night dragged.

The morning sun peered over the flat horizon, gilding the rocks spotting the desert carpet. The biggest stones are little more than one hundred fifty feet high. Right after breakfast I ran into John Bachar, who at the time was probably the world's foremost free climber. For several years he'd tooled around the country in his old VW van, abiding for a time at the crag where the sun shined the brightest. All climbs were easy for Bachar, and he had to make his own difficulties. He completely dominated the cliff with his grace and confidence. He never got rattled, never lost control, and you knew if he ever got killed climbing, it wouldn't be his fault; it would be a gross transgression of all taste and would prove that climbing was absurd and all wrong. You'd sell all your gear and curse God for the rest of your life—on aesthetic, not moral grounds. Bachar had been out at Joshua Tree for about two months, and his soloing feats astonished everyone.

It was winter, when college checked my climbing to weekends, so my motivation was there, but my fitness was not. Straightaway, Bachar suggested a "Half Dome day." Yosemite's Half Dome is two thousand feet high, call it twenty rope lengths. Hence, we'd have to climb twenty pitches (or twenty climbs) to get in our Half Dome day. In a wink, Bachar was shod, cinching the sling on his chalk bag. "Ready?" Only then did I realize he intended to climb all two thousand feet solo, without a rope. To save face, I agreed, thinking: "Well, if he suggests something too asinine, I'll just draw the line. I was the first to start soloing at Josh, anyway..."

We embarked on vertical rock, twisting feet and jamming hands into bulging cracks; smearing the toes of our skin-tight boots onto tenuous bumps; pulling over roofs on bulbous holds; palming off rough rock and marveling at it all. A little voice inside occasionally asked me just how good a flexing, quarter-inch hold could be. If you're solid, you set curled fingers or pointed toes on that quarter-incher and push or pull perfunctorily. And I was solid.

After three hours, we'd disposed of a dozen pitches, and felt invincible. We upped the ante to stiff 5.10, or extreme difficulty. We slowed considerably, but by early afternoon, we'd climbed twenty pitches: The Half Dome day was history. As a finale, Bachar suggested we solo a 5.11—an exacting thing even for Bachar, for back then, the 5.11 grade moved us onto world-class terrain, just a tick below the technical limit. I was already exhausted from racing up twenty different climbs in about five hours, having cruised the last four or five on rhythm and momentum. Regardless, I followed Bachar over to Intersection Rock, the "hang" for local climbers and the site for Bachar's final solo.

He wasted no time and scores of milling climbers froze like statues when he started up. He moved with flawless precision, plugging his fingertips into shallow pockets in the 105-degree wall. I scrutinized his moves, making mental notes on the intricate sequence. He paused at fifty feet, directly beneath the crux bulge. Splaying his left foot out onto a slanting edge, he pinched a tiny flute and pulled through to a gigantic bucket hold. Then he walked up the last one hundred feet of vertical rock like it was nothing. From the summit, Bachar flashed down that sly, candid snicker, awaiting my reply.

I was booted up and covered in chalk, facing a notorious climb. Fifty impatient eyes gave me the once over, as if to say: "Well?" That little voice said, "No problem," and I believed it. I drew several deep breaths, if only to convince myself. I didn't consider the consequences, only the moves. I started up.

A body length of easy stuff, then those pockets, which I finger adroitly before yarding with maximum might. The first bit passes quickly. Everything is clicking along, severe but steady, and I glide into the "coffin zone" (above fifty feet) faster than I can reckon. Then, as I splay my foot out onto the slanting edge, the chilling realization comes that, in my haste, I've bungled the sequence, that my hands are too low on the puny flute that I'm pinching with waning power. My foot starts vibrating and I'm instantly desperate, wondering if and when my body will freeze and plummet. There is no reversing any of this. The only way off is up. A montage of black images floods my brain.

I glance down between my legs. My gut churns at the thought of a free fall onto the boulders, of climbers later pausing and cringing at the red stains and tufts of hair. They glance up and say, "Yeah, he popped from *way* up there. Never had a chance."

That little voice is bellowing: "Do something! Pronto!" My breathing is frenzied while my arms, gassed from the previous two thousand feet, feel like concrete. Pinching that little flute, I suck my feet up so as to extend my arm and jam my hand into the bottoming crack above. But the crack is too shallow, accepts but a third of my hand. I'm stuck, terrified, my whole life focused down to a single move.

Shamefully, I understand the only blasphemy—to willfully jeopardize my life, which I have done, and it sickens me. I know that wasted seconds could...then the world stops, or is it preservation instinct kicking my brain into hypergear? In a heartbeat I've realized my implacable desire to live, not die! My regrets cannot alter my situation: arms shot, legs wobbling, head on fire. Then my fear overwhelms itself, leaving me hollow and mortified. To concede, to quit, would be easy. The little voice calmly intones: "At least die trying." I hear that, and punch my hand deeper into the bottoming crack. If only I can execute this one crux move, I'll get an incut jug hold and can rest off it before the final section. I'm afraid to eyeball my crimped hand, scarcely jammed in the shallow crack. It *must* hold my 205 pounds, on an overhanging wall, with scant footholds, and this seems ludicrous, impossible.

My body has jittered in this spot for minutes, forever. My jammed hand says "No way!" but the little voice adds, "Might as well try it..."

I pull up slowly—my left foot still pasted to that sloping edge—and that big bucket hold is *right there*. I almost have it. I do! Simultaneously, my right hand rips from the crack and my foot flies off the edge: all my weight hangs from an enfeebled left arm. Adrenaline powers me atop the "Thank God" bucket, where I press my chest to the wall, get my 205 pounds over my feet, and start shaking like no simile can depict.

Ten minutes pass before I can press on. I would rather yank out my wisdom teeth with vice grips. Dancing black orbs dot my vision as I claw up the last one hundred feet and onto the summit.

"Looked a little shaky," laughs Bachar, flashing that candid snicker.

That night I drove into town and got a bottle. The next day, while Bachar went for an El Cap day (three thousand feet, solo, of course), I wandered listlessly through dark desert corridors, scouting for turtles, making garlands from wildflowers, relishing the skyscape—doing all those things a person does on borrowed time.

The Other Side of Luck

Greg Child

from Thin Air, chapter 12. published by Perigrine-Smith by Gibbs-Smith
Publishing Co. Reprinted with permission from Gibbs-Smith Pub. Co.

Greg Child is both a literary talent and one of the most accomplished all-around climbers in the history of the sport. His many climbing articles and stories are some of the best of the genre. The following account, taken from Greg's book Thin Air, *chronicles his attempt on 26,400-foot Broad Peak, the thirteenth highest mountain in the world. Greg's story here, and Joe Simpson's short-form version of* Touching the Void, *are two of the finest and most powerful modern renditions of the classic mountaineering epic. We join Greg and partner Pete Thexton shortly after their remarkable first ascent of Lobsang Spire.*

Throughout the calm, clear morning of June 25 we watch the figures of Alan, Andy, Roger, and Jean leave their high bivouac and head toward the summit of Broad Peak. A thousand feet below them, two Polish women follow their tracks. Even through an eight-hundred-millimeter lens they appear as mere specks beneath the rocky black pyramid of the main summit. The slant of the sun highlights their tracks as they zigzag across the great snowy terrace. They negotiate a small serac, then a steep chute, then gain the col at 25,591 feet between the main and central summits.

"They'll be on the summit in two hours," Doug forecasts.

As the figures move south on the long summit ridge, they disappear behind a rocky promontory. Below them we see the Polish women turn around and descend from 24,500 feet, evidently deciding that the time is not ripe to push on. As the women descend they sway and stumble with fatigue. From a distant part of the mountain a savage crack rents the air as a huge avalanche cuts loose and blows up a thick cloud of debris.

Soon it will be time for us to leave for Broad Peak too. Pete and I decide to leave in late afternoon to climb Broad Peak's initial couloirs by moonlight and reach Camp One while the snow is firmly frozen. Doug and Steve, with Don and Gohar, decide to leave at dawn on the 26th, after a full night's sleep. An hour before sunset, as the afternoon begins to gather and the light on the peaks around base camp softens to a gentle glow, Pete kisses Beth goodbye and we bid the camp farewell, heading across the glacier. Out in the center of the icy wastes I pause to photograph K2, majestic and clear in the twilight.

"There'll be plenty of time for that," Pete says, hurrying me along toward the base of the three-crowned giant ahead of us.

Between base camp and the foot of Broad Peak lie two miles of glacier, crevassed and forested with a maze of ice towers, or penitents. As Pete and I pick our path across suspect snow patches, moving from one rubbly island to another, we probe the snow with our ice axes to check for crevasses. We talk of the route ahead and check off items to ensure that nothing has been forgotten. As we make our way we talk about Lobsang. Yes, it had been perfection, and there would be more. We spoke of more climbs—he'd come to Yosemite and we'd climb El Capitan; I'd visit the Alps in winter; and maybe, if Broad Peak went well, we'd find ourselves together on K2. A great warmth radiated from Pete onto me, like the alpenglow clinging to the mountains. His small kindnesses and carefully chosen words told me that I was at last breaking through the carefully guarded barrier with which he surrounded himself.

At a snow patch I probe forward, poking my ice axe shaft into the snow ahead. The snow feels firm. Nothing thuds or tinkles to imply a hollow surface. I deem it safe, but the very moment I assure Pete it is so and move forward, the surface gives way with a crash and I drop into a slot.

"Crevasse," I understate, feeling the foolish surprise one would feel standing on a glass-topped table that suddenly shatters. More surprising is that the crevasse has a false floor and I have stopped just a body-length down. Beneath me I can see cracks in the floor that drop into a black emptiness.

"Thought I'd lost you already," Pete says, seating himself on his pack as I grapple out. Scalpel-sharp fins of ice have sliced hairline cuts into my arms and face. I look as if I've had a tussle with a wildcat.

Pete points over his shoulder. "You'll be pleased to know you've got an audience. Some trekkers watched the whole display from their camp a few hundred feet away."

"Embarrassing..."

"Don't worry," Pete adds. "No one from our camp saw it."

As we enter the forest of penitents the sun drops, leaving the air breathless and the summit rocks of K2 burning orange. The gurgle and rush of streams fall suddenly silent, choked by night's freeze. As we emerge from the ice maze, Broad Peak towers suddenly before us, its silhouette well defined as the Baltoro grows quickly black with night. On a bed of scree beneath the mountain we pause for a drink and a bite to eat. On the scree lies a cluster of old wooden wedges and hemp slings. We fiddle with these artifacts left by some predecessor, perhaps the Austrians Hermann Buhl, Kurt Diemberger, Fritz Winterstellar and Marcus Schmuck, who pioneered the first ascent of Broad Peak in 1957, or perhaps they belong to the tragic Polish expedition who'd made the first ascent of the 26,247-foot-high Central Peak.

In late July 1975, six Poles set off up the face above us, climbing a more direct variation of the Austrian Route to the 25,591-foot col between the main and central summits. That variation has become the *voie normale*, but from the col they planned to climb the south ridge of the central summit. Snow conditions were poor, the going slow. Beneath the col, as night and storm approached, one man, Roman Bebak, descended, leaving five to complete the climb. As the storm grew stronger and the five rushed to complete the route, three men—Bohdan Nowaczyk, Marek Kesicki and Andrej Sikorsk—took shelter from the wind on the final rock step below the summit, while Kazimierz

Glazek and Janusz Kulis persevered to the top. At 7:30 P.M. Glazek and Kulis reached the summit, then descended to the others. The storm was now upon them. As the last man, Nowaczyk, made the final abseil to the col, the anchor pulled and he fell to his death, taking vital ropes with him. Trapped in a raging storm with no way to descend the steep, avalanche-prone chute beneath the col, the climbers bivouacked out in the open, wearing only the clothes on their backs.

At first light they resumed their search for Nowaczyk and the ropes, finding neither. In desperation, they tied all their slings and harnesses together to construct a makeshift rope. In the afternoon Glazek descended the gully to the snowfields, and three hundred feet below found a bivouac site. But behind him the weakened Sikorski slipped, knocking Kesicki and Kulis from the face. Sikorski fell six hundred feet; Kesicki slid down the snowfields and plummeted thousands of feet over the huge seracs; Kulis, the only one of the three to survive the fall, stopped one hundred fifty feet below Glazek. Glazek and Kulis endured a second terrible night in a snowhole, then continued down the next morning, their fingers and feet blackened by frostbite. Kulis would subsequently lose most of his fingers and toes. On the descent they found Sikorski, partially buried in snow. Attempts to revive him proved fruitless: he was dead. The only traces of Kesicki were a few tufts of hair and some blood stains in the snow.

As we enter the first couloirs of Broad Peak the full moon rounds the mountain and douses the west face in a silvery light that bounces bright as daylight off the snow. We crampon our way quickly over the firm, crystalline surface until a rocky promontory appears, at 18,543 feet. Here sits a small tent—Camp One, established by the Polish women. Anna and Krystyna were climbing with bivy gear, food and fuel. We rest here an hour, make tea, then continue into the moonlight.

Step after step, breath after breath, every hour the atmosphere thins just a little. Behind us, the first hint of dawn turns the Karakoram every shade of blue and gold imaginable, while the moon sits fixed in the sky, great and white, refusing to evaporate. The mountain glows, changing color by the minute, like a horizon of chameleons. With this view over our shoulders, we zigzag through the gullies and towers of yellow limestone. As we reach the crest of a rocky spur at about twenty thousand feet, blinding daylight and heat flood the mountain. Day reveals further relics of past expeditions: shredded tents, bits of fixed rope and an old oxygen cylinder poking out of the snow. I pick up the steel cylinder to feel what it would be like to hump its weight up a mountain. Weighing at least twenty pounds, it feels like an unexploded bomb, but my lungs wish they could have a taste of the cylinder's juicy contents.

The half-melted tracks of our four team members pit the slope. As I slot my feet into their footsteps I pretend that I am following Buhl's tracks, back in 1957, the year of my birth, and the year too that he died, on Chogolisa. Heat dries our throats so we keep chewing handfuls of snow. Tiny black gnats, blown in from the plains, dot the surface of the snow. At first they look dead, but as the sun warms them they spring to life and crawl around.

At about 20,500 feet on the morning of June 26, we meet Alan, Andy, Roger and Jean, returning from their successful ascent the previous day. They look wasted.

"Well done," Pete says to Andy and Alan, who reach us first and describe their windless summit day.

"It's no punter's peak up there," Andy says. "The summit ridge is at twenty-six thousand feet and is bloody long. Technical too. Andy felt sick all the way along the ridge. And Roger nearly bought it on the descent—he tried to glissade down from the col, got out of control, lost his ice axe, and went sliding down. By a miracle he stopped in some soft snow."

Andy considers us wearily. "Now I know what they mean when people say 'eight thousand meter.' " And down they go, sucking at an atmosphere that grows thicker each step.

From our position on the spur, we can see the jet-black central and main summits far above. To the north is K2. To our left, the three-hundred-foot tall ice cliffs at the foot of the west face's great snow terrace, above which our route will skirt, appear to threaten our path. This is, however, an optical illusion, for the cliffs are far to the side. Even so, whenever there is a crack and rumble of falling ice we look up in alarm.

At about 21,600 feet Pete stops and points ahead. "Hey, I see numbers!"

"What? You're hallucinating!"

"No. Look—on the side of the Central Peak—three numbers—666."

I scan the wall and just as I feel certain that Pete is succumbing to hypoxia I too see a chance play of sunlight on white snow and black rock that bears a perfect resemblance to three sixes.

"Looks as though Crowley left his mark here too," says Pete, referring to Alister Crowley, the Irish mountaineer and satanist who'd been on the flanks of K2 in 1902. Crowley believed that the number 666 had magical powers. On K2's Northeast Ridge his party had reached twenty thousand feet with a contingent of Balti porters, but steep ice had halted them. Angered at the decision to retreat, Crowley, who referred to himself as "The Great Beast," got into a violent quarrel with his partner, Guy Knowles, and threatened him with a revolver that he pulled from his pack. A fight ensued that almost dragged the two men over the precipice until Knowles wrested the weapon from Crowley. Seventy-six years later, a strong American expedition climbed the northeast ridge, shortly after a Polish team had pioneered the route to over eight thousand meters.

We reach Camp Two, at 21,998 feet, late that morning, just as the heat becomes stifling and the snow turns to mush. Here stands another tent left by the Polish women. We slip into it and begin to melt snow to fend off dehydration. Doug and Steve reach us in the early afternoon and pitch a tent nearby, while we begin to sleep off our long night shift.

The next morning, June 27, is again clear. We climb a long, low and angled spur of snow and ice until noon, when at 22,802 feet we find a third ragged and fluttering Polish tent. Here, we all rest and brew up for an hour. Wind cuts fiercely across the slope and rams into the tent's nylon walls. As we set off again, Don and Gohar arrive. Don moves in sprightly fashion for all of his fifty years. These two decide to bivy here, while Doug, Steve, Pete and I set off to camp higher. We agree that while we go to the summit the next day, Don and Gohar will move up and occupy our high camp for their own summit bid the following day.

"Better keep climbing if we're going to make it up this hill," Doug says, and we set off.

As we gain elevation, K2 disappears behind Broad Peak's squarish central summit. Occasional clouds now wander across our path, engulfing us and creating eerie contrasts of diffuse light over the stark neutrals of white snow and black rock. We spread out over the slope, carving a diagonal route upward, Doug striding powerfully in front, then Steve, me and finally Pete. At 3:00 P.M., at the site of Alan's and Andy's bivouac, we pause for another brew. Their snow cave resembles less a cave than a rabbit hole. Steve checks the altimeter.

"Twenty-four thousand three hundred feet," he announces. It is the highest Steve and I had ever been, short of flying.

We set off again, trudging and gasping at the altitude until twilight begins to darken the mountain. At 24,500 feet, near a jumble of one-hundred-foot tall seracs, I clear a platform to place our tent, light the stove to melt a pan of snow, and await Pete. Doug and Steve climb through the serac and bivy three hundred feet above. Twenty minutes pass. Pete approaches slowly, coughing raucously.

"Hurry up Pete—you've got the tent!" I call, feeling the cold night bite into my fingers and toes. He staggers up to me, panting at the unsubstantial air, then dumps his pack and sits on it. I hand him a hot brew. He guzzles it and quickly revives.

"How are you feeling?" I ask.

"Just tired. I'll be better with a rest."

It is late into the night before we finish melting snow for drink. Even then we feel we could have consumed a gallon more. Our stomachs feel queasy with altitude. Out of the sweets, chocolate, Grain Bars and tinned fish we carry, it is a salty can of sardines that sates us most; with the huge fluid loss through breathing and exertion at altitude our body salts are dropping low. Pete's cough disappears as he rehydrates, then sleep takes us. I begin to realize the deficit in sleep we have amassed by climbing around the clock for so many hours and by pushing ourselves up the mountain so late into the day.

During the night, altitude creeps into our heads. By morning it is bashing away inside our skulls. Waking is a long and difficult process, cloudy and drug-like. The crack of wind on the tent walls and the crinkle of our frost-covered Gore-Tex sleeping bags are soon accompanied by the hiss of the stove. While I melt snow I hear Pete mumbling in his sleep, in between the sporadic gasping of Cheynes-Stokes breathing.

"What about this rope then?" he asks.

"Rope? Our rope is in the pack."

"Noooo, not that rope," he chides.

"Then what rope?"

"The rope we're all tied into."

"We're not tied in Pete, we're in the tent, Camp Four, Broad Peak."

"Noooo, you don't understand," and I began to feel like a thickheaded schoolboy giving all the wrong answers. I plied him for more clues to his sleepy riddle and got this:

"It's the rope that all of us are tied to."

"Fixed rope?"

"Nooooo," he whined.

"Umbilical cord?" Any wild guess now.

"Noooo!"

"Then you must be speaking of a metaphysical rope eh, one that everyone is tied to but no one is tied to?" But before I can get an answer the smell of sweet tea wakes him. "How is your head?" I ask, as I try to force some hot oatmeal down my throat.

"Terrible." Both of us squint from the pounding pain in our temples.

"Mine too. Maybe we should go down."

"No. Mornings are always the worst. We're nearly there. Give me some aspirin. We'll be OK."

We quaff down three aspirins each and set off, carrying nothing in our packs but a stove. The steep ice of the serac gets our blood flowing and clears our heads. As I pull onto the slope above the serac I see Doug and Steve stomping out the last few feet of the final chute to the col. Following their tracks I enter the steep chute two hours later, wade through soft snow, and arrive at the 25,591-foot col.

Here, on Broad Peak's first ascent in 1957, Buhl had almost given up, slumping in the snow until his doggedness and Diemberger's enthusiasm had urged him onto his feet and on to the summit. A strong wind gusts from the north, splashing spindrift over the summit ridge. Ahead, the prow-like summit juts toward Sinkiang, China. Beneath me, in Sinkiang, lie the North Gasherbrum Glacier, and deep within a fold of valley, the Shaksgam River. China's rust-colored landscape contrasts sharply with the blinding white of the Godwin-Austen Glacier and the peaks of Karakoram.

Pete labors up to me via the chute the Austrians in '57 had found to be verglassed, the Poles in '75 had found a bed of ice, and we in '83 find a ribbon of steep snow. While awaiting Pete I've fallen asleep long enough for the lump of ice I'd dumped in the pan to melt and boil. As I make a brew, Doug and Steve wave from their position on the ridge a few hundred feet away. We signal back. All is well, the summit a few hours away, and within sight.

The sky is intensely clear all across Baltistan. Nanga Parabat, one hundred fifty miles away, stands on the southwest horizon. Straddling the border of Pakistan and China, as Broad Peak itself does, lies the pyramidal Gasherbrum IV, immediately to our south, and visible to the left of Broad Peak's main summit. Gasherbrum IV is an impressive sight, with its unclimbed northwest ridge directly before us and the northeast ridge of the first ascent on the left. I recall that an American team is working on the northwest ridge, and wonder if they are gasping away somewhere on the final rocky head wall capping the mountain.

"That's a beautiful mountain down there," Pete remarks of Gasherbrum IV. "We ought to give that northwest ridge a shot next season, if it isn't climbed this year."

I agree and we set off along Broad Peak's mile-long summit ridge at ten o'clock.

Along the summit ridge lies the most technical climbing yet; short steps of compact snow interspersed with rock outcrops. We rope up and move together, pausing to belay over tricky sections. The first difficulties of the ridge lie in skirting a large limestone block, across which an old piece of bleached rope is strung, knotted to a rusting piton. As I lead across, in crampons, mitts and down suit, I squint at the rock and check my eyes to be sure I'm not hallucinating, for the rock over which I climb is pitted with the fossils of seashells. Eons ago, this piece of the earth lay on the ocean floor; now it stands at 8,000 meters.

As we near the summit the strain of altitude grows. Each step becomes increasingly harsh. When we pass through the door of eight thousand meters and enter the region climbers call the "death-zone," disorientation and fatigue take an exponential leap. At perhaps one o'clock, Doug and Steve pass us on their return from the summit.

"We summited at 11:30 A.M. It's even windier and colder up there," Doug says, shouting above the wind. Plumes of spindrift curl over the ridge ahead.

"How far away?" I ask.

"An hour."

"Doug, let's go. I can't feel my feet," shouts Steve.

Doug yells into my ear: "We'll get as far down the mountain tonight as we can. Good luck, kid." They move off, their steps jerky and tired. Pete and I are now as alone as we would ever be.

Moving at 8,000 meters is like wading through treacle.[1] I gradually become aware of a peculiar sense of disassociation with myself, as if a part of me is external to my body, and is looking on. I feel this most when setting up boot axe belays or making difficult moves, a strong feeling as if someone invisible is peering over my shoulder keeping an eye on me, or even as if I have a second, invisible head on my shoulders.

We traverse for another half hour to the false summit, an icy, corniced dome at 26,382 feet. There we sit, looking toward the tantalizingly close

[1] Molasses.

main summit. By now those sensations of disassociation are punctuated by feelings of total absence: momentary blackouts, when neither I nor the guy over my shoulder seem to be around. I would emerge from these absences a few paces from where they'd struck me, leading to concern over stepping off the narrow ridge. "Like a dream," I mutter to Pete, but the wind snatches my words away before he hears them.

I look ahead: The corniced ridge dips down and curves left in a final long, easy slope to the summit, only eighteen feet higher than our position. We are nearly there, thirty minutes away. But my fears about what is happening to me double. A vicious headache rings in my ears and pounds at my temples, and a tingling in my arms grows so intense that my fingers curl into a tight fist, making it hard to grip my ice axe. My last shred of rational consciousness raises a cry of concern over the possibility of stroke, or cerebral edema. But to articulate this to Pete is difficult, as speech and thought seem to have no link in my mind. Exhaustion I can understand, and given that alone I might crawl to the summit, but something alien is going on within me and I'm not prepared to push my luck with it. I get it out that I want down. Pete kneels beside me and gazes at the summit, so near yet so far.

"Go down? But we're so close! Just half an hour!"

The idea of turning away from success when it is so close is maddening to me too, and Pete's ever-present determination nearly gets me going. I try to ascertain whether the sensations I feel are imaginary, or are really the beginning of some short-circuiting of my body chemistry.

There is a state of mind that sometimes infects climbers in which the end result achieves a significance beyond anything that the future may hold. For a few minutes or hours one casts aside all that has been previously held as worth living for, and focuses on one risky move or stretch of ground that becomes the only thing that has ever mattered. This state of mind is what is both fantastic and reckless about the game. Since everything is at stake in these moments, one had better be sure to recognize them and have no illusions about what lies on the other side of luck. It is one of those times. I have to weigh up what is important and what is most important.

"It'd be nice to reach the top, you and I," Pete says. And so it would be, to stand up there with this man who has become such a strong friend in such a short time.

"Didn't you say that summits are important?" he adds. Those are my words he is throwing back at me, shouting above the wind and his own breathlessness, harking back to my determination of a few weeks before that we should succeed on Lobsang Spire. I struggle to compose an intelligible sentence.

"Only important when you're in control.... Lost control.... Too high, too fast. You go on. I'll wait below."

"No—we stay together," he replies.

Strain is written on Pete's face as much as mine. In sixty hours, we've climbed from 15,500 feet to over 26,000 feet. We've found our limits. The decision to descend comes without a word. We just get up and begin the long path down, seeing that those red hills in China are now covered in cotton wool clouds, encircling K2 and lapping at Broad Peak's east face.

A few hundred feet from our high point I feel a sensation like a light blinking out in my brain. I have just enough time to kneel down before I slump backwards onto a patch of snow, then black out into a half-world of semiconsciousness and inaction.

"So this is it," I think with a strangely detached curiosity as the day turns pitch black. "This is where the plunge into senselessness and apathy begins, where the shades of death descend." Yet at the same time I am conscious of my swaying head and my incoherent mumbling. I think of Sally, whom I have no right to inflict such folly upon. "Get up you idiot, get up," I keep telling myself, until vision gradually returns. How long have I been out? I cannot tell.

Next to me sits Pete, observing my state as a good doctor should. He wears a white lab coat with a stethoscope draped around his neck; I double-check; nonsense. He is wearing his red high-altitude suit. I am beginning to imagine things. A minute later I regain control of myself, as suddenly as I'd lost it. Pete puts a brew of hot grape drink in my hands. As soon as I drink the liquid I throw it up.

"See. Told you I was sick." The purple stain in the snow forms intricate arabesque designs that grow onto the snow crystals glinting in the afternoon light. I could watch these hallucinations all day, but Pete urges us onto our feet. Rapidly, I begin to improve. My strength and mental faculties return. I've made it back through the 8,000-meter door before it slammed shut and locked me in. But I've cut it close.

In the warm glow of evening I take Pete's photo as we reach the col: the summit stands behind him. Have we made the right decision? Should we go on? Would we have the strength to return later? I feel remorse at having let Pete down, but then the tables suddenly turn: Pete appears over a crest on the col, lagging on the end of the rope. He takes short steps and looks stressed.

"I can't breathe properly," he says in a whisper. "It feels as if my diaphragm has collapsed."

A bolt of fear runs up my spine.

"Are my lips blue?" he asks.

"Yes," I say, noting the indication of oxygen starvation.

"We'll get down," I blurt out, and we turn and crunch tracks to the edge of the wind-blown col. Things are wrong. We have to shed altitude, and fast, but a snail's pace is the best Pete can manage in this thin soup of air. We reach the steep chute that we'd climbed to reach the col. The hour is late, about 7:00 P.M., but we seem outside of time: we are simply there. I wrap a sling around a spike, double our short rope, and abseil sixty feet to the start of the snowfield. Pete follows.

On the snowfield, wind and driving snow have covered all sign of our tracks. "I'll go ahead and break trail. Follow as fast as you can," I say, and Pete nods in response. Dragging the rope behind me I begin loping down the slope. After three hundred feet I turn to see Pete has barely moved.

"Pete!"

No answer.

By the time I fight my way back through the soft snow the last gleam of twilight peters out in the sky and night is upon us. Where have the hours gone? Pete has his headlamp on. It shines out to the windy night. He doesn't speak. When I turn toward the glacier I see a pinpoint of light shining up from base camp, eleven thousand feet below. It's Beth, his girlfriend, far below, giving the eight o'clock signal as arranged, and Pete is returning it.

Conversation is superfluous. We know we're going to be on the move all night, very high, and in rising wind and storm. Already, clouds block out the stars. I tie the rope to Pete's harness and begin belaying him down, length after length, till his strength begins to ebb. Then I talk him down, ordering and cajoling every step out of him. At about 10:00 P.M. he collapses in the snow and whispers he can no longer see. So I guide him, traversing forty-five degrees right, or straight down. Even on the easiest ground he has to face in. Without tracks it's all instinct anyway. All the time wind and spindrift swirl across the slope, and the bastard moon shines everywhere but on the upper slopes of Broad Peak. There is no time to think of what might happen to us, but only that we must move down, move down, move down.

The hours melt into a pastiche of endless, dreamlike movement. Pete becomes too weak to walk, so somehow I support him, dragging him, lowering him, whatever it takes to move. The sensation of being outside of myself is more prevalent than ever. My watcher checks my every move and decision. I keep turning around, expecting to see someone. As I mechanically work toward getting us down, part of my mind begins to wander. I find myself thinking of that first ascent of the central summit, by the Poles. The account I'd read called their stormy descent a "struggle for survival." Accompanying the story was a photo of Broad Peak, littered with crosses where climbers had perished. Those crosses are now underfoot, and the ghosts of history are hiding in the shadows. I find that agnostics also pray.

The slope steepens, indicating that somewhere nearby is the band of ice cliffs we'd climbed that morning. We need to find the low spot in them by which we'd ascended, but where that is is anyone's guess. We link arms and shuffle toward what I hope is our earlier position. The wind howls and Pete inches around uncertainly.

"If only I could see."

"I'm your eyes, Pete—move right ten steps!"

And he does.

It soon becomes too steep to blunder about as we are, so I begin making twenty-foot leads, shoving my axe into the soft snow and belaying Pete in to me. At the last belay he lets go of everything and swings down to the edge of the ice cliff. The shaft of my axe droops alarmingly. I lose my cool and curse at him as I haul him back up.

"Sorry," he whispers calmly. Throughout the ordeal he has remained composed, conserving his energy for matters of survival, rather than letting fear take hold. I clip him to his axe and wrap his arms around it.

"Just don't lose it now, brother. Please."

The wind attacks with unprecedented malice. Waves of spindrift hiss down around us, burning our faces. If my backtracking is correct, then somewhere in the darkness at the bottom of the ice cliff is our tent, and if things have gone as planned, Don and Gohar are in it. I call till my throat is raw, then shove my ice axe in to the hilt, from which to lower Pete. Confusion reigns in the seconds it takes to lower him; he is so disoriented that he cannot tell whether he is at the bottom of the cliff or not. I am blinded by spindrift, and feel the axe shifting out of the snow. I wrap the rope around my arm to distribute some of the weight, while holding the axe in with my knee. Pete gasps in distress as the rope pinches his waist.

"Are you down?"

"Can't... tell."

"For God's sake, you gotta be down!"

He comes to a stop and digs his hands into the snow. I abseil off my second short tool, moving quickly before it slides out. At the bottom of the serac we again link arms to negotiate some broken ground. I glance about, searching with my headlamp for a familiar lump of ice to tell me that we have descended the ice cliffs in the right spot. Then, suddenly, a light appears, illuminating the form of a tent.

"We've got a sick man here, Don," I call to the light. Pete crawls a few feet along a crest of snow, then stops completely. A bobbing headlamp approaches. It is Gohar, himself groggy, woken from a deep sleep. I lie on my back, sit Pete on my shoulders, and slide us down the last sixty feet to the tent, while Gohar belays us. As Don drags Pete into the tent it comes around to 2:00 A.M. We have been moving for 22 hours.

I stagger out to repitch our tent, the tent that Pete and I had collapsed and weighted with snow blocks that morning so it wouldn't blow away. It is filled with snow and the foam pads are gone. I throw the rope down for insulation and crawl into my sleeping bag. It seems that a million years have passed since we set out. We've gone beyond mental and physical barriers that we didn't even know existed within us. We've become a single entity, fighting to survive. Nothing will stop us from getting down now. In a couple of days this will be just an experience we have shared to become closer. All the bullshit of ethics, ego, competition, and the glamour of big summits has been scraped aside to reveal that in the end everything boils down to one thing—life! My eyelids close under the weight of exhaustion and I dream of grassy places.

But those words of Pete's are the last we ever share.

At dawn on June 29, Pete awakes to ask Gohar for water. Gohar presses a cup of warm liquid to Pete's lips, but Pete doesn't drink from it. Don and

Gohar look at each other for a few seconds, then call me. I awoke with a throbbing headache. "Dead," they are saying. But that is impossible! We'd made it through that hellish descent! We were going to make it down! Then sense prevails like a sledgehammer. I rush into the tent and try to force life into him, through his mouth, with mine, forcing my own thin, tired air into him. His lungs gurgle loudly, saturated with the soup of pulmonary edema. I tear his jacket open and rhythmically pound my palms against his chest to squeeze a beat from his heart, but he will have none of it. He will only lie there with an expression of sublime rest on his face, as if dreaming the same grassy dream I had been.

We sit in silence, our heads full of sad thoughts, our eyes registering that the unthinkable has happened. Don lies back on one elbow, looking at Pete.

"It's always the good blokes that go," Don says.

Suddenly I hate this mountain and its heartless geology. What about the people at home and below who love Pete, what about them? Outside, the Karakoram is ablaze with a clear and calm light.

"Notice that the wind has suddenly dropped?" asks Don. "Not a breath. It's always the same when death is about, always a lot of noise and wind, but as soon as it gets what it's after it quiets down. I've seen it before and it's always the same."

I'm still thinking about that, still wondering.

The wind returns a few minutes later, stronger than before, and threatens to tear the tent apart with its claws, like an evil predator, now searching for us. I sit staring at Pete. He can't be dead. I won't accept it. But he is gone and I know it. I close his partially opened eyelids with my hand and wrap his sleeping bag around him. Gohar clenches my arm. "Greg Sahib, we must go," he says with a look of natural fear. I look around, thinking there must be something we should do—a place to bury him, some words, perhaps get him down the mountain for...for what?

"We've got to see to ourselves now," says Don sternly. "You're in a terrible state, youth."

One last glance at Pete. Gohar's lips move as he softly speaks a prayer in Urdu, then we bid our friend farewell. I crawl out of the tent, zip it shut, turn into the maelstrom of blowing snow, and start down. We leave everything as it was. Gear lay strewn about; none of it possessed of value any longer. It is a long descent, every step full of a great sense of loss and perhaps a strange feeling of guilt at having to leave our friend as we did. But the snow will soon settle over him and set firm as earth. The snowfield will inch inexorably to the ice cliffs and peel away in bursts of avalanche to the glacier, which will carry him within it to the fast-flowing Braldu. His journey will outlive us and no ashes could be scattered more thoroughly, nor a monument exist more lasting than Broad Peak.

Weary legs take us down to the Polish tent at 23,000 feet by late morning. Doug and Steve, two specks 3,000 feet below, move down ahead of us. We tumble into the tent, laying about.

"I thought he'd make it," I say for the tenth time.

"No. I could tell the moment I laid eyes on him he was bad," says Don. I keep thinking of what death means, of how none of us will ever know Pete again. Then there are voices outside the tent. A party of Swiss, heading up, appear and greet us happily. I form words to explain the tragedy, but somehow words have no feeling, no reality. One of the Swiss looks at us with pity. "Yes, I was on Everest last year and lost a member. We also had to leave him on the mountain." By God, that's not a member who has died, that's a man, a friend. I curse him entirely; what can he say?

The Swiss have a radio. They call their base camp and carry the message to ours. In a few hours Doug, himself just off the mountain, will break the news to Beth and she would burst into tears. Then the Polish women arrive. I tell them too, but the news doesn't seem to sink in. They can only complain that Don had accidentally taken one of their stoves from Camp One, and when he'd realized his mistake had left it in Camp Two. They harp about this, while I mouth words to try and make them see exactly what had happened above.

"But don't you think it's important that there be a stove in every camp?" one of them asks rhetorically. I toss them our stove and set off down the mountain. Words. They had meaning no longer. No one really understands what we've been telling them. No one is thinking correctly. Nothing is the same up here. It's the thin air.

On June 30 we trace our way down the final narrow couloir of the mountain. Slipping clumsily with snow balling up under our feet, we see four figures on the glacier below. Andy, Alan, Roger and Nebi look up and count four figures descending—we have been joined by one of the Swiss—and hope beyond hopes that a mistake has been made and we are all coming down alive. I lope through soft snow across the final stretch, sinking up to my thigh with each step.

It is Alan who comes forward to meet me halfway. We look at each other, point-blank. Our gazes penetrate more than flesh and blood.

"Then you know," I say.

"Yeah. Pete is dead."

I throw my axe on the scree. I can no longer contain myself. Roger supports me and holds me tightly. "It's not worth it, it's not bloody worth it," I say.

"No. It's not," Roger answers.

As the afternoon falls on that last day of June, we look into one another's eyes and for the first time know each other. I have learned the real rule of this beautiful, reckless, terrible game, the only rule: The mountains are beautiful but they are not worth dying for.

from The White Spider

Heinrich Harrer

In unquestionably the most famous mountaineering account ever told, Heinrich Harrer chronicles a 1936 attempt on Switzerland's Eiger North Wall. This colossal, crumbling limestone cliff, leading 6,000 feet straight up to the 13,042-foot summit, was the last climbed of the six Great North Walls of the Alps. The steepest, biggest and most dangerous of these faces, it finally fell to Harrer and three companions in 1938. By then, the cliff had already killed eight people, with dozens more to follow. With a tourist hotel at its base, the Eiger became one of the world's most famous mountains, while the climbs on its face became headline news across the globe. While Harrer disparaged the tawdry and sensational public outpouring to his mountain, it no doubt colored the heroic tone of his classic tale recounting the tragic events of 1936.

As is often the case with mountain folk, whose features have been carved by wind and storm so that they look older in their youth, younger in their old age, Albert von Allmen's face is ageless. He might be in his middle thirties or middle fifties.

The mountains have been von Allmen's strict teachers and loyal friends, even if his profession leads him more into than onto the peaks. For Albert is a sector guard on the Jungfrau Railway. He is responsible for everything along the line inside the Eiger, and sees to it that nothing goes wrong in that long tunneled section; but he is equally interested in everything that goes on outside. True, he doesn't quite understand the young people who are trying to climb the terrific Eiger precipice, but, even if he thinks them a little deranged, he has a soft spot for them. Von Allmen's eyes are surrounded by many little creases which record not only cares and the hard life of the mountains, but also the joy of laughter.

At noon on July 21, 1936, Albert was standing outside the gallery entrance at Kilometer 3.8, after opening the heavy wooden door. It was a Tuesday. Ever since Saturday the eighteenth, there had been four climbers on the north face: two Austrians, Edi Rainer and Willy Angerer, and two Bavarians, Anderl (Andreas) Hinterstoisser and Toni Kurz. Everyone had fallen for the fresh-faced, clean-limbed Toni Kurz, not only because he was himself a professional guide, but because of his laugh. When Toni laughed, it was as if life itself were laughing. All young men, these: Angerer, the eldest, was twenty-seven, Kurz and Hinterstoisser just twenty-three. They had already climbed almost as high on the face as Sedlmayer and Mehringer the year before, on their ill-fated attempt from which they did not return. But surely these four would come back safely. What had been seen of them during the last few days gave solid grounds for hope that this time there would be no disaster.

None of those present had seen such magnificent climbing. True, one of the climbers, apparently Angerer, seemed to have been struck by a stone.

44

That was why the party had been moving so slowly for the last two days; and that was probably why they had decided to turn back. The descent over ice fields and rock cliffs swept by falling stones and avalanches looked ghastly enough, but the four men were descending steadily, in obvious good heart and without a moment's hesitation, toward the safety of the easier ground below. The three fit ones were continually attending to the one who had clearly been hurt. They couldn't be bad, these lads who looked after each other so well. They must be fine fellows, even if a bit crackpot.

Albert von Allmen thought of the Sunday tourists and excursionists, the blasé men and the ladies in high heels who went to the tunnel window at Eigerwand Station and uttered their "ahs" and "ohs" as they gazed at the terrifying gulfs and immeasurable heights of the Eiger's precipice. It was people like those, hungering for sensation, who were now crowding around the telescopes at Grindelwald and Kleine Scheidegg. And then, too, there were the pronouncements of the know-it-alls, busy weighing up the chances of another catastrophe or of the safe return of four living men to the valley.

They *must* get back safely, thought Albert. His sympathy lay with youth, youth generally, but particularly these four youngsters on the face. It would be a good idea to take a look at them and hear for himself how they were getting on. Allmen pushed back the bolts of the heavy wooden doors and stepped out into the open, as he had done a hundred times before. He was used to the grim aspect of the face; but that day, perhaps because there were people on it, it seemed particularly horrific. A layer of glassy ice overlaid the rock; here and there stones clattered past, lethal bullets humming menacingly down for thousands of feet quite clear of the face. Then, too, there was the roaring of snow avalanches as they slid down, whole cascades of snow and ice. The very thought that there were living men somewhere up in that vertical hell was oppressive. Could they still be alive? Von Allmen shouted, listened, shouted again.

Then the answer reached him. A cheery, gay answer. The voices of four young people shouting, yodelling. Albert couldn't see them, but judging by the sound, they couldn't be more than three or four hundred feet above him. It seemed incredible to him that anyone could climb down those icy perpendicular or even overhanging rocks, continually swept by falling stones; but these crazy kids had so often shown how possible it is to climb impossible things. And, above all, there was that cheery shout coming down from above:

"We're climbing straight down. All's well!"

All well with all of them. Albert's heart beat faster for joy.

"I'll brew you some hot tea," he shouted back.

Smiling with pleasure, Albert von Allmen went back through the gallery door to his shelter inside the mountain and put a huge kettle on for tea. He could already see, in his mind's eye, the arrival of the four lads, exhausted, injured perhaps by stones, maybe seriously frostbitten, but alive and happy.

He would meet them with his steaming tea. There was no better drink than hot tea for frostbitten, exhausted men. He was slightly cross at the time it was taking the water to start bubbling; the lads would be here in a minute or two.

But the lads didn't come in a minute or two.

Long after the tea was ready, they hadn't come. Albert set the golden-brown drink on a low flame, just enough to keep it hot without getting stewed.

Still the lads didn't come; and the sector guard, this man whose age it was impossible to guess, had time for second thoughts.

On Saturday, July 18, 1936, the two ropes, Angerer-Rainer and Hinter-stoisser-Kurz, started up the face. At first they moved independently. At the level of the bivouac previously occupied by the two Austrians, they roped up as a foursome. The rope joining them was no longer a dead length of hemp for them but, as it were, a living artery, seeming to say: "For better or for worse, we belong together." This was an uncommonly daring but in no sense featherbrained undertaking. They successfully climbed the exceptionally severe crack below the Rote Fluh. Above it, Andreas Hinterstoisser was the first to achieve the traverse to the First Ice Field, climbing in textbook fashion with the help of the rope. This technique of the "rope traverse" had been discovered and developed before World War I by that master of rock climbing, Hans Dulfer, during his first ascents of the East Face of the Fleishbank and the West Wall of the Totenkirchl in the Kaisergebirege. In this way Dulfer showed how to link climbable pitches by the use of a diagonal "lift" from the rope on unclimbable ones. The current joke about the Dulfer technique ran: "You go as long as it goes, and when it doesn't go anymore, you just do a traverse and go on."

It was this kind of traverse which Hinterstoisser did on the Eiger face. He had discovered the key to the climb. When they had all completed the traverse, he retrieved the traversing rope. In doing so he threw away the key. If it came to a retreat, the door to the way back was now locked behind them forever. But who was thinking of a retreat?

Many were watching the four men through field glasses. And the spectators forgot their criticisms in admiration, even astonishment, at the speed and assurance with which the two ropes crossed the First Ice Field, climbed up beyond it, and reached the barrier between it and the Second—the greater—Ice Slope. Since the Sedlmayer-Mehringer attempt, everyone knew how difficult those rocks must be.

But what had happened? Suddenly the second pair, Rainer and Angerer, were seen following the leaders slowly and hesitantly. Hinterstoisser and Kurz were already moving up to the rocks above the Rote Fluh. The other two remained motionless for a long time. Then it could be seen that one was supporting the other. Had there been an accident?

It will never be known exactly what happened, but it seems almost certain that Angerer was struck by a stone and Rainer was busy tending him. Presently Hinterstoisser and Kurz could be seen letting a rope down from their stance, which was plainly safe from bombardment by stones. Their joint efforts succeeded in bringing Angerer up to them. Then Rainer followed quickly, without making use of the emergency rope.

The tiny nest in the rocks above the Rote Fluh thus became the first bivouac place for this party of four. They had reached an incredible high level on their first day—more than halfway up the face.

On the morning of Sunday the nineteenth there were more crowds around the telescopes. They saw the four men leave the bivouac at about seven o'clock. And how was the injured man? Obviously better, for instead of retreating, they were climbing on, across the huge slope of the Second Ice Field. All the same, they were moving more slowly than on the first day. Were they all tired, then, or was it all because of the injured man? Why didn't they turn back?

One fact stands out for certain: the four men were a united, indissoluble party. Kurz and Hinterstoisser, climbing in the lead again, never thought of leaving Rainer behind with the injured man. The Austrians didn't want to rob the other two of their chance of reaching the top. And so they all stayed together, though the leaders had frequently to wait for quite a time.

The weather was neither fine nor definitely bad. In the context of the Eiger, conditions were bearable. By the end of this Sunday the party had reached the Third Ice Field; a little below the bivouac which had proved fatal to Sedlmayer and Mehringer, the four men made ready to spend their second night in the open. It had been a good day's work, but they had not gained enough height to make sure of a successful push to the top on the following day. What kind of night would it be? In what condition was Angerer and how were the other three? The spectators down in the valley didn't know any of the answers. They withdrew for the night, rubbernecks, reporters, guides, and mountaineers. Tomorrow would show.

The next day was Monday, July 20. Once again no movement could be seen in the bivouac till seven o'clock. It was a tiny place, with hardly room to sit down. Once again Kurz and Hinterstoisser began to climb the steep ice slope leading to the "Death Bivouac." After about half an hour they stopped. The others were not following them. Nobody knows what the four men said to each other. Whatever it was, the decision taken was crucial and bitter for the leaders, a matter of life and death for the other two. It was clear that Angerer was no longer in condition to climb any farther.

All of a sudden the Hinterstoisser party could be seen climbing down to the bivouac, where they remained for some time; then they all began the descent together. A human being was more important than the mere ascent of a mountain face. Perhaps the united strength of the whole party would succeed in bringing the injured man down?

They crossed the great slope of the Second Ice Field comparatively quickly, but the descent of the rock step, on the doubled rope, to the first, took several hours to accomplish. Once again the watchers were amazed at the care and assurance with which the ropes were handled. But night fell, just as the men reached the lower ice field, close to where Sedlmayer and Mehringer's second bivouac had been; they camped for their third night on the face. There could not be a stitch of dry clothing on their bodies and this third bivouac must needs sap their strength; yet three must now have enough strength for the fourth. They had only managed to come down about one thousand feet during the whole day; fully another three thousand feet of the face still gaped below them. Still, once the traverse and the Difficult Crack were behind them, the safety of the valley would not be so far away. They knew that part of the wall from having climbed down it once already.

Yes, but that traverse.

It would be the crux of this new day, Tuesday, July 21. All four seem to have stood the bivouac quite well, for they came down the ice slope to the start of the traverse at a good pace; but at that point those watching could suddenly see only three men at work. Had one of them fallen off?

Mists wreathed about the face, the wind rose, the rattle of falling stones grew sharper, avalanches of powder snow swept the track of yesterday's descent. The worst danger from falling stones would be over as soon as the four men were safely across the traverse. But where had the fourth got to?

When the cloud curtain parted again, the men at the telescopes could see all four climbers again, but Angerer, apparently *hors de combat,* was taking no part in the attempts to master the traverse. One man seemed to be taking the lead in these efforts—surely it must be Hinterstoisser, the man who first dealt with this key point on the way up. But now there is no traversing rope fixed to the rock. And the rock doesn't seem to be climbable without artificial aids.

The weather was worsening; it had in fact already broken. The water which had all along been pouring down the rocks must have hardened into ice. All the experts with field glasses could sense the fearsome tragedy to come. Retreat was cut off; nobody could move over the glassy film overlaying the rock, not even an Andreas Hinterstoisser. The precious hours of the entire morning were consumed by vain, frustrating, incredibly exhausting and dangerous attempts. And then came the last desperate decision: to climb straight down the vertical rock face, some six hundred or seven hundred feet high, which at some points bulged far out even beyond the vertical.

The only way led directly through the line of fire from stones and avalanches. Sedlmayer and Mehringer had taken a whole day to climb that pitch, and that in fine weather on dry rock. Now all hell had broken loose on the mountain. But it was their only chance. They began to get the ropes ready for the descent through thin air. It was at this moment that they heard Albert von Allmen's shouts coming up from below.

Someone shouting, so close at hand? Then things could not go wrong! A man's voice, giving strength and courage and the certainty that the bridge back to the living world was still there. And in spite of the dangers and their awareness of the seriousness of their situation, they all joined in yodeling back: "All's well!" Not a single cry for help, not even an admission of their terrifying peril. All's well.

Albert von Allmen was getting cross. How long was he expected to keep their tea warm? Presently his irritation changed to apprehension. Two whole hours had gone by since he had spoken to the climbers, and still no movement at the entrance to the gallery. Could they have climbed down past it? Could they have missed the ledge, which runs across to the window?

The sector guard went back to the door. The face was looking grim and ghastly now; visibility was very restricted; mists were steaming up everywhere. Stones and avalanches were singing their pitiless song. Albert shouted.

And back came an answer.

This time no cheery yodel, but a shocking answer coming now from one man, the last lone survivor, crying for help... Toni Kurz.

The voice of a brave, unbelievably tough young guide, cradled in Bavaria in the shadow of the Watzmann; a man who had rescued many in distress on the mountains, but who had never yet shouted for help. But now he was shouting desperately for his very life.

"Help! Help! The others are all dead. I am the only one alive. Help!"

The wind, the avalanches, and the whistling stones forbade a more exact exchange of information. In any case, Albert von Allmen by himself could bring no aid. He shouted, "We'll be coming," and hurried back into the gallery to telephone. Eigerglestcher Station, down below, answered his call.

"Allmen speaking. There's been a fearful disaster on the face. There's only one survivor. We must fetch him in. Have you any guides with you?"

Yes, there were guides down there—Hans Schlunegger, with Christian and Adolf Rubi, all from Wengen. Yes, they could come up, of their own accord even in face of instructions. It was a case of humanity triumphing over regulations. For Bohren, the chief guide of Grindelwalds, in his concern for the guides under his command, had issued a communication to the Guides' Commission in Bern, and to the Central Committee of the Swiss Alpine Club, which had also been repeated in the *Grindelwald Echo*. It ran:

> One cannot help regarding the contemplated climbing attempts on the North Face of the Eiger with serious misgivings. They are a plain indication of the great change which has taken place in the conception of the sport of mountaineering.
>
> We must accept that the visitors who take part in such attempts are aware of the dangers they are themselves risking; but no one can expect the dispatch of guides, in unfavorable conditions, on a rescue operation, in case of any further accidents on the Eiger's North Face. We should find it impossible to force our guides to take a compulsory part in the kind of acrobatics which others are undertaking voluntarily.

That was the chief guide's stated position. Nobody could have held it against the guides at Eigergletscher Station if they had refused to take a single step onto the face when they heard of the accident. But there was one man still alive. They were all determined to rescue him, to snatch him, if possible, from the clutches of that fatal wall.

The railway provided a train, which immediately took them to the gallery window at Kilometer 3.8; through it they stepped onto the face, glistening under its coat of ice. Clouds of snow dust blew into their faces as they quietly traversed diagonally upward on the slippery, treacherous ledges, till they reached a point about three hundred feet below where Toni Kurz was hanging from the rope in a sling.

There was mixed despair and relief in his voice—still astonishingly strong—as he heard his rescuers and answered them.

"I'm the only one alive. Hinterstoisser came off and fell the whole way down. The rope pulled Rainer up against a carabiner. He froze to death there. And Angerer's dead, too, hanging below me, strangled by the rope when he fell."

"All right, pal. We've come to help you!"

"I know," shouted Toni. "But you've got to come from above, to the right, up through the crack where we left some pitons on the way up. Then you could reach me by three descents on the doubled rope."

"That's impossible, pal. Nobody could climb it with this ice about."

"You can't rescue me from below," Kurz shouted back.

Day was drawing to its close. The guides would have to hurry if they were to get back safely to the gallery window before dark. They shouted up the wall, "Can you stick it for one more night, pal?"

"No! No! No!"

The words cut the guides to the quick. They were never to forget them. But any aid was out of the question in the dark, on this face, in this weather.

"Stick it, pal!" they shouted. "We'll be back first thing in the morning!"

They could hear Toni's shouts for a long time, as they climbed back down to the gallery window.

The young Berchtesgaden guide must have despaired of seeing the night through. But life had a strong hold on him; in spite of the gale, the volleys of stone, the fearsome cold, he survived the night, swinging backward and forward in his rope sling. It was so cold that the water thawed by the warmth of his body froze again immediately. Icicles eight inches long formed on the points of the crampons strapped to his boots. Toni lost the mitten from his left hand; his fingers, his hand, then his arm, froze into shapeless, immovable lumps. But when dawn came, life was still awake in his agonized body. His voice, too, was strong and clear, when the guides got in touch with him again.

Arnold Glatthard had by now joined Schlunegger and the Rubi brothers. The four guides together were ready to fight this merciless wall for the life of their young colleague from Bavaria. The rocks were covered with an appalling glaze of ice. It seemed almost impossible to climb at all. And there was Toni pleading again: "You can only rescue me from above. You must climb the crack."

It was impossible. Even Kurz and Hinterstoisser in their full strength could not have climbed the crack in such conditions. It was a pitch which even in fine weather would have seriously tested these four men, first-class guides, brought up in a great tradition, master climbers all, but little versed in the technique of modern, artificial climbing. It would have called for just that kind of "acrobatics" against which Chief Guide Bohren had taken such a strong stand.

However, the four guides succeeded in reaching a point only about one hundred thirty feet below where Toni Kurz was hanging on the rope. So far did the overhang beetle out over the abyss that they could no longer see him from there. If Kurz had another rope on which to rope himself down, he would be saved. But how to get one to him? Attempts with rockets failed. The rope went shooting past Kurz, far out from the face. There was only one thing left.

"Can you let a line down," they asked him, "so that we can attach a rope, rock pitons, and anything else you need?"

"I have no line," came the reply.

"Climb down as far as you can and cut away Angerer's body. Then climb up again and cut the rope above you. Then untwist the strands of the rope you have gained, join them, and let the resulting line down."

The answer was a groan: "I'll try."

A little while later they heard the strokes of an axe. It seemed incredible that Kurz could hold on with one frozen hand and swing the axe with the other. Yet he managed to cut the rope away; only, Angerer's body didn't fall, for it was frozen solid to the rock. Almost in a trance, answering the last dictates of the will to live, Kurz climbed up again, cut away the rope there. The maneuver had won him twenty-five feet of rope, frozen stiff. And then began the unbelievable work of untwisting the strands. Every climber knows how difficult that is, even on firm ground, with two sound hands. But Toni Kurz was suspended between heaven and earth, on an ice-glazed cliff, threatened by falling stones, sometimes swept by snow slides. He worked with one hand and his teeth for five hours.

A great avalanche fell, narrowly missing the guides. A huge block whizzed close by Schlunegger's head. And then a body came hurtling past. Toni's? No, it wasn't Toni's, but Angerer's, freed from the imprisoning ice. Those were hours of agony for Toni, fighting for his life, agonizing too for the guides, who could do nothing to help, and could only wait for the moment when Kurz might still achieve the incredible.

Presently the fabricated line came swinging down to the rescue party. They fastened a rope to it. Toni Kurz's strength was ebbing fast; he could hardly draw up the line, but somehow he managed it. Even now the rope wasn't long enough. The guides attached a second to it. The knot where the two ropes were spliced swung visible but unreachable out there under the great overhang.

Another hour passed. Then, at last, Toni Kurz was able to start roping down, sitting in a sling attached to the rope by a carabiner. Inch by inch he worked his way downward. Thirty, forty, fifty feet down. A hundred feet, a hundred and twenty. Now his legs could be seen dangling below the overhang.

At that moment the junction knot jammed in the carabiner of the sling in which Toni was sitting. The knot was too thick and Toni could not force it through the carabiner. They could hear him groaning.

"Try, lad, try!" the frustrated rescuers cried to encourage the exhausted man. Toni, mumbling to himself, made one more effort with all his remaining strength, but he had little left; his incredible efforts had used it almost all up. His will to live had been keyed to the extreme so long as he was active; now the downward journey in the safety of the rope sling had eased the tension. He was nearing his rescuers now; now the battle was nearly over, now there were others close at hand to help. And now this knot. Just a single knot.

But it won't go through.

"Just one more try, pal. It'll go!" There was a note of desperation in the guides appeal. One last revolt against fact, one last call on the last reserves of strength against this last and only obstacle. Toni bent forward, trying to use his teeth just once more. His frozen left arm with its useless hand stuck out stiff and helpless from his body. His last reserves were gone.

Toni mumbled unintelligibly, his young face dyed purple with frostbite and exhaustion, his lips just moving. Was he still trying to say something, or had his spirit already passed over to the beyond? Then he spoke again, quite clearly. "I'm finished," he said.

His body tipped forward. The sling, almost within reach of the guides, hung swinging gently far out over the gulf. The man sitting in it was dead.

A Short Walk
with Whillans

Tom Patey

from Summit Magazine, Summer 1991 Text © 1991 by Tom Patey Introduction ©
1991 by Summit Magazine Reprinted with permission by Mrs. T. Patey and Summit.

Don Whillans cut a wide swath in the climbing community. His notoriety came in equal measure from his prowess in getting up hard routes and his acerbic wit. The former made him one of the leading figures in British climbing during the 1950s. Whillans's crowning climbing achievement was his 1970 first ascent of Annapurna's South Face. He died of a heart attack in 1984, at the age of fifty-two. "A Short Walk with Whillans," written in 1963, comes from Tom Patey's hilarious book, One Man's Mountains *(1971). Patey achieved outstanding success in the Scottish hills, the Alps and the Himalayas and was a family physician in Ullapool until his tragic death on a British sea stack in 1970.*

"Did you spot that great long streak of blood on the road over from Chamonix? Twenty yards long, I'd say."

The speaker was Don Whillans. We were seated in the little inn at Alpiglen, Don's aggressive profile framed against an awe-inspiring backdrop of the Eiger Nordwand.

"Probably some unfortunate animal," I ventured without much conviction.

Whillans's eyes narrowed. "Human blood," he said. "Remember, lass?" (appealing to his wife Audrey), "I told you to stop the car for a better look. Really turned her stomach, it did. Just when she was getting over the funeral."

I felt an urge to inquire whose funeral they had attended. There had been several. Every time we went up on the Montenvers train we passed a corpse going down. I let the question go. It seemed irrelevant, even irreverent.

"Ay, it's a good life," he mused, "providing you don't weaken."

"What happens if you do?"

"They bury you," he growled, and finished his pint.

Don has that rarest of gifts, the ability to condense a whole paragraph into a single, terse, uncompromising sentence. But there are also occasions when he can become almost lyrical in a macabre sort of way. It depends on the environment.

We occupied a window table in the inn. There were several other tables, and hunched round each of these were groups of shadowy men draped in black cagoules—lean-jawed, grim, uncommunicative characters who spoke in guttural monosyllables and gazed steadfastly toward the window. You only had to glimpse their earnest faces to realize that these men were "Eiger Candidates"—martyrs for the "Mordwand" (an Eiger pseudonym coined by the German press—literally "Murder Wall").

"Look at that big black bastard up there," Whillans chuckled dryly, gesturing with his thumb. "Just waiting to get its claws into you. And think of all the young lads who've sat just where you're sitting now, and come back all tied up in sacks. It makes you think."

It certainly did. I was beginning to wish I had stayed at Chamonix, funerals or no funerals.

"Take that young blonde over there," he pointed toward the sturdy Aryan barmaid who had just replenished his glass. "I wonder how many dead men she's danced with? All the same," he concluded after a minute's reflection, "T'wouldn't be a bad way to spend your last night."

I licked my lips nervously. Don's philosophic discourses are not for the fainthearted.

One of the Eiger Candidates detached himself from a neighboring group and approached us with obvious intent. He was red haired, small and compact and he looked like a Neanderthal man. This likeness derived from his hunched shoulders and the way he craned his head forward like a man who had been struck repeatedly on the crown by a heavy hammer, and through time developed a protective overgrowth of skull. His name was Eckhart, and he was a German. Most of them still are. The odd thing about him was his laugh. It had an uncanny hollow quality. He laughed quite a lot without generating a great deal of warmth, and he wore a twisted grin which seemed to be permanently frozen onto his face. Even Whillans was moved.

"You—going—up?" he inquired.

"Nein," said Eckhart. "Nix gutt! You wait here little time, I think. Now there is much vatter." He turned up his coat collar ruefully and laughed. "Many, many stein fall....All day, all night....Stein, stein." He tapped his head significantly and laughed uproariously. "Two nights we wait at Tod Bivouac." He repeated the name as if relishing its sinister undertones. ("It means Dead Man," I said to Whillans in a hushed whisper.) "Always it is nix gutt....Vatter, stein....Stein, vatter. So we go down. It is very funny."

We nodded sympathetically. It was all a huge joke.

"Our two Kameraden, they go on. They are saying at the telescopes, one man he has fallen fifty meters. Me? I do not believe this." (Loud and prolonged laughter from the company.)

"You have looked through the telescope?" I inquired anxiously.

"Nein," he grinned, "Not necessary...tonight they gain summit... tomorrow they descend. And now we will have another beer."

Eckhart was nineteen. He had already accounted for the North Face of the Matterhorn as a training climb and he intended to camp at the foot of the Eigerwand until the right conditions prevailed. If necessary, he could wait until October. Like most of his countrymen he was nothing if not thorough, and finding his bivouac tent did not measure up to his expectations, he had hitchhiked all the way back to Munich to secure another. As a result of this, he had missed the spell of settled weather that had allowed several rivals to complete the route, including the second successful British team, Baillie and Haston, and also the lone Swiss climber, Darbellay, who had thus made the first solo ascent.

"Made of the right stuff, that youngster," observed Don.

"If you ask me I think he was trying to scare us off," I suggested. "Psychological warfare, that's all it is."

"Wait till we get on the face tomorrow," said Whillans. "We'll hear your piece then."

Shortly after noon the next day we left Audrey behind at Alpiglen, and the two of us set off up the green meadows which girdle the foot of the Eigerwand. Before leaving, Don had disposed of his Last Will and Testament. "You've got the car key, lass, and you know where to find the house key. That's all you need to know. Ta, for now."

Audrey smiled wanly. She had my profound sympathy.

The heat was oppressive, the atmosphere heavy with menace. How many Munich Bergsteigers had trod this very turf on their upward path never to return to their native Klettergarten? I was humming Wagner's Valkyrie theme music as we reached the lowest rocks of the face.

Then a most unexpected thing happened. From an alcove in the wall emerged a very ordinary Swiss tourist, followed by his very ordinary wife, five small children and a poodle dog. I stopped humming immediately. I had read of tearful farewells with wives and sweethearts calling plaintively, but this was ridiculous. What an undignified send-off! The five children accompanied us up the first snow slope scrambling happily in our wake, prodding our rucksacks with inquisitive fingers. "Go away," said Whillans irritably, but ineffectively. We were quite relieved when, ultimately, they were recalled to base and we stopped playing Pied Pipers.

"Charming, I must say," remarked Don. I wondered whether Hermann Buhl would have given up on the spot—a most irregular start to an Eiger epic and probably a bad omen.

We started climbing up the left side of the shattered pillar, a variant of the normal route which had been perfected by Don in the course of several earlier attempts. He was well on his way to becoming the Grand Old Man of Grindelwald, though not through any fault of his own. This was his fourth attempt at the climb and on every previous occasion he had been turned back by bad weather or by having to rescue his rivals. As a result of this, he must have spent more hours on the face than any other British climber.

Don's preparations for the Eiger—meticulous in every other respect—had not included unnecessary physical exertion. While I had dragged my weary muscles from Breuil to Zermatt via the Matterhorn, he whiled away the days at Chamonix, sunbathing at the Plage until opening time. At the Bar Nationale he nightly sank five or six pints of "heavy," smoked forty cigarettes, persuaded other layabouts to feed the jukebox with their last few francs and amassed a considerable reputation as an exponent of "Baby Foot," the table football game which is the national sport of France. One day, the heat had been sufficiently intense to cause a rush of blood to the head and a subsequent inspiration, because he had walked four miles up to the Montenvers following the railway track, and had acquired such enormous blisters that he had to make the return journey by train. He was nevertheless just as fit as he wanted to be, or indeed needed to be.

First impressions of the Eigerwand belied its evil reputation. This was good climbing rock with excellent friction and lots of small incuts. We climbed unroped, gaining height rapidly. In fact, I was just starting to enjoy myself when I found the boot.

"Somebody's left a boot here," I shouted to Don.

He pricked up his ears. "Look and see if there's a foot in it," he said.

I had picked it up: I put it down again hurriedly.

"Ha! Here's something else—a torn rucksack," he hissed. "And here's his water bottle—squashed flat."

I had lost my newfound enthusiasm and decided to ignore future foreign bodies. (I even ignored the pun.)

"You might as well start getting used to them now," advised Whillans. "This is where they usually glance off, before they hit the bottom."

He's a cheery character, I thought to myself. To Don, a spade is just a spade—a simple trenching tool used by grave diggers.

At the top of the Pillar, we donned our safety helmets. "One thing to remember on the Eiger," said Don, "never look up, or you may need a plastic surgeon."

His advice seemed superfluous that evening, as we did not hear a single ricochet. We climbed on up, past the Second Pillar and roped up for the traverse across to the Difficult Crack. At this late hour the crack was streaming with water, so we decided to bivouac while we were still dry. There was an excellent bivouac cave near the foot of the crack.

"I'll have one of your cigarettes," said Don. "I've only brought Gauloises." This was a statement of fact, not a question. There is something about Don's proverbial bluntness that arouses one's admiration. Of such stuff are generals made. We had a short discussion about bivouacking, but eventually I had to agree with his arguments and occupy the outer berth. It would be less likely to induce claustrophobia, or so I gathered. I was even more aware of the sudden fall in temperature. My ultra-warm Terray duvet failed by a single critical inch to meet the convertible bivvy-rucksack which I had borrowed from Joe Brown. It had been designed, so the manufacturers announced, to Joe's personal specifications, and as far as I could judge, to his personal dimensions as well.

Insidiously and from nowhere it seemed, a mighty thunderstorm built up in the valley less than a mile away. Flashes of lightning lit up the whole face and grey tentacles of mist crept out of the dusk, threatening to envelop our lofty eyrie.

"The girl in the tourist office said that a ridge of high pressure occupying the whole of central Europe would last for at least another three days."

"Charming," growled Whillans. "I could give you a better forecast without raising my head."

"We should be singing Bavarian drinking songs to keep our spirits up," I suggested. "How about some Austrian yodeling."

"They're too fond of dipping in glacier streams. That's what does it," he muttered sleepily.

"Does what?"

"Makes them yodel. All the same, these bloody Austrians."

The day dawned clear. It seemed a miracle had happened and a major thunderstorm had cleared the Eiger, without lodging on the face. Don remained inscrutable and cautious as ever. Although we were sheltered from any prevailing wind, we would have no advance warning of the weather, as our horizons were limited by the face itself.

There was still a trickle of water coming down the Difficult Crack as Don launched himself stiffly at the first obstacle. Because of our uncertainty about the weather and an argument about who should make breakfast, we had started late. It was 6:30 and we would have to hurry. He made a bad start by clipping both strands of the double rope to each of the three pitons he found in position. The rope jammed continuously and this was even more disconcerting for me, when I followed carrying both rucksacks. Hanging down the middle of the pitch was an old frayed rope, said to have been abandoned by Mademoiselle Loulou Boulaz, and this kept getting entangled with the ice axes.

By the time I had joined Don at this stance I was breathing heavily and was more than usually irritated. We used the excuse to unrope and get back into normal rhythm before tackling the Hinterstoisser. It was easy to find the route hereabouts: you merely followed the pitons. They were planted everywhere, with rotting rope loops (apparently used for abseils) attached to most of them. It is a significant insight into human psychology that nobody ever stops to remove superfluous pegs on the Eiger. If nothing else, they help to alleviate the sense of utter isolation that fills this vast face, but they also act as a constant reminder of man's ultimate destiny and the pageant of history written into the rock. Other reminders were there in plenty—gloves, socks, ropes, crampons and boots. None of them appeared to have been abandoned with the owner's consent.

The Hinterstoisser Traverse, despite the illustrations of prewar heroes traversing á la Dulfer, is nothing to get excited about. With two fixed ropes of unknown vintage as an emergency handrail, you can walk across it in three minutes. Stripped of scaffolding, it would probably qualify as Severe by contemporary British standards. The fixed ropes continued without a break as far as the Swallow's Nest—another bivouac site hallowed by tradition. Thus far I could well have been climbing the Italian Ridge of the Matterhorn.

We skirted the First Ice Field on the right, scrambling up easy rubble where we had expected to find black ice. It was abnormally warm, but if the weather held we had definite grounds for assuming that we could complete the climb in one day—our original intention. The Ice Hose which breaches the rocky barrier between the First and Second Ice Fields no longer merited the name because the ice had all gone. It seemed to offer an easy alley but Don preferred to stick to known alternatives and advanced upon an improbable-looking wall some distance across to the left. By the time I had confirmed our position on Hiebeler's route description, he had completed the pitch and was shouting for me to come on. He was well into his stride, but still did not seem to share my optimism.

His doubts were well founded. Ten minutes later, as we were crossing the water-worn slabs leading to the Second Ice Field, we saw the first falling stones. To be exact we did not see the stones, but merely the puffs of smoke each one left behind at the point of impact. They did not come bouncing down the cliff with a noisy clatter as stones usually do. In fact they were only audible after they had gone past—WROUFF!—a nasty sort of sound halfway between a suck and a blow.

"It's the small ones that make that sort of noise," explained Whillans. "Wait till you hear the really big ones!"

The blueprint for a successful Eiger ascent seems to involve being at the right place at the right time. According to our calculations the face should have been immune to stonefall at this hour of the morning.

Unfortunately, the Eiger makes its own rules. An enormous black cloud had taken shape out of what ought to have been a clear blue sky, and had come to rest on the Summit Ice Field. It reminded me of a gigantic black vulture spreading its wings before dropping like lightning on unsuspecting prey.

Down at the foot of the Second Ice Field, it was suddenly very cold and lonely. Way across to the left was the Ramp; a possible hideaway to sit out the storm. It seemed little more than a stone's throw, but I knew as well as Don did that we had almost fifteen hundred feet of steep snow-ice to cross before we could get any sort of shelter from stones.

There was no question of finding adequate cover in the immediate vicinity. On either side of us steep ice slopes, peppered with fallen debris, dropped away into the void. Simultaneously with Whillans's arrival at the stance, the first flash of lightning struck the White Spider.

"That settles it," he said, clipping the spare rope through my belay carabiner.

"What's going on?" I demanded, finding it hard to credit that such a crucial decision could be reached on the spur of the moment.

"I'm going down," he said. "That's what's going on."

"Wait a minute! Let's discuss the whole situation calmly." I stretched out one hand to flick the ash of my cigarette. Then a most unusual thing happened. There was a higher-pitched "WROUFF" than usual and the end of my cigarette disappeared! It was the sort of subtle touch that Hollywood film directors dream about.

"I see what you mean," I said. "I'm going down too."

I cannot recall coming off a climb so quickly. As a result of long ac- quaintance, Don knew the location of every abseil point and this enabled us to bypass the complete section of the climb which includes the Hinterstoisser

Traverse and the Chimney leading up to the Swallow's Nest. We merely abseiled directly downward from the last abseil point above the Swallow's Nest and reached a key piton at the top of the wall overlooking the start of the Hinterstoisser Traverse. From here, a straightforward abseil of one hundred forty feet goes vertically down the wall to the large ledge at the start of the traverse. If Hinterstoisser had realized that, he would probably not now have a traverse named after him, and the Eigerwand would not enjoy half its present notoriety. The idea of a "Point of No Return" always captures the imagination, and until very recent times, it was the fashion to abandon a fixed rope at the Hinterstoisser to safeguard a possible retreat.

The unrelenting bombardment, which had kept us hopping from one abseil to the next like demented fleas, began to slacken off as we came into the lee of the Rote Fluh. The weather had obviously broken down completely and it was raining heavily. We followed separate ways down the easy lower section of the Face, sending down volleys of loose scree in front of us. Every now and again we heard strange noises, like a series of muffled yelps, but since we appeared to have the mountain to ourselves, this did not provoke comment. Whillans had just disappeared round a nearby corner when I heard a loud ejaculation.

"God Almighty," he said (or words to that effect). "Japs! Come and see for yourself!"

Sure enough, there they were. Two identical little men in climbing uniforms, sitting side by side underneath an overhang. They had been crouching there for an hour, waiting for the bombardment to slacken. I estimated that we must have scored several near misses.

"You—Japs?" grunted Don. It seemed an unnecessary question.

"Yes, yes," they grinned happily, displaying a full set of teeth. "We are Japanese."

"Going up?" queried Whillans. He pointed meaningfully at the grey holocaust sweeping down from the White Spider.

"Yes, yes," they chorused in unison. "Up. Always upwards. First Japanese ascent."

"You-may-be-going-up-Mate," said Whillans, giving every syllable unnecessary emphasis, "but-a-lot-'igher-than-you-think!"

They did not know what to make of this, so they wrung his hand several times, and thanked him profusely for the advice.

" 'Appy little pair!" said Don. "I don't imagine we'll ever see them again."

He was mistaken. They came back seven days later after several feet of new snow had fallen. They had survived a full-scale Eiger blizzard and had reached our highest point on the Second Ice Field. If they did not receive a medal for valor, they had certainly earned one. They were the forerunners of the climbing elite of Japan, whose members now climb Mount Everest for the purpose of skiing back down again.

We got back to the Alpiglen in time for late lunch. The telescope stood forlorn and deserted in the rain. The Eiger had retired into its misty oblivion, as Don Whillans retired to his favorite corner seat by the window.

The Green Arch

John Long

We came from nowhere towns like Upland, Cucamonga, Ontario and Montclair. None of us had done anything more distinguished than chase down a fly ball or spend a couple of nights in juvenile hall, but we saw rock climbing as a means to change all that. *The Lonely Challenge, The White Spider, Straight Up*—we'd read them all, could recite entire passages by heart. It is impossible to imagine a group more fired up by the romance and glory of the whole climbing business than we were. There was just one minor problem: there were no genuine mountains in Southern California. But there were plenty of rocks. Good ones, too.

Every Saturday morning during the spring of 1972, about a dozen of us would jump into a medley of the finest junkers two hundred dollars could buy and blast for the little mountain hamlet of Idyllwild, home of Tahquitz Rock. The last twenty-six miles to Idyllwild follows a twisting road, steep and perilous in spots. More than one exhausted Volkswagen bus or wheezing old Rambler got pushed a little too hard, blew up and was abandoned, the plates stripped off and the driver, leaden with rope and pack, thumbing on toward Mecca. We *had* to get to a certain greasy spoon by eight o'clock, when our little group, the Stonemasters, would meet, discuss an itinerary, wolf down some food and storm off to the crags with all the subtlety of a spring hailstorm.

The air was charged because we were on a roll, our faith and gusto growing with each new route we bagged. The talk within the climbing community was that we were crazy, or liars, or both; and this sat well with us. We were loud-mouthed eighteen-year-old punks, and proud of it.

Tahquitz was one of America's hot climbing spots, with a pageant of pivotal ascents reaching back to when technical climbing first came to the States. America's first 5.8 (The Mechanic's Route) and 5.9 (The Open Book) routes were bagged at Tahquitz, as was the notion and the deed of the "first free ascent," a route first done with aid but later climbed without it (The Piton Pooper, 5.7, circa 1946). John Mendenhall, Chuck Wilts, Mark Powell, Royal Robbins, Tom Frost, T. M. Herbert, Yvon Chouinard, Bob Kamps and many others had all learned the ropes there.

The Stonemasters arrived about the same time that the previous generation of local hardcores—a high-blown group consisting of would-be photographers and assistant professors—was being overtaken by house payments and squealing brats. They hated every one of us. We were all ninety cents away from having a buck, ragged as roaches, eating the holes out of doughnuts—and we cared nothing for their endorsement. We'd grappled up many of their tougher climbs, not with grace, but with pure gumption and fire, and the limelight was panning our way.

The old guard was confounded that we of so little talent and experience should get so far. When it became common knowledge that we were taking a bead on the hallowed Valhalla (one of the first 5.11 routes in America)—often tried, but as yet unrepeated—they showed their teeth. If we so much as dreamed of climbing Valhalla, we'd have to wake up and apologize. The gauntlet was thus thrown down: if they wouldn't hand over the standard, we'd rip it from their hands. When, after another month, we all had climbed Valhalla, some of us several times, the old boys were stunned and saw themselves elbowed out of the opera house by kids who could merely scream. And none could scream louder than Tobin Sorenson, the most conspicuous proponent of a madman to ever lace up Varappes.

Climbing had never seen the likes of Tobin, and probably never will again. He had the body of a welterweight, a lick of sandy brown hair and the faraway gaze of the born maniac; yet he lived with all the precocity and innocence of a child. He would never cuss or show the slightest hostility. Around girls he was so shy he'd flush and stammer. But out on the sharp end of the rope he was a fiend in human form. Over the previous summer he'd logged an unprecedented string of gigantic falls that should have ended his career, and his life, ten times over. Yet he shook each fall off and clawed straight back onto the route for another go, and usually got it. He became a world-class climber very quickly, because someone that well formed and savagely motivated will gain the top in no time—if he doesn't kill himself first. Still, when we started bagging new routes and first free ascents, Tobin continued defying the gods with his electrifying peelers. The exploits of his short life deserve a book. Two books.

One Saturday morning five or six of us hunkered down in our little restaurant in Idyllwild. Tahquitz was our oyster. We'd pried it open with a piton and for months had gorged at will; but the fare was running thin. Since we had ticked off one after another of the old aid routes, our options had dwindled to only the most grim or preposterous ones. But, during the previous week, Ricky Accomazzo had scoped out the Green Arch, an elegant arc on Tahquitz's southern shoulder. When Ricky mentioned he thought there was an outside chance that this pearl of an aid climb might go free, Tobin looked as though the Hound of the Baskervilles had just heard the word "bone," and we nearly had to lash him to the booth so we could finish our oatmeal.

Since the Green Arch was Ricky's idea, he got the first go at it by rights. Tobin balked, so we tied him off to a stunted pine and Ricky started up. After fifty feet of dicey wall climbing, he gained the arch, which soared vertically above for another eighty feet before curving right and disappearing in a field of big knobs and pockets. If we could only get to those knobs, the remaining three hundred feet would go easily and the Green Arch would fall. But the lower corner and the arch above looked bleak. The crack in the back of the arch was too thin to accept even fingertips, and both sides of the corner were blank and marble-smooth. Yet by pasting half his rump on one side of the puny corner, and splaying his feet out on the opposite side, Ricky stuck to the rock—barely—both his butt cheek and his boots steadily oozing off the steep, greasy wall. It was exhausting duty just staying put, and moving up was accomplished in a grueling, precarious sequence of quarter-inch moves. Amazingly, Ricky jackknifed about halfway up the arch before his calves pumped out. He lowered off a bunk piton and I took a shot.

After an hour of the hardest climbing I'd ever done, I reached a rest hold just below the point where the arch arched out right to melt into that field of knobs. Twenty feet to pay dirt. But that twenty feet didn't look promising.

There were some sucker knobs just above the arch, but those ran out after about twenty-five feet and would leave a climber in the bleakest no-man's-land, with nowhere to go, no chance to climb back right onto the route, no chance to get any protection, and no chance to retreat. We'd have to stick to the arch.

Finally, I underclung about ten feet out the arch, whacked in a suspect knifeblade, clipped the rope in—and fell off. I lowered to the ground, slumped back, and didn't rise for ten minutes. I had matching and weeping strawberries on both ass cheeks, and my ankles were all rubbery and tweaked from splaying them out on the far wall.

Tobin, unchained from the pine, tied into the lead rope and stormed up the corner like a man fleeing Satan on foot. He battled up to the rest hold, drew a few quick breaths, underclung out to that creaky, buckled, driven-straight-up-into-an-expando-flake knifeblade, and immediately cranked himself over the arch and started heaving up that line of sucker knobs.

"No!" I screamed up. "Those knobs don't go anywhere!" But it was too late.

Understand that Tobin was a born-again Christian, that he'd smuggled Bibles into Bulgaria risking twenty-five years on a Balkan rock-pile, that he'd studied God at a fundamentalist university, and that none of this altered the indisputable fact that he was perfectly mad. Out on the sharp end he not only ignored all consequences, but actually loathed them, doing all kinds of crazy, incomprehensible things to mock them. (The following year, out at Joshua Tree, Tobin followed a difficult, overhanging crack with the rope noosed around his neck.) Most horrifying was his disastrous capacity to simply charge at a climb pell mell. On straightforward routes, no one was better. But when patience and cunning were required, no one was worse. Climbing, as it were, with blinders on, Tobin would sometimes claw his way into the most grievous jams. When he'd dead-end and have to stop, with nowhere to go and looking at a Homeric peeler, the full impact of his folly would hit him like a wrecking ball. He would suddenly panic, wail, weep openly, and do the most ludicrous things. And sure enough, about twenty-five feet above the arch those sucker knobs ran out, and Tobin had nowhere to go.

He was, in fact, looking at a fifty-foot fall—*if* that blade I'd bashed under the roof held. But I *knew* it would not. At best, it might sufficiently break his fall for the next lower piece to stop him. That piece was ten feet below the shitty blade, at the rest hold, so Tobin was looking at a seventy-footer, a tad more with rope stretch.

As Tobin wobbled far overhead, who should lumber up to our little group but his very father, a minister, a quiet, retiring, imperturbable gentleman who hacked and huffed from his long march up to the cliff side. After hearing so much about climbing from Tobin, he'd finally come to see his son in action. He couldn't have shown up at a worse time. It was like a page from a B-movie script—us cringing and digging in, waiting for the bomb to drop; the good pastor, wheezing through his moustaches, sweat-soaked and confused, squinting up at the fruit of his loins; and Tobin, knees knocking like castanets, sobbing pitifully and looking to plunge off at any second.

There is always something you can do, even in the grimmest situations, if only you keep your nerve. But Tobin was gone, totally gone, so mastered by terror that he seemed willing to die to be rid of it. He glanced down. His face was a study. Suddenly he screamed, "Watch me! I'm gonna jump." We didn't immediately understand what he meant.

"Jump off?" Richard yelled.

"Yes!" Tobin wailed.

"NO!" we all screamed in unison.

"You can do it, son!" the pastor put in.

Pop was just trying to put a good face on it, God bless him, but his was the worst possible advice because there was no way Tobin could do it. Or anybody could do it. There were no holds! But inspired by his father's urging, Tobin reached out for those knobs so very far to his right, now lunging, now hopelessly pawing the air like a falling man clasps for the cargo net.

And then he was off. The blade shot out and Tobin shot off into the grandest fall I've ever seen a climber take and walk away from—a spectacular, cartwheeling whistler. His arms flailed like a rag doll's, and his blood-curdling scream could have frozen brandy. He finally jolted onto the rope, hanging upside down and moaning softly. We slowly lowered him off and he lay motionless on the ground and nobody moved or spoke or even breathed. You could have heard a pine needle hit the deck. Tobin was peppered with abrasions and had a lump the size of a pot roast over one eye. He lay dead still for a moment longer, then wobbled to his feet and shuddered like an old cur crawling from a creek.

"I'll get it next time," he grumbled.

"There ain't gonna be no next time!" said Richard.

There was, but it came four years later. In one of the most famous leads of that era, Ricky flashed the entire arch on his first try. Tobin and I followed.

Tobin would go on to solo the north face of the Matterhorn, the Walker Spur and the Shroud on the Grandes Jorasses (all in Levis), would make the first alpine ascent of the Harlin Direct on the Eiger, the first ascent of the Super Couloir on the Dru, would repeat the hardest free climbs and big walls in Yosemite, and sink his teeth into the Himalaya. He was arguably the world's most versatile climber during the late 1970s. But nothing had really changed: he always climbed as if time were too short for him, pumping all the disquietude, anxiety, and nervous waste of a normal year into each route.

I've seen a bit of the world since those early days at Tahquitz, have done my share of crazy things, and have seen humanity with all the bark on, primal and raw. But I've never since experienced the electricity of watching Tobin out there on the very quick of the long plank, clawing for the promised land. He finally found it in 1980, attempting a solo ascent of Mount Alberta's north face. It was a tragedy, of course. Yet I sometimes wonder if God Himself could no longer bear the strain of watching Tobin wobbling and lunging way out there on the sharp end of the rope, and finally just drew him into the fold.

from Annapurna

Maurice Herzog

from "ANNAPURNA", published 1952 by Lyons and Burford,
31 W. 215 Street, NY, NY, 10010

The French ascent of Annapurna was the first ascent of the mountain; the first ascent of an eight-thousand-meter peak, a feat attempted over thirty times by parties of various nations; the first successful French Himalayan expedition; and the last time leader Maurice Herzog would ever climb. After battling through avalanches and cold so horrendous that "it absolutely perished me" (according to fellow climber Lionel Terray), Herzog and partner Louis Lachanal summited on June 3, 1950. The victory cost both climbers their toes; loosing his gloves on the descent to the highest camp cost Herzog all of his fingers. Their ghastly retreat off the mountain and back to Kathmandu—both Herzog and Lachanal were carried out on the backs of porters—was no less remarkable and chilling than their ascent, entailing perilous crossings over raging rivers, torturous injections and almost daily amputations. Months later, in the American Hospital at Neuilly, Herzog dictated "the story of a terrible adventure that we survived only by an incredible series of miracles." Told in a straightforward style tempered with the heroic decorum unique to that era, Annapurna remains the quintessential mountaineering epic, unsurpassed in power and effect. We here excerpt the last two pages of Herzog's timeless narrative, dictated during his penultimate day in Nepal before the long voyage home.

On July 12, 1950, we left Kathmandu. According to custom, our shoulders were draped with magnificent garlands of sweetly scented flowers. The Maharajah, full of thoughtful attentions, had ensured that my return should be effected as comfortably as possible, and I was borne out on a luxurious litter carried by eight men; the all too familiar jerky movements resumed as we wound up toward the pass.

G. B. accompanied me as far as the first turn. He had served us most loyally and as an expression of my personal appreciation I made him a gift of my revolver which, during all the desperate war years, had never left my side. It is an unknown weapon in these parts and he was deeply touched by this memento. For the rest of his life, it would remind him of our joint adventure. G. B. saluted me with an expression of infinite sadness, the tears running down his brown face. He continued walking beside me for a time, and then gradually dropped behind.

The path wound up toward the hill and soon lost itself in the jungle. The garland of flowers spread its fragrance around me. I gazed one last time at the mountains in the blue distance, where the great giants of the earth were gathered in all their dazzling beauty.

The others were far ahead. The jolting began anew, bearing me away from what would soon be a land of memories. In the gentle languor into which I sank, I tried to envisage my first contact with the civilized world, of landing at Orly and meeting family and friends. In fact, I could not then imagine the violent emotional shock I would experience nor the sudden nervous depression that would take hold of me. The countless surgical operations in the field—that sickening butchery that shook even the toughest natives—had gradually deadened our souls, and we were no longer able to value the true horror of it all. A toe carved off and tossed away; blood flowing and spurting; the unbearable stench of suppurating wounds—all this left us unmoved.

In the airplane before landing, Lachanal and I would put on fresh bandages for our arrival. But the minute we started down that iron ladder, all those generous eyes looking up at us with such pity would at once tear aside the masks behind which we had steeled ourselves for so long. We were not to be pitied—and yet, the tears in those eyes and the expressions of distress would suddenly bring me face to face with reality. Such a strange consolation for my sufferings to have brought me!

Rocking in my litter, I meditated on our adventure now drawing to a close, and on our unexpected victory. Men often talk of an ideal as a goal toward which one strives but never attains; yet for each of us, Annapurna was an ideal realized. In our youth we had not been misled by fantasies, nor by the bloody battles of modern warfare that pervert the imaginations of the young. For us the mountains formed a natural field of activity where, playing on the frontiers of life and death, we had found the freedom we had sought without knowing it and which was the ultimate need of our nature. The mountains had bestowed on us their beauty and grace and we adored them with a child's simplicity and revered them with a monk's veneration.

The Annapurna we approached in spiritual poverty is now the treasure on which we live. With this realization, we turn the page: A new life begins.

There are other Annapurnas in the lives of men.

The South Face
of Mt. Watkins

Chuck Pratt

Originally appeared in the 1965 American Alpine Journal
from Ascent Magazine, winter 1970 © 1970 by the Sierra Club
Reprinted with permission by the Sierra Club

The historic first ascent of Yosemite Valley's El Capitan in 1958 opened a new era in Yosemite climbing. In subsequent years, three additional routes, each more than twenty-five hundred feet in height, were established on the great monolith. El Capitan's great height, the sustained nature of the climbing and the resulting logistical problems required that the first ascents of these routes be accomplished in stages, with the use of fixed ropes to facilitate a retreat to the valley floor. Since the initial ascent of El Capitan, eight ascents of the various routes have been made, and climbers involved in the latter-day pioneering have gained great confidence and experience in sustained, multi-day climbing. By the summer of 1964, with new improvements in hauling methods and equipment, the time seemed ripe for someone to attempt a first ascent of such a climb in a single, continuous effort.

One of the few walls that had remained unclimbed by the summer of 1964, and that afforded a challenge comparable to El Capitan, was the south face of Mount Watkins. Rising twenty-eight hundred feet above Tenaya Creek at the east end of Yosemite, Mount Watkins rivals in grandeur even nearby Half Dome. Despite the obvious and significant challenge presented by the face, the mention of Watkins only bored the resident climbers of Camp 4. Though many of them, including me, speculated on who would climb it, none of us were moved into action. Then, one pleasant July evening at Warren Harding's High Sierra camp on the shore of Lake Tenaya, when the wine and good fellowship were flowing in greater quantity than usual, Warren produced a flattering photograph of the south face and invited me to join him. We enthusiastically shook hands, confident that the fate of Mount Watkins had been sealed.

Several days later we were strolling through Camp 4, two rash climbers looking for a third, having agreed that on this climb a three-man party was a fair compromise between mobility and safety. However, our recruiting was unrewarded. The experienced were not interested; those interested lacked the necessary experience. By evening we had resigned ourselves to a two-man party when Yvon Chouinard walked out of the darkness. He had ten days to spare and wondered if there were any interesting climbs planned.

Within the week, after a reconnaissance trip to study the face and plan a route, we were assembling food, climbing equipment and bivouac gear for a four-day attempt on the face. The three-mile approach to Mount Watkins began at Mirror Lake. As we unloaded packs at the parking lot, two young ladies approached us and asked if we were some of *the* Yosemite climbers. Yvon pleaded guilty and pointed out our destination. They asked if it were true that Yosemite climbers chafe their hands on the granite to enable them to friction up vertical walls. We assured them that this was true as well. Then, with perfect timing, Harding yanked a bottle of wine and a six-pack out of the car, explaining that these were our rations for four days. We left the young ladies wondering about the good judgment of Yosemite climbers. And so the legends grow.

After following the Sierra Loop Trail for two miles, we eventually began contouring the slopes above Tenaya Creek until we reached the base of Mount Watkins, where we sought out a suitable camping spot for the night. In the darkness, we noted with apprehension that the granite bulk of Mount Watkins completely obliterated the northern quadrant of the sky. The following morning we awoke grim and silent. With lowered eyes we approached the base of the wall.

Unlike most major Yosemite climbs, Mount Watkins had very little climbing history. Warren had been seven hundred feet up some years before, and climbers had studied the face from the southern rim of the valley, but ours would be the first and all-out push for the summit. On his brief reconnaissance, Warren had been stopped by an eighty-foot head wall above a large, tree-covered ledge. During our study of the face three days before, we had elected to follow his route as it involved only third- and fourth-class climbing and would allow us to gain a great deal of altitude on the first day. By climbing a prominent corner at the left end of the tree-covered ledge, we could gain enough height to execute a series of pendulums in order to reach a comfortable-looking ledge at the top of the head wall, thus eliminating the necessity of bolting eighty feet. This ledge would then access an eight-hundred-foot dihedral system on the right side of the face. The dihedral eventually connected with a thin, curving arch leading westward across the wall. We hoped this arch would take us to the great buttress in the center of the face and that the buttress would in turn take us the remaining five hundred feet to the summit. However, these speculations would be resolved only after several days of sustained, technical climbing. The personal challenge, the unsuspected hardships, the uncertainty; in short, the unknown, which separates an adventure from the commonplace, was the most appealing and stimulating aspect of the climb to which we had committed ourselves.

Our immediate concern was transporting one hundred pounds of food, water and equipment up to Warren's previous high point. Loading everything into two large packs, Warren and I struggled up the hand lines left by Yvon as he led ahead of us up an intricate series of ledges and ramps. By noon we reached the tree-covered ledge and the base of the head wall where Warren had turned back before. Having volunteered to haul the first day, I began repacking our loads into three duffel bags while Warren and Yvon worked their way up the shallow corner at the left end of the ledge. Two free-climbing pitches brought them to a ledge where they analyzed the problems of the long pendulums necessary to reach our goal for the first day—the comfortable-looking ledge eighty feet above me at the top of the head wall. By midafternoon, Yvon had descended seventy-five feet, climbed across a delicate face and after trying for half an hour to place a piton, then resigned himself to a bolt. Descending once more, he began a series of spectacular swings trying to reach the ledge above the head wall. After numerous failures he finally succeeded by lunging for the ledge after a sixty-foot swing across the face. Warren rappelled to Yvon, and after dropping me a fixed rope, joined him in an effort to reach the great dihedral which we hoped to follow for four hundred feet.

Prusiking up the fixed rope, I could watch Yvon leading an overhanging jam crack in the dihedral. From the ledge, I began hauling all three bags together. I was using a hauling method developed by Royal Robbins for the El Capitan routes. It consisted of a haul line passed through a pulley at the hauler's anchor. By attaching a prusik knot or a jumar to the free end of the line, it was possible for me to haul the loads by pushing down with my foot in a sling instead of hauling up with my arms. The method was highly efficient and far less tiring than hauling hand-over-hand.

Yvon and Warren returned to the ledge after leaving two hundred feet of fixed rope, and we settled down for the first bivouac of the climb. After only one day on the wall it was evident to all that our greatest difficulty would be neither the climbing nor the logistics, but the weather. It was the middle of July and temperatures in the valley were consistently in the high nineties. We had allowed ourselves one and one-half quarts of water per day per person—the standard quantity for a sustained Yosemite climb. Still, we were not prepared for the intense, enervating heat in which we had found ourselves sweltering for an entire day. Those mountaineers who scorn Yosemite and its lack of alpine climbing would find it an interesting education to spend a few days on a long valley climb in midsummer. Cold temperatures and icy winds are not the only adverse kinds of weather.

The following morning Warren and I ascended the fixed ropes and continued climbing the great dihedral, hoping to reach its top by the end of the day. The climbing was both strenuous and difficult, as we resorted more and more to thin horizontal pitons and knifeblades driven into shallow, rotten cracks. However, our biggest problem continued to be the unbearable heat; we were only occasionally relieved of it by a slight breeze. Although we tried to refrain from drinking water during the day so as to have at least a full quart each to sip at night, we were all constantly digging into the climbing packs for water bottles. Every few minutes we found it necessary to moisten our throats, since even a few breaths of the dry, hot air aggravated our savage thirst. Even the hauling, which should have been a simple task, became a major problem. Yvon, who was hauling that day, exhausted himself on every pitch, becoming increasingly tired as the day wore on.

In the early afternoon, we were surprised by the passing of a golden eagle across the face. Welcoming the chance for a brief respite, we stopped climbing and watched as the magnificent bird glided effortlessly high above us. Although he presented an inspiring sight, we hoped his nest didn't lie on our route. In the days to come, this eagle would make a ritual of crossing the face, sometimes as often as three or four times a day, as though he were a silent guardian appointed to note the progress of the three intruders who labored so slowly through his realm of rock and sky.

By the end of the second day, we reached a group of ledges so large and comfortable that we named them the "Sheraton-Watkins." It was here that we were faced with the first major setback in our carefully planned route. The top of the dihedral was still some two hundred feet above us, and those two hundred feet presented not only rotten, flaky rock and incipient cracks, but also the probability of requiring placement of a large number of bolts. Now that we were within two hundred feet of the prominent arch we had seen from the ground, we could see clearly that it did not connect with the large buttress in the center of the face, but that a gap of one hundred feet or more separated them. The prospect of bolting across one hundred feet of blank wall so appalled us that we began searching for other avenues of approach to the middle of the face. We were in a deep corner, the left wall of which presented messy but continuous cracks leading eighty feet to a ledge on the main wall. From this ledge, it appeared that a short lead would end on the first of a series of broken ramps sweeping west across the face. It seemed the only reasonable alternative, and we had just enough light left to ascend one pitch to the ledge eighty feet above before settling down on "Sheraton-Watkins."

We were up early the morning of the third day in order to accomplish as much as possible before the sun began its debilitating work. From our high point, Yvon began the next lead. It was here that we began to literally walk out on a limb. We could see the broken ramps leading several hundred feet across the face. Once we left the dihedral, retreat would become increasingly more difficult. Not only would the route beyond have to be possible, but we would have to consistently make the correct decisions as to which route to follow. Using every RURP and knifeblade we had brought, plus three bolts, Yvon succeeded in reaching the start of the first ramp. Then I began the first of three leads that were to carry us three hundred feet across the face. Although the climbing was moderate fifth class, it required a great deal of effort. After nearly three days of climbing, the heat had reduced our strength and efficiency to the point where we moved at a snail's pace. Warren was barely able to manage hauling the bags without assistance, and most of the afternoon was spent getting our little expedition across the traverse. Although we had not gained much altitude, our efforts were finally rewarded when the traverse carried us into the buttress in the center of the face. Once again resorting to the indispensable RURPs and knifeblades, I led a delicate and circuitous pitch past a dangerously loose flake to a curving arch. After following the arch as far as possible, I descended, leaving what I thought would be a simple pendulum for tomorrow's climbing team. We were now situated on widely spread but comfortable ledges, and as we nibbled on our ever-decreasing supply of cheese, salami and gorp, we caught a glimpse of our friend the eagle as he passed on his daily rounds.

At the end of this, the third day of climbing, we were well aware of our critical situation. We had brought enough water for four days. It was now obvious that we could not reach the summit in less than five. Seven hundred feet remained between us and the giant ceiling at the lip of the summit and the route remained uncertain. We reluctantly agreed that it would be necessary to reduce our ration of water to provide enough for at least one additional day on the face. We did not yet consider the possibility of retreating although the prospect of facing the unbearable heat with less than an inadequate supply of water filled us with dismay.

The fourth day proved to be one of the most difficult and uncertain any of us had ever spent on a climb. The sun continued its merciless torture as Yvon and Warren returned to the struggle. Warren found that I had underestimated the pendulum. After an agonizing effort, he finally succeeded in swinging to a ledge and I proceeded up to haul. By midafternoon, after climbing as slowly as turtles up the central buttress, we reached the most critical point of the climb. Above us a blank, sixty-foot head wall topped by an overhang blocked further progress. Warren had nearly fainted several times from the heat, Yvon was speechless with fatigue and I was curled up in a semistupor trying to utilize a small patch of shade beneath an overhanging boulder. In an effort to provide more shade we stretched a bivouac hammock over our heads, but it provided little protection. For the first time we considered the possibility of retreating, but even that would require another day on the wall. It seemed that those very qualities which had made the climb so appealing might now prove to be our undoing.

Warren investigated the possibility of rappelling one hundred feet to the opposite corner of the buttress. However, we did not want to lose one hundred feet of hard-earned altitude, especially since we could not be certain that the left side of the buttress continued to the summit. After a barely audible consultation, we decided to try the head wall above us, eventually hoping that we would find cracks leading to the summit, still five hundred feet above us.

Warren volunteered to go up first. After placing three bolts, he came down, too exhausted to continue. I went up next and with extreme difficulty placed two more, the first direct aid bolts I had ever placed, barely adequate, even for aid. Yvon took my place, and after breaking two drills was able to place one more before relinquishing the lead to Warren. Instead of placing more bolts, Warren lassoed a small tree and prusiked fifteen feet to a horizontal crack. In a magnificent display of spirit and determination, he continued the lead over the head wall, did some extremely difficult free climbing and reached a ledge adequate for a belay. Refreshed in spirit if not in body, Yvon followed the lead in semidarkness, marveling at Warren's endurance. Leaving a fixed rope, they returned and we all collapsed gratefully on barely adequate ledges.

By the fourth day, Yvon had lost so much weight from dehydration that he could lower his climbing knickers without undoing a single button. For the first time in seven years, I was able to remove a ring from my finger. And Harding, whose resemblance to the classical conception of Satan is legendary, took on an even more gaunt and sinister appearance.

We slept late the fifth morning and awoke somewhat refreshed. Confident that we would reach the summit by nightfall, we ascended the fixed rope to study the remaining four hundred feet. Once again, we were faced with a critical decision. Continuous cracks led to within one hundred feet of the summit, but it appeared that they would involve nailing a long, detached flake. Yvon led an awkward pitch that curved to the left around a corner. After joining him, I dropped down and swung to the left corner of the buttress. Still, I was unable to see if that corner of the buttress continued to the summit. I decided to climb the cracks above Yvon. They were of jam crack width and I pushed the free climbing to my limit to conserve the few bongs we had brought. After a fierce struggle through bushes, I was able to set up a belay in slings. That morning we had had two full quarts of water for the three of us. Yvon and I had already finished one quart, and when he joined me I was surprised to find he still had a full quart. Warren had refused to take any water that day, preferring to give the climbing team every advantage. His sacrifice was a display of courage and discipline that I have rarely seen equaled.

With added incentive, Yvon led a mixed pitch up a strenuous and rotten chimney, executing some gymnastics at its top to gain a narrow ledge. He joyfully announced that the next pitch appeared to be easy aid climbing and that the summit was only two hundred feet above him. Anxious now for the top, I climbed as rapidly as I could, while Warren struggled resolutely below with the bags. What we thought was a detached flake turned out to be a one-hundred-foot column, split on either side by a perfect angle crack. The right-hand crack seemed to require fewer bongs, so I quickly nailed my way to the column's top, a flat triangular ledge only eighty feet from the summit. It appeared that the next lead would just skirt the gigantic ceiling at the lip of the summit.

Yvon, resorting one last time to RURPs and knifeblades, tapped his way to the crest of Mount Watkins just as the sun went down. His triumphant shout told me what we had all waited five days to hear. When Warren reached the ledge, he asked to clean the last pitch as he felt that he had not contributed enough that day! Warren Harding, who had been the original inspiration for the climb, whose determination had gotten us over the head wall below and who had sacrificed his ration of water after five days of intense thirst, felt that he had not done enough! I passed him the rope and as he began cleaning the last pitch of the climb, I settled down on the ledge with my thoughts.

In the vanishing twilight, the valley of the Yosemite seemed to me more beautiful than I had ever seen it, more serene than I had ever known it before. For five days the south face of Mount Watkins had dominated our lives as only nature can dominate the lives of men. With the struggle over and our goal achieved, I was conscious of an inner calm that I had experienced only on El Capitan. I thought of my incomparable friend Chouinard and of our unique friendship—a friendship now shared with Warren—for we were united by a bond far stronger and more lasting than any we could find in the world below. I wondered what thoughts were passing through the minds of my companions during the final moments. My own thoughts rambled back through the entire history of Yosemite climbing—from that indomitable Scotsman Anderson, who first climbed Half Dome, to John Salathe, whose philosophy and climbing ethics had dominated Yosemite climbing for nearly twenty years, to Mark Powell, Salathe's successor, who showed us all that climbing can be a way of life and a basis for a philosophy. These men, like ourselves had come to the Valley with a restless spirit and the desire to share an adventure with their friends. We had come as strangers, full of apprehension and doubt. Having given all we had to the climb, we had been enriched by a physical and spiritual experience few men can know. Having accepted the hardships as a natural consequence of our endeavor, we were rewarded by a gift of victory and fulfillment for which we would be forever grateful. It was for this that each of us had come to Yosemite, and it was for this that we would return, season after season.

My reverie was interrupted by a shout from above and in the full, rich moonlight I prusiked to the top where Yvon was waiting for me. Warren had hiked to the summit cap to see if anyone had come to meet us. He returned alone and the three of us shared some of the happiest moments of our lives. As we turned away from the rim to hike to Snow Creek and some much-needed water, I caught a last glimpse of our eagle, below us for the first time. In the moonlight, he glided serenely across the face as majestic as always, and as undisturbed by our presence as he had been five days before.

Glacier Driving

Jim Sharp

I miscalculated, and it was too late to recover. My airplane hit hard on a wing and cartwheeled up the canyon. The landing gear smashed through the floor in a cloud of dust and flying Plexiglass™. Flung hard against the sides of the cockpit, I hit the instrument panel.

I reached up to turn off the master switch so we wouldn't explode, but the upper part of the cockpit was missing. So much for that familiar ritual.

Rain drummed onto the fabric of the fuselage. Drops hit the hot cylinders—crack, sizzle, pop. Three of the four bolts holding the seat had sheared; I was pitched forward, against the shoulder harness. The landing gear had broken my leg. My head ached and my chest hurt like hell.

My passenger appeared through the rain. I told him about the emergency equipment that had flown out early in the crash; he went down into a draw and retrieved it. His name was Don Lee. He didn't know it yet, but he had five compressed vertebrae among other injuries. Lee had been living in the bush. He was young, he was strong, and he was undoubtedly in shock. He returned with the sleeping bags, helped me out of the wreck, and set up camp under the wing. It pays to choose your passengers carefully in Alaska.

We ended up at "Providence Hotel," as that old bold pilot Don Sheldon called the Anchorage hospital. Lee had been living in the wild, doing what he pleased, and he didn't much cotton to hospital life. He mended as quickly as he grew tired of what he perceived to be the most constraining form of life short of jail. To make the time pass, he took to flirting with the nurses. They loved him, and he loved them.

I was bedeviled, stalling and spinning in my sleep. Word came that the two people in the other plane, the missing craft we had searched for and found, had been killed. The dead pilot's wife called to thank me for helping, and then she kept wondering why it had to be her husband. Both planes crashed on separate sides of the same draw; by some strange coincidence, both had traveled the exact same distance from the point of impact. But we had lived and they had died. Why? I told her I didn't know.

It didn't take long to realize that the Providence Hotel was doing us no good, so they finally let us out. We rode north in the company station wagon, flat on our backs, listening to Willie Nelson, rolling gently over the frost heaves of the Parks Highway, rolling home to Talkeetna.

A week or so later, some tourists came by and wanted a scenic flight around the Ruth Glacier. Kitty Banner was working in the office and she gave me a wink. I donned a turtleneck over my upper body cast and, using a brace, hoisted myself into the cockpit while Kitty kept the passengers entertained. Everything went fine, except that on landing I couldn't quite reach the flaps lever. Finally I asked my passenger, "Ma'am, do you mind pulling that lever down there, between the seats, yes, that's the one." Later, on the ground, she allowed as how she had never met a more barrel-chested man in her life, and with such good posture, too, not since the passing of her late husband, a career man in the Corps.

When it comes to Alaskan air crashes, the name that comes to mind is Sheldon. He went through thirty-nine airplanes in thirty years of flying. Most of them wore out and got traded in, though seven or eight experienced "accelerated depreciation." But during his last decade Sheldon didn't bust up a single airplane. Economics was a factor, probably. It's hard enough to make money in the air-taxi business. Even without accidents.

I first met Sheldon in the late sixties when he flew our expedition to the south buttress of Denali. I had a pretty fresh pilot's license, and Sheldon broke all the rules I had just taken the trouble to learn. He flew a Cessna 180, loaded to the ceiling with climbers and gear. He hugged ridges, made cowboy turns and spun yarns—all at the same time. It was a good show, complete with sleight of hand, defiance of gravity and vaudeville antics. His flying impressed me.

Not long afterward, I came across an old Cessna 180 in New Mexico. I flew it around for a couple of years, landing in hayfields, on beaches and dirt roads practicing for my return north. In the fall of 1974, I returned to Talkeetna in my own plane. Sheldon had just endured a pretty heavy bout with cancer, and he looked a lot older than I remembered, thin and drawn.

It was hunting season and lots of customers were waiting to be flown in—squinty-eyed, radiator-shop types out for blood. Sheep season started after the glaciers softened up in August. Most of the flying was Super Cub work, with desperate little sandbars and hillside strips, and long hours skimming ridges looking for rams. Sometimes it was real hard to find a place to land. One pilot I knew, old Fred Potts from McCarthy, used to find a likely spot from the air and parachute out an assistant with a shovel to build him a strip. "Adios, amigo, happy landings. Build me a good one and we'll eat in town tonight!"

Moose season followed sheep season. There's considerably more to a moose than there is to a sheep. I remember standing on a slippery float trying to horse a big chunk of moose meat into the cabin, watching the floats sink under the weight of the moose and three great white hunters, wondering just how we were going to get off that small lake now that the wind had died down.

Don Sheldon seemed to thrive under this kind of adversity. He chatted on as he gassed the plane, sitting up on the wing in white coveralls and watch cap, full of his famous boyish exuberance. It was this eternal enthusiasm that I found hard to account for after putting in a few seasons myself. Much of a glacier pilot's life is dull, repetitive, hard work. For every hour in the air you must spend two on the ground, loading the airplane, fueling, cleaning the windshield and filling out paperwork. That old adage about flying—long hours of boredom punctuated by moments of sheer terror—holds true.

None of this side of flying troubled Sheldon, though. Not after thirty years and tens of thousands of hours in the air, not after lugging moose meat and headhunters and smelly climbers around south-central Alaska, and not even under the shadow of terminal illness did he ever lose his enthusiasm. He was one of the few men I have met who seemed entirely fulfilled by his work.

As good as Sheldon was at flying, he was not a teacher. I would ask him a question and halfway through the explanation he would launch into a yarn. It took Mike Fisher, a Talkeetna Pilot who had flown for Sheldon, to unravel the mysteries of glacier flying. "Why, it's just like landing in a big snowy cow pasture," he began. And then he would modulate into a well-thought-out theoretical explanation.

Glaciers, of course, have gradients. The steeper the gradient, the shorter the distance the aircraft will be able to land and take off in. Hermann Geiger demonstrated this principle forty years ago in the Alps with a Piper Cub. The heavier Cessna 180s and 185s we used on Denali couldn't maneuver as easily on steep terrain, but they took us to some amazing nooks and crannies nevertheless. Still, it was scary business. Takeoffs could be especially exciting—sometimes the terrain just dropped out from beneath the airplane. We would go negative gravity and float up in our seat belts as we began to free-fall, down, down, until the airspeed picked up, the wings generated lift, and we were flying.

Reading the gradient of a glacier as you fly toward it is hard because of the lack of visual clues. I was with Sheldon once when he dropped some spruce boughs onto the glacier. Then, on final pass, he lined up on the boughs. As we touched down, the engine was roaring with full power, not a setting you usually associate with landing.

The axiom that best explains this scenario is the "point of no relative movement" theory, a military technique. You pick an object in the distance and keep it in a fixed place on the windshield as you approach. If the object drops below your windshield mark, you know you are overshooting; if it rises, you are getting low. If it remains stationary, you're doing great. Full power is required with a fully loaded airplane, flaps down, to achieve a zero descent rate at 7,000 feet. You aren't coming down to the glacier; it's coming up to you.

When I left Talkeetna that fall of 1974, Sheldon offered me a job flying for him the following season. "I'll teach you all my trade secrets," he said. It was a dream that never came true. Alas, Sheldon returned to the Providence Hotel, where he died in February 1975, taking with him his yarns and secrets. He was buried at the village cemetery across the railroad tracks. Ray Genet stuck an ice axe in his grave. It was stolen. Genet got another ice axe and set it in concrete. Genet was a stubborn man.

Sheldon had introduced me to both Genet and Martin Schliessler, a German filmmaker from Baden-Baden. I flew Schliessler to Bethel, way out in western Alaska. Most film crews I have known head for the nearest

Holiday Inn, but we ended up camping out in a fuselage of a wrecked de Havilland Otter at the airport. ("We make us a bewack here, eh?") In his youth Schliessler had climbed with Hermann Buhl; he now spent most of his time adventuring around, "bewacking" here and there, always putting on a houndstooth sports jacket for a drink come evening. We became good friends.

A few months later I traveled to Baden-Baden to edit some footage in Schliessler's studio. There, only a few months before Sheldon's death, we got a letter from him. On the advice of his doctors he was selling the air service, the new hangar, and the Mountain House on the Ruth Glacier. Sheldon offered these to Martin and his investors, saying, "Sharp has the tiger drive to get the work done on the glaciers, sandbars and lakes."

The Germans had just lost money investing in an air service run by an old Lufthansa pilot in Ecuador. So, instead, they purchased a hunting lodge in the bush north of Talkeetna. I hired on in the spring to fly with the Germans. Meanwhile, Don's widow, Roberta, sold the service to an airline pilot from Anchorage.

The lodge had a notorious little airstrip cut into a swamp. It was originally designed for a Super Cub, but if you were careful and took off with light loads, you could operate a 180 from it. The strip paralleled the lake and sported a nasty crosswind; even Sheldon had had a lot of respect for it. More than once the Germans ran out of beer late in the evening and persuaded me to make a run to Talkeetna before the Fairview Hotel shut down. I made countless flights in and out, often in that spooky northern twilight, carrying heavy loads. On one run back from Anchorage, I managed 1,440 bottles of Beck's. It was good training.

I went back to Europe that fall to edit film again with Schliessler. While we were in Baden-Baden, word came that Roberta Sheldon had repossessed the air service. I lost no time in writing to ask her for a job. When I got back to the States in the spring, I got in my 180 and headed up north with my good friend John Ruger. We departed Boulder on April Fool's Day, 1976. That night, in southern Idaho, we encountered a storm. The plane started to ice up, so I headed down to a lower altitude. During the descent, the windshield exploded into the cabin. My nose was broken, and my glasses and everything in the front of the cabin flew into the night. A wall of wind blowing at one hundred fifty miles an hour hit us. I looked over and saw Ruger, his hair peeled back from his scalp. I yelled, "I can't see."

The plane was buffeting violently. I turned on the landing lights. It was snowing. I saw a couple of hills ahead, turned, extended the flaps and set her down. We rolled a ways, hit a snowdrift, and flipped over. Exiting where the windshield once was, we stood together in the snow, shaking hands. Then we pitched our tent off the tail and spent a pretty comfortable night.

The next morning we heard some dogs barking. Following the noise, we dropped into a hollow with a ranch house. There, Sherm Swim fixed us up with some coffee. "Yeah, boys," he began, "I've had four crashes on my place here; sits right under the airway, see. Why one ol'boy in a Bonanza, he lit so hard, buried his watch halfway through his wrist. Never did find the band. Another one, first the wings came off up there somewhere in the clouds and here come the fuselage. Yep, you boys are the lucky ones; yessir, you're the only ones who survived. Here, have some more coffee."

We finished the trip on the airlines. Shortly after arriving in Talkeetna, I bought the air service from Roberta along with a brand new Cessna 185 to replace the 180. I rented Sheldon's new silver hangar and set up housekeeping there in "Talkeetna's largest living room" with Kitty, whom I'd met gassing up at the Boulder Airport. We slept around—some nights between the 185 and the 180, others between the skis of one of Sheldon's silver 180s. We'd never slept in the same room with a bunch of airplanes before, never smelled the eighty-octane drifting out of the fuel vents, the lingering dope of fabric wings. We'd never been surrounded by so much polished aluminum, so many compound curves, so many struts and braces, flying wires and flush rivets. Here was the past and the future, the mountain, adventure and true love.

When it became necessary to sally forth, Kitty strolled to the button on the wall nearest the door and pushed it. Within seconds the door revealed air and clouds, much like the shutter on the Nautilus revealed the mysteries of the ocean depths to Captain Nemo. We'd roll out the flying machine and away we'd go.

During the bicentennial year it seemed everyone was climbing Denali. All the air services were busy. Ray Genet, who had been on the first winter ascent of Denali in 1967, was my biggest customer. In the summer he guided large groups up the West Buttress; in the fall he took hunters out for sheep and moose. Genet had been to the summit of Denali more often than any man on the planet. The summit was everything for Genet, and by extension, it became everything for all those accountants, attorneys and bankers who comprised his clientele.

It was Genet's practice to have his assistant guides take his expeditions in a few days before he met them himself. He would then race up to meet them near Kahiltna Pass, where he would exhort the group upward and onward. On one trip, the weather had been so bad we hadn't been able to fly. The rest of the expedition had been in for over a week, and Genet was even more impatient than usual. We landed on the glacier to encounter the unthinkable: the clients and guides were still at base camp. They hadn't moved in a week. Genet was onto the glacier before the prop stopped. He walked over to his guides for a talk. Then he addressed the whole group.

The storm had dumped a lot of snow; the avalanche danger was high. Several of Genet's guides were fundamentalist Christians. God had spoken, told them not to advance. Genet disagreed. It took half an hour of sermonizing in his lilting Swiss accent. Genet may not have convinced his guides, but he swayed the majority of the congregation. Only a few clients, suddenly remembering important appointments back in L.A., flew back with me. The remainder prepared to follow their leader.

Whether you are traveling one hundred fifty miles an hour or 55 miles an hour, whether you wear white overalls or black livery, there's not much difference between being somebody's glacier pilot and being somebody's chauffeur—except there's no sliding glass window between the front and the back of a Cessna 185.

Genet once received an inquiry from a young lady in Boulder who wanted to experience the summit. He asked if I knew Janie. I replied that I wasn't sure but that I thought I did. "Well, tell me," he asked, "does she have any fire?"

I thought this over for a while. I really didn't want to become too involved, other than driving. I had wintered in Boulder and knew word traveled fast in that town. I told him what little I knew about Janie—ten or twenty times. Genet sent her a plane ticket, and we flew down to Anchorage to pick her up. As soon as he saw her, Genet became entranced. He growled, "Ah, green eyes! Come with me." He even gave her the front seat on the return flight back to Talkeetna.

Janie had been recommended by a former client who had paid Genet $5000 for a private trip up Denali. She wanted very much to reach the summit. Genet was thinking of conquest of a different sort. For the next few days she parried and sidestepped quite deftly, being nimble both in body and mind. I knew all this because Janie and I played pool together. I became her confidante and counselor and, knowing all parties involved (the chauffeur always knows), hoped she could attain her goal on her own terms.

Finally, the day came for the flight in. Excitement was in the air. The day was perfect, and off they flew to the mountain. Several days later I spotted Janie in town, sunburned and downcast. "He ran my ass off up the west buttress," she said, "and when I couldn't keep up, he offered some Germans fifty bucks to take me back down."

Cliff Hudson, who'd been operating out of Talkeetna since the late fifties, was another legendary local, and after Sheldon's death, he became the new dean of Talkeetna pilots. One day we all flew over to Mount Hayes to pick up various expeditions. We took off from Talkeetna, a flight of three, in loose echelon formation with old Hudson in his battle-scarred 185 out in front.

This act of cooperation was definitely a first for the Talkeetna air services. Intense rivalry had always existed between Hudson and Sheldon. At one point, Sheldon reported Hudson to the FAA for buzzing him in midair; another time "the rat" (as Sheldon called Hudson) and "the world-famous bush pilot" (as Hudson referred to Sheldon) got into a regular knock-down, drag-out fight in front of a local grocery. Fists, tomatoes, paper towels and insults went flying.

The enmity between Hudson and Sheldon lasted for years; other grudges persist among most of the Talkeetna air services to this day. Some say it has to do with a curse the Indians placed on the area many years ago.

Doug Geeting, another Talkeetna regular, is a natural pilot, easygoing and friendly. Partway through his first season, he hit some mud on the end of a runway and put one of Hudson's planes up on its nose. I ran into him in the Fairview soon afterward and he gave me Hudson's reaction: "You dumb shit, you dumb shit, you dumb shit."

Ah, the Fairview. The village airstrip lies adjacent to his green-and-white clapboard hotel/bar. In the summer, after the ground dries out, a great cloud of sandy dust blows out behind departing planes, which usually take off toward the south. The drinks get gritty and the lies get thicker.

Every now and then the wind will shift and a plane will take off northward toward the Fairview, giving those at the bar a somewhat different perspective. (Take into account that serious drinkers abound in Talkeetna. It's well into the afternoon and they have invested substantially in a pleasant buzz.) An airplane roars in the distance and they look up, seeing a speck getting bigger and bigger. An angry prop grows louder, followed by the ear-splitting crackle of a flat-out Continental engine. At the last possible moment, the pilot pulls up. The building shakes and the glasses rattle.

"Make me another, George; I got to start all over."

"Did you get the tail number off that one?"

"Who does he think he is, Sky King?"

"Hey, I bet it was your wife that put him up to it."

I thought about Sheldon a lot. Of all his feats, the most dramatic were his landings at 14,300 feet on Denali's west buttress. Most light planes get sickly above 14,000 feet—the air is thin, controls are sloppy, and engine performance is anemic. Brad Washburn had suggested this semilevel place to Sheldon in the midst of the Helga Bading rescue in 1960. Sheldon went up in his Super Cub and plucked Bading out; since then the shelf had not seen any fixed-wing landings.

Ten people died on Denali during the 1976 season. The park service spent vast sums of money on helicopters and twin-engined planes chartered out of Anchorage for rescues and body retrievals. Public outrage over the costs, as well as a feeling in the climbing community that such reaction could lead to restrictions, led to many questions. Was there a low-tech, low-cost solution?

For several months I tried to get approval for a simulated emergency landing at 14,300 feet. The park service wanted to know when. I tried to explain that the weather and snow conditions had to be right and I couldn't say exactly when. They couldn't quite grasp the idea that things happen impromptu on Denali. So, one day I just went up and landed in my Super Cub. I stepped off the plane in cowboy boots. Genet was there with a big group, and I calculated they could all help me stamp out a runway if the snow was soft. I was striding pretty well in my Tony Lamas, though, and there was enough room to land a DC3. Contrary to what I had read, however, the gradient wasn't as steep as I would have liked.

I took off all right, leaving a bunch of surprised folks. When I arrived back in Talkeetna, I jokingly told climbing ranger Bob Butts I had been making a low pass, hit a downer, and landed at 14,300 feet. Then I squared with him and told him conditions were just right and that we should go back up there in the Cessna 185. He called park headquarters and got permission.

We were slightly heavy on gas, to simulate a flight direct to Anchorage with an injured climber. As we climbed to 14,000 feet, I glanced at the manifold pressure gauge. We were pulling fourteen inches—less than 50 percent power. I looked over at Butts, sitting calmly with sunglasses and oxygen mask. We looked like we were heading out to rob a 7-Eleven. The truth was that we were about to make the first landing ever in a Cessna 185 above 14,000 feet on Denali.

The conditions seemed unchanged since my last flight, but it was now close to the warmest time of day. I turned up the flow on my oxygen and inquired after Bob's. We flew across the south buttress, banked over the west buttress, then saw Windy Corner. The terrain came up fast, the air was smooth. The crevasses below yawned wide. The tents got larger and larger in the featureless white. The skies touched. We slowed, turned and took off again without stopping, landed again, got out, took pictures, and congratulated ourselves.

The very next day the phone rang, a patch from Radio Anchorage. Genet's gravelly voice came in from altitude. A mishap on the west buttress; the injured climber would be at the 14,300-foot camp. It had snowed the night before, but otherwise conditions were good.

I cranked up the 185 and took off. My nose was all dried out from the necessary supplemental oxygen during the previous day, but the landing went without a hitch.

Two large mountaineers walked up to the plane supporting a huge man between them. He must have weighed 240 pounds. I took a draw of oxygen, looked him over, and told his pards to put him in. I started the engine and looked over at my man. He nodded.

I shoved the coal to her and we started down, slowly, through the new snow. I moved the elevators, playing with the angle of the skis so they would plane up on the snow. Get it just right and you can feel that extra acceleration in the pit of your stomach. Get it wrong and everybody is in for some heavy work pushing you back up the slope.

We went forever down the slope without accelerating. The slope steepened near the large crevasses. We were committed by then. The plane staggered off, and the crevasses dropped out from beneath us.

My oversized passenger was a Seattle dentist, and he had torn a knee cartilage. I flew him directly to Anchorage, where he caught a connecting flight home. My bill was $655 and he gave me a check, saying he'd just have to go home and pull a few more teeth. The average park service evacuation was running $3,000.

During the next two seasons, I landed for rescues a half dozen times at 14,300 feet. Once, to refute conventional wisdom, I landed down glacier, stopped, loaded up, and took off without turning the plane.

Another time I ran out of gas on the flight home and had to put the plane down on the Parks Highway. I radioed Hudson to bring me some fuel. While a trooper directed traffic, Hudson landed. As he handed me the gas can, he muttered something—I think they were the same words he had earlier said to Doug Geeting.

In the late seventies the government decided that operations at 14,300 with a Cessna 185 were unsafe, contending there was not enough margin for error. They were probably right. But I was young and hardheaded and fought and ran afoul of both the FAA and the park service, law and order on the Last Frontier.

So I sold out and headed south.

In Central America, an old airline pilot and I liberated a Twin Beech. The plane had been impounded by a government for at least two years. There were bird nests in the engine nacelles and there was water in the fuel tanks. The airplane needed liberating badly.

Just before we took off, the old man popped a couple of pills. Nitroglycerin, I figured; he sure better keep that ticker going. He opened the throttles and nine hundred horsepower thundered out. The fuselage shook. We were rolling. Just then a car full of Federales screeched onto the taxiway, gesturing frantically. We kept rolling. The tail came up—sixty, seventy, eighty knots.

The runway had a slight downhill grade, sort of like a glacier, down to where it ended, none too subtly against the flanks of a good-sized hill covered with palms. Toward this obstacle we sped at ninety knots.

"Gear up," yelled the old man.

The engines roared, the wheels swung into the nacelles, the hill loomed larger and larger. We cleared it and laughed all the way to Panama.

Tis-Sa-Ack

Royal Robbins

First attempted by Royal Robbins, Dennis Hennek and Chuck Pratt in 1968, the previously untouched central section of the great face of Yosemite's Half Dome was completed in October 1969 by Robbins and Don Peterson. In the following account the author has attempted to reconstruct the thought and attitudes of his companions. Any resemblance....

HENNEK: It was Robbins' idea, mainly. It was on a lot of guys' minds. Had been for a long time. I had thought of it, and when I loaned him my glass I figured he was taking a look. Meant more to him than anyone. He already had two routes on the face, and couldn't bear to see anyone else get this one. He wanted to own Half Dome.

ROBBINS: In the afternoon Marshall—I call him Marshall because Roper started that. Roper likes to call people by their middle names, and such. Like he calls me "Roy," because he hates the pretentiousness of my first name. And I can't help that. Anyway he likes to call Pratt Marshall, so I will try it for a while. Marshall led a nice pitch up into this huge slanting dihedral of white rock streaked with black lichen; the Zebra. Those black streaks, legend tells us, were made by the tears of the Indian girl for whom I named the route.

PRATT: I belayed in slings at the top of this pitch which wasn't too bad, except at the start where you're thirty feet out with nothing in and then you start aiding with a couple of shitty pins. Royal liked the next pitch because it was loose and gave him an excuse to play around with those damn nuts and feel like they were really doing some good, which I doubt. But I am, it's true, rather conservative. Then we came down on fixed ropes and slept on a big ledge we called the Dormitory.

HENNEK: We would have been all right in the Zebra but we didn't have enough big pitons, even though we were carrying two sets of hardware. We needed about ten two-inch and a dozen inch-and-a-half pitons. The reason we had two sets of hardware is so one guy could be climbing all the time while another was cleaning. I led to the top of the Zebra and Pratt came up and started leading around the overhang at the top while Robbins cleaned the last pitch.

ROBBINS: From Hennek's hanging belay the crack widened to five inches. So Marshall used a four-inch piton, our biggest, endwise. It was weird, driven straight up like that. Then he got in a couple of good pins and used two nuts behind a terrible flake. Pitons would have torn it off. He didn't like it. Marshall hates nuts. He was talking about how it was shifting and then lodging again, just barely. I think he wanted it to come out so he could say, Robbins I told you so. But it held long enough for him to place a bolt, but it wasn't very good because he wanted to get off that nut before the nut got off the flake.

HENNEK: We couldn't see Chuck bolting above the overhang, but Glen Denny, who was taking pictures from across the way, got some good shots of us hanging there and Pratt working away. About dusk I lowered Royal out to jümar up and then I started cleaning the pitch.

ROBBINS: When I got up there I saw Marshall had managed to bash three pins into unlikely cracks. There was nothing to stand on. When I pictured the three of us hanging from those pitons I immediately got out the drill. Marshall isn't known as an anti-bolt fanatic—it's true about that thing on Shiprock, but that was mainly Roper—he isn't known as a fanatic, but there is no one slower on the bolt gun draw than Marshall Pratt. I got in a good solid bolt and we settled down for the night.

HENNEK: Royal says settled down, but he didn't get settled very fast. He was screwing around and cursing in the blackness, and then I heard this rip. He had put too much weight on one end of his hammock, and he ought to know better having designed the mothers, and then there was this explosion of screeching and shouting and terrible foul language that would have done credit even to Steve Roper. I thought it was funny. It went on and on. Fulminations in the darkness. I was amazed that he so completely lost control because he always seemed like such an iceberg.

ROBBINS: I had a unique experience the next day: placing sixteen bolts in a row. It was just blank and there was no way around. But it was a route worth bolting for, and after a time I began to take an almost perverse joy in it, or at least in doing a good job. I put them in all the way, so they're good solid reliable bolts, and I put them quite far apart, so I think that it's perhaps the most craftsmanlike ladder of that many bolts in the world. Still, I was really happy to reach with the aid of a skyhook a crack descending from a ledge fifty feet higher. When Marshall came up he was raving. He raved a lot on that wall. He's an outstanding ravist, often shouting at the top of his lungs like Othello in heat. "Why, why, why," he shrieked, "Why didn't I re-up?" "Christ, I could be a sergeant by now, with security and self-respect. Why did I start climbing in the first place? Shit, I could have been a physicist, with a big desk and a secretary. A secretary!" he repeated, brightening, a leer breaking across his face. "But, no, no, I couldn't do that. I had to drop out of college. Because I...I," his voice rising in a crescendo, "I, like Christian Bonington, chose to climb." I was convulsed. We were having a good time. Nobody uptight. No ego trips. But we were low on bolts and low on water. We would have to go down the next day. It was late afternoon and....

HENNEK: I'll take over here to save all of us from another of Royal's glowing descriptions of how the sun goes down. After a night on the ledge—and a rather long October night at that—we rappeled, placing bolts and dropping from one hanging stance to another. We all wanted to return. It was going to be a good route and we left a lot of hardware at the base, to save carrying it up next time.

PRATT: But when next time came, in June, the summit snowfield was still draining down the face. It had been a heavy winter. So we put it off until the fall and I went to the Tetons. Robbins went to Alaska to stroke his alpine hang-up, and Dennis went fun-climbing in Tuolumne Meadows and re-damaged an old injury so he was out of the running for the year. In October I got a card from Robbins saying he'd be up in a few days for the Dome, and when he didn't arrive it really pissed me off, and when days later he still hadn't arrived I said fuck it and made plans to go on El Cap with Tom Bauman. Christ, when Robbins didn't show, people were looking for him on Half Dome, solo. And then when he finally came up several days late his mood really turned me off. He was tense and cold. He said he couldn't wait until Tom and I had done our climb; he was taking the Dome too seriously, so I decided not to go.

ROBBINS: When Chuck said he wouldn't go I was almost relieved. At least now he couldn't make me feel like I was dirtying the pants of American Mountaineering. I feel guilty with a camera when Pratt is on the rope. It's like asking a Navajo to pose, and I would never do that. Marshall hates cameras as much as he hates my puns and 5.10 psychos. He doesn't want anything to get between him and the climbing experience. He suggested I ask Don Peterson. Peterson had been up the Dihedral Wall and was hot to go on anything as long as it was difficult. Although he had never studied the wall, it didn't take much persuading.

PETERSON: We agreed to go up in the morning. Robbins was like a man possessed. He was totally zeroed in on Half Dome. He had a lecture date soon and he had to squeeze it in. It rained like hell that night and looked bad in the morning but Robbins figured we might as well go up because it might not storm. I didn't like it but I didn't say anything and we started walking up expecting to get bombed on any minute.

ROBBINS: Our loads were murderous. We stopped where the great slabs begin and gazed upward. "Didn't know what you were getting into, did you?" I asked, facetiously. "Well," replied Don, "it can't be any harder than things I've already done." I turned absolutely frigid. The tone of the next eight days was set right there.

PETERSON: What I didn't like was his assumption of superiority. Like he figured just because he was Royal Robbins he was the leader. I didn't buy that. Christ, I had done climbs in the Valley as hard as he'd done, and I did the Dihedral faster. Yet when we got up to the base of the wall he sent me to fetch water. I just don't buy that crap.

ROBBINS: On the way up Don asked if there was anything on the North American Wall harder than the third pitch. I told him no—as hard but not really harder. Well then, he said, we shouldn't have any trouble with the rest of it. Mead Hargis and I have been up the third pitch and it wasn't too bad. Oh, really, I said. It might be a little easier now because Hennek and Lauria had to place a bolt. Oh no, he said, we chopped it. We went right on by.

In a few hours we were at the Dormitory. It was strange climbing with Don. Like many young climbers he was intensely impatient. He was used to great speed and just going. Speed is where it's at. It's not the noblest thing in climbing, but it moves many. Still, I didn't expect to feel the pressure of Don's impatience running up the rope like a continually goading electric current. And I didn't expect a generation gap, but there it was. For eight days we would be locked in sullen conflict, each too arrogant to understand the other's weaknesses.

PETERSON: On the second day we reached the top of the Zebra. Royal belayed in slings while I led the pitch over the top. Right away there was the wide crack. Robbins told me Pratt had knocked a four-incher endwise into the five-inch crack. I screwed around for a while, wondering why he hadn't brought a bigger bong this time. I couldn't get it to work, so I took three bongs and put them one inside the other and that filled the crack okay, but God was it spooky. Still, I thought it was a pretty clever piece of engineering.

ROBBINS: After Don made this strange bong maneuver, he reached the flake where Marshall had had his wild time with those tiny wired nuts. "It's been a long time since I've used nuts," said Don, to cut the power of any criticism I might have of his chocking ability. After he had put his weight on the second one it pulled and he ripped out the other, falling fifteen feet. He didn't like that and this time he nested two pins first. But he still couldn't drive a pin higher as the flake was too loose so he put the nut back in and got on it. It was holding so he started to take in rope and as he was reaching for Pratt's bolt the chock came out and down he came, pulling the pins and falling twenty feet this time. I feared he might be daunted but he swarmed right back up the rope and got the top nut in and got on it and pulled in a lot of rope and got the bolt this time. Fighting spirit, I thought. I reflected how Don was a football player and how he must charge the line the way he charges up those pitches.

PETERSON: Robbins was rather proud of his bolt ladder and bragged about it while he was leading it. I passed his belay in slings and led on up to the previous high point which Robbins called Twilight Ledge. In the morning he took a long time leading around several lips of rock. I was getting pretty antsy by the time he finished. Christ, was it all going to be like this?

ROBBINS: Above us rose a deceptive five-inch crack. Don went up to look at it and said do you want to try it? It won't hurt to try I replied, but when I got up there I wouldn't do it without a bolt, and we had no bolts to spare. So for about an hour I played with bongs driven lengthwise, and with four-inch bongs enlarged by one-inch angles driven across their spines. It was distasteful as hell, and if anything came out I'd be right in Don's lap. I was trembling with more than exertion when I finally clawed my way to Sunset Ledge. When Don came up I was gratified to hear him say he didn't think he could have done it. Maybe now the tension would be eased between us. He probably wanted me to say, "Sure you could," but I couldn't give up the one point I had won.

PETERSON: It was a good ledge. We were halfway or more. It was my lead but Royal had a lot more bolting experience so he led off, placing a bolt ladder diagonally across a blank section. In the morning I finished the ladder, nailed a big loose flake and put in a bolt and belayed in slings. When Robbins came up three or four pins just fell out.

ROBBINS: The first thing I did was put in another bolt, for above Don's belay rose another of those vile five-inch cracks, too big for our pins and too small to get inside. I launched an all-out effort, struggling and thrashing desperately in the slightly overhanging crack. Four months later I still bear the scars. The top of the flake was like a big stone fence without mortar, but I got across that and placed a few bolts and then nailed a thin horizontal flake. I placed seven pins there and four fell out before I had finished. With two good bolts for a belay and hanging bivouac I was safe and happy with nothing on my mind but the next 800 feet. Don wanted to try the jamcrack because I had said it was probably the hardest free climbing I had done on a big wall, but I told him we don't have time man, which we didn't. I was very relieved, for I was afraid he would come up easily and go down and tell the fellows I said it was hard but he didn't find it so. What the hell, that would happen in the next ascent anyway. Let the pitch have a reputation for a year.

PETERSON: At about this point I wasn't feeling too happy. Robbins had taken almost a whole day to lead one pitch. I just didn't see how we could make it at this rate. I knew he had to place a lot of bolts, but it drove me out of my skin waiting for him to finish. I felt I could have gone faster. We were using too many bolts when we still had this big blank section above us. What if we didn't have enough? But the only thing Robbins had to say was "We can always turn back, or else they can pull us off." I didn't think we were going to make it. I had never gone so slowly on a climb in my life.

ROBBINS: I hated drilling those bolts. We had these extra-long drills that were all we could get at the last minute, and we had a long drill holder too, so I was bending over backwards drilling, and drilling is plenty bad enough without that. Here I was working away and always this mumbling and bitching from below, and finally the shocking ejaculation, "This is a lot of shit." From then on I felt I was battling two opponents, the wall and Peterson. I had learned to expect a grumble whenever I made the slightest error, such as not sending up the right pin ("Goddamn it, everything but what I need"), or forgetting the hauling line. I began to feel incompetent. It wasn't really so much what Don said, it was that he said it. It was a new experience climbing with someone who gave his emotions such complete freedom of expression. I was shocked and mildly terrified by Peterson's dark passions bubbling repeatedly to the surface. It probably would have been healthier to have responded in kind, to have shouted "Fuck you, Peterson," every time I felt scorn, real or imagined, coming my way. I didn't lack such feelings. The things I was calling Don were far worse than anything he said, direct or implied. But when I said them I kept my mouth shut.

PETERSON: On the fifth morning I had to use up three more bolts because there was another five-inch overhanging crack. I finally got into it and went free for a hundred feet completely inside a huge flake for half the way. Then we had three straightforward pitches before some bolting brought us to a great ledge, where a ramp led up to a huge blank area below the summit. That night our water froze. In the morning I led up the ramp to a tight little alcove. The blank wall started about thirty feet up. It looked awfully big.

ROBBINS: As I nailed up to the blank area, I thought hard about our remaining thirty bolts. We would place some so they were barely adequate, allowing us to pull and re-use them. We had now traversed too much to descend. Those long drills were murder. I had three Rawl drills and another holder, and I used them to start the holes. They were extremely brittle, but I soon learned that a broken Rawl worked fine, and if they didn't break well, I would re-break them with the hammer. I was saving three short Star drills for the end. I didn't get far that day. It was slow going. I used one drill seven times before discarding it. Don spent the night scrunched in his cave while I bivouaced in a hammock. The weather, which had been threatening, was holding well. The next day was an ordeal. Sometimes it took nearly an hour for one bolt. Whenever I wasn't drilling I had my head against the rock in despair and self-pity. And always that electricity along the rope, that distracting awareness that Peterson must be going mad. Poor Peterson, but poor me too. Besides the hard work, there's something mentally oppressive about being in the middle of a large, totally blank piece of rock. I was sorry I had disdained bat-hooks, believing as I had that if you're going to drill a hole you ought to fill it with a good bolt. I was so far gone now that anything went. I just wanted to get up. But there was nothing to do but what we were doing. When Don came up to my hanging belay the first thing he said was, "I was sitting down there for twenty-four hours!" That's energetic youth. Don had suffered as much sitting as I had drilling. That afternoon, Don placed a few bolts, more quickly than I had, but with no more enthusiasm. The next day I again took over the bolting, inexorably working toward the barely visible lower corner of the dihedral leading to the summit overhangs. That edge of rock was our lodestone, drawing us like a magnet.

PETERSON: Robbins had hoped to do the wall in six days, but this was the eighth. We really wanted to get off and thought maybe we could. The bolting was going a little faster now with Robbins using the short drills and not putting the bolts in very far. He would place one fairly well and then two poor ones and then another good one and then come down and take out the two bad ones and re-place them above. He did this about twenty times. Robbins rarely said anything while he was working on a pitch. He was like a beaver working away on a dam, slow and methodical. At times I felt I was going to burst, just sitting in one place doing nothing. I like to climb. This wasn't climbing, it was slogging. But I had to admire Robbins' self-control. He had about as much unmanageable emotion as an IBM machine.

ROBBINS: We reached our lodestone just as the sun was reaching us. Don eagerly grabbed the lead, nailing up from the last bolt. Thin nailing it was, too. By stretching a long way from a rurp, he drove a knifeblade straight up behind the rottenest flake imaginable. It seemed impossible it could have held. I had vowed that I wasn't going to give Peterson an inch, but I weakened. I told him it was a damn good lead. It would have been too flagrant not to have done so. We were now on a ledge beneath the final overhangs. Above, gently pivoting with grotesque finality in the afternoon breeze, dangled a gangly form, mostly arms and legs, with a prophet's head of rusty beard and flowing locks. It was the artist, Glen Denny. He and the rock around him had already taken on a golden hue as I started up in an all-out effort to reach the top before dark. It didn't look far, but using two rurps just to get started was a bad omen. I went as fast as possible, but not fast enough to escape Peterson's urging to greater speed. The summit tiers overlapped one another, building higher and higher like the ninth wave. On several, reaching the crack separating the folds was barely possible. On one, a hook on the wire of a nut saved a bolt. Everything happened at once as I neared the top. The cracks became bad, the light went, pulling the rope was like a tug-of-war, and I was running out of pins. I had just gotten in a piton and clipped in when the one I was on popped. As I got onto the next one the piton below dropped out and then I was off the aid and onto a sloping smooth slab in the blackness, realizing I was really asking for it and picturing the fall and the pulled pins and hanging in space above Don. I backed down and got into my slings and cleaned the top pin with a pull, then began nailing sideways. Glen Denny is watching silently as I start to crack but I realize I am getting melodramatic and find myself looking at it through Glen's eyes, completely objectively and so cool down and feel with fingers the cracks in the darkness and bash away with the hammer smashing my fingers and pins coming out and me complaining in the darkness putting fear into the heart of my companion and asking him to send up his anchors so I can use them but he refusing and me saying to Glen that's the way it's been all the way up.

The Devil's Thumb

Jon Krakauer

I'd been okay on the winding, two-lane blacktop between Fort Collins and Laramie, but when I eased the Pontiac onto the smooth, unswerving pavement of Interstate 80, I couldn't keep my eyes open.

That afternoon, after nine hours of humping two-by-tens and pounding nails, I'd told my boss I was quitting: "No, not in a couple of weeks, Steve; right now." It took me three hours to clear my belongings out of the rusty construction trailer I'd called home in Boulder, Colorado. I loaded everything into the car, drove up Pearl Street to Tom's Tavern, and downed a beer. Then I was gone.

At 1 A.M., thirty miles east of Rawlins, fatigue overtook the euphoria of my quick escape; suddenly I felt tired to the bone. The highway stretched straight and empty to the horizon and beyond. The lights of an oil rig twinkled in the distance. Outside the night air was cold, and the stark Wyoming plains glowed in the moonlight like Rousseau's "Sleeping Gypsy." I wanted badly to be that gypsy, conked out on my back beneath the stars. I shut my eyes—just for a second, but it revived me somewhat. The Pontiac, a sturdy behemoth from the Eisenhower years, floated down the road on its long-gone shocks like a raft on an ocean swell. I closed my eyes a second time, and kept them closed a few moments longer. A little later, I let my eyelids fall again. I'm not sure how long I nodded off—maybe five seconds, maybe thirty—but I awoke to the rude sensation of the Pontiac bucking violently along the dirt shoulder at seventy miles per hour, the rear wheels fishtailing wildly. By all rights, the car should have sailed off into the rabbitbrush and rolled, but I managed to wrestle the old machine back onto the pavement without so much as blowing a tire, and let it coast gradually to a stop. I loosened my death-grip on the wheel, took several deep breaths to quiet the pounding in my chest, then slipped back into drive and continued down the road. Pulling over to sleep would have been the sensible choice, but I was on my way to Alaska to change my life. Patience was a concept well beyond my twenty-three years.

Sixteen months earlier I'd graduated from college with little distinction and no marketable skills. In the interim, an off-again, on-again four-year relationship—the first serious romance of my life—had come to a messy, long-overdue end. Nearly a year later, my love life was still a wasteland. To support myself I worked on a house-framing crew, grunting under crippling loads of plywood, counting the minutes till the next coffee break, scratching at the sawdust stuck to the back of my neck. Blighting the Colorado landscape with condos and tract houses for $3.50 an hour wasn't the career I'd dreamed of as a boy.

Late one evening, I was mulling all this over on a barstool at Tom's when an idea came to me, a scheme for righting what was wrong in my life. Laudably uncomplicated, the more I thought about it, the better the plan sounded. By the bottom of the pitcher, its merits seemed unassailable. The plan consisted, in its entirety, of climbing a mountain in Alaska called the Devil's Thumb.

The Devil's Thumb is a prong of exfoliated diorite that presents an imposing profile from any point of the compass, but especially from the north: Its great north wall, which had never been climbed, rises sheer and clean for six thousand vertical feet from the glacier at its base. Twice the height of El Capitan, the north face of the Thumb is one of the biggest granite walls on the continent. I would go to Alaska, ski across the Stikine Icecap to the Devil's Thumb, and make the first ascent of its notorious nordwand. It seemed, midway through the second pitcher, like a particularly good idea to do all of this solo.

Writing these words more than a dozen years later, it's not clear just *how* I thought soloing the Thumb would transform my life. My reasoning—if one can call it that—was fueled by the scattershot passions of youth, and from reading too much Nietzsche. I was dimly aware that I might be getting in over my head, but I was convinced that if I could somehow climb the Thumb, everything that followed would turn out all right. So I pushed the accelerator to the floor and, buoyed by the jolt of adrenaline that followed the Pontiac's brush with destruction, sped west into the night.

You can't get close to the Devil's Thumb by car. The peak stands in the Boundary Ranges on the Alaska-British Columbia border, not far from the fishing village of Petersburg, a place accessible only by boat or plane. There is regular jet service to Petersburg, but the sum of my liquid assets amounted to the Pontiac and two hundred dollars in cash—not even enough for one-way airfare. So I took the car as far as Gig Harbor, Washington, then hitched a ride on a northbound seine boat short on crew. Five days out, when the *Ocean Queen* pulled into Petersburg to take on fuel and water, I jumped ship, shouldered my backpack, and walked down the dock in a steady Alaskan rain.

Back in Boulder, without exception, every person with whom I'd shared my plans about the Thumb had been blunt: I'd been smoking too much pot; it was a monumentally bad idea; I was grossly overestimating my climbing abilities; I'd never be able to hack a month completely by myself; I would fall into a crevasse and die.

The residents of Petersburg reacted differently. Being Alaskans, they were accustomed to people with screwball ideas. A sizeable percentage of the town's population cultivated half-baked schemes to mine uranium in the Brooks Range, or sell icebergs to the Japanese, or market moose droppings by mail. Most of the Alaskans I met, if they reacted at all, simply asked how much money there was in climbing a mountain like the Devil's Thumb.

In any case, one of the appealing things about climbing the Thumb—and to my mind, one of the appealing things about climbing in general—was that it didn't matter a rat's ass what anyone else thought. Getting the scheme off the ground didn't hinge on winning the approval of some personnel director, admissions committee, licensing board, or panel of judges. If I felt like taking a shot at some unclimbed alpine wall, all I had to do was get myself to the foot of the mountain and start swinging my ice axes.

Petersburg sits on an island; the Devil's Thumb rises on the mainland. To gain the foot of the Thumb, it was first necessary to cross twenty-five miles of salt water. For most of a day I walked the docks, trying without success to hire a boat to ferry me across Frederick Sound. Then I bumped into Bart and Benjamin.

Both were ponytailed constituents of a Woodstock Nation tree-planting collective called the Hodads. We struck up a conversation. I mentioned that I, too, had once worked as a tree planter. "It's your lucky day, kid," Bart said. "For twenty bucks you can ride over with us. Get you to your fuckin' mountain in style." The Hodads had chartered a float plane to fly them to their camp on the mainland the next morning. On May 3, a day and a half after arriving in Petersburg, I stepped off the Hodads' Cessna, waded onto tidal flats at the head of Thomas Bay, and began the long trudge inland.

The Devil's Thumb pokes up out of the Stikine Icecap, an immense, labyrinthine network of glaciers that hugs the crest of the Alaskan panhandle like an octopus, its myriad tentacles snaking down to the sea from the craggy uplands along the Canadian frontier. In putting ashore at Thomas Bay, I gambled that one of these frozen arms, the Baird Glacier, would lead me safely to the bottom of the Thumb, thirty miles distant.

An hour of gravel beach led to the tortured blue tongue of the Baird. A logger in Petersburg had suggested I keep an eye out for grizzlies along the shoreline. "Them bears is just waking up this time of year," he smiled. "Tend to be kinda cantankerous after not eatin' all winter. But you keep your gun handy, you shouldn't have no problem." Problem was, I didn't have a gun. As it turned out, my only encounter with hostile wildlife involved a flock of gulls who furiously dive-bombed my head. Between the birds and my anxiety, it was with no small relief that I turned my back on the beach, donned crampons and scrambled up onto the glacier's broad, lifeless snout.

After three or four miles I gained the snow-line, where I exchanged crampons for skis. Putting the boards on my feet cut fifteen pounds from the awful load on my back and made the going much faster. But now that the ice was covered with snow, many of the glacier's crevasses were hidden, making solitary travel extremely dangerous.

In Seattle, anticipating this hazard, I'd stopped at a hardware store and purchased a pair of stout aluminum curtain rods, each ten feet long. Upon reaching the snowline, I lashed the rods together at right angles, then strapped the rig to the hip-belt on my backpack so the poles extended horizontally over the snow. Were I to break through the snow over a hidden crevasse, the curtain rods would—I hoped mightily—span the slot and check me from dropping into the frozen bowels of the Baird.

The first climbers to venture onto the Stikine Icecap, circa 1937, were Bestor Robinson and the legendary German-American alpinist, Fritz Wiessner. The duo spent a stormy month in the Boundary Ranges, but failed to reach any major summits. Wiessner returned in 1946 with Donald Brown and Fred Beckey to attempt the Devil's Thumb, the nastiest-looking peak in the Stikine. Fritz wrenched a knee during a fall on the hike in and limped home in disgust, his teammates in tow. Beckey returned that same summer with Bob Craig and Cliff Schmidtke. On August 25, after several abortive attempts and some exceedingly hairy climbing on the peak's east ridge, Beckey and company sat on the Thumb's wafer-thin summit tower in a tired, giddy daze. Far and away the most technical climb ever done in Alaska, their ascent was a milestone in the history of American mountaineering.

In the ensuing decades, three other teams also climbed the Thumb, but all steered clear of the big north face. Reading accounts of these expeditions, I'd wondered why none of them had approached the peak by what appeared, from the map at least, to be the easiest and most logical route—the Baird. I wondered a little less after coming across an article by Beckey in which the distinguished mountaineer cautioned, "Long, steep icefalls block the route from the Baird Glacier to the icecap near Devil's Thumb." But, after studying aerial photographs, I decided Beckey was mistaken, that the icefalls weren't so big or so bad. The Baird, I was certain, was the best way to reach the mountain.

For two days I slogged steadily up the glacier without incident, congratulating myself for discovering such a clever path to the Thumb. On the third day, I arrived beneath the Stikine Icecap proper, where the long arm of the Baird joins the main body of ice. Here, the glacier spills abruptly over the edge of a high plateau, dropping seaward through a gap between two peaks in a phantasmagoria of shattered ice. Seeing the icefall in person resulted in an altogether different impression than the photos had left. As I stared at the tumult from a mile away, the thought crossed my mind for the first time since leaving Colorado that maybe this Devil's Thumb trip wasn't the best idea I'd ever had.

The icefall was a maze of crevasses and teetering seracs. From afar it resembled a bad train wreck, as if scores of ghostly white boxcars had derailed at the lip of the icecap to tumble down the slope willy-nilly. The closer I got, the more unpleasant it looked. My ten-foot curtain rods seemed a poor defense against crevasses that were forty feet across and two hundred fifty feet deep. Before I could finish figuring out a course through the icefall, the wind came up, and snow began to slant hard out of the clouds, stinging my face and reducing visibility to almost nothing.

I carried on anyway.

For the better part of the day I groped blindly through the labyrinth in a whiteout, retracing my steps from one dead end to another. Time after time I thought I'd found a way out, only to wind up in a deep blue cul de sac, or stranded atop a detached pillar of ice. A madrigal of creaks and sharp reports underfoot—the sort of protests a large fir limb makes when slowly bent to the breaking point—served as a reminder that it is the nature of glaciers to move, the habit of seracs to topple.

As much as I feared getting flattened by a wall of collapsing ice, I was even more afraid of falling into a crevasse, a fear that intensified when I put a ski through a snow bridge spanning a slot so deep I couldn't see the bottom of it. A little later, I broke through another bridge to my waist. The curtain rods kept me out of the hundred-foot hole, but after I extricated myself, I bent double with dry heaves thinking about lying in a pile at the bottom of the crevasse, waiting for death to come, with nobody even aware of how or where I'd met my end.

Night had nearly fallen by the time I emerged from the top of the serac slope onto the empty, wind-scoured expanse of the high glacial plateau. In shock and chilled to the core, I skied far enough past the icefall to put its rumblings out of earshot, pitched the tent, crawled into my sleeping bag and shivered myself to a fitful sleep.

I had planned on spending between three weeks and a month on the Stikine Icecap. Not relishing the prospect of humping a month's rations, heavy winter camping gear, and a small mountain of climbing hardware all the way up the Baird, I had paid a Petersburg bush pilot one-hundred fifty dollars—the last of my cash—to have six cardboard cartons of supplies air-dropped once I'd reached the foot of the Thumb. I showed the pilot exactly where, on his map, I intended to be, and told him to give me three days to get there; he promised to fly over and make the drop as soon thereafter as weather permitted.

On May 6 I set up base camp on the icecap just northeast of the Thumb and waited for the airdrop. For the next four days it snowed, nixing any chance for a flight. Too terrified of crevasses to wander far from camp, I occasionally went out for a short ski to kill time, but mostly I lay silent in the tent—the ceiling was too low to sit upright—with my thoughts, fighting a rising chorus of doubts.

As the days passed, I grew increasingly anxious. I had no radio, no means of communicating with the outside world. It had been many years since anyone had visited this part of the Stikine Icecap, and many more would likely pass before anyone did so again. I was nearly out of stove fuel, and down to a single chunk of cheese, my last package of Ramen noodles, and half a box of Cocoa Puffs. This, I figured, could sustain me for three or four more days, but then what? It would take only two days to ski back down the Baird to Thomas Bay, but a week or more might pass before a fishermen happened by who could give me a lift back to Petersburg. (The

Hodads were camped fifteen miles down the impassable, headland-studded coast, and could be reached only by boat or plane.)

When I went to bed on the evening of May 10, it was still snowing and blowing hard. I was going back and forth on whether to head for the coast in the morning or stick it out on the icecap, gambling that the pilot would show before I starved or died of thirst, when, just for a moment, I heard a faint whine, like a mosquito. I tore open the tent door. Most of the clouds had lifted, but there was no airplane in sight. The whine returned, louder this time. Then I saw it: a tiny red-and-white speck, high in the western sky, droning my way.

A few minutes later the plane passed directly overhead. The pilot, however, was unaccustomed to glacier flying and he'd badly misjudged the scale of the terrain. Worried about winding up too low and getting nailed by unexpected turbulence, he flew a good thousand feet above me—believing he was just off the deck—and never saw my tent in the flat evening light. My waving and screaming were to no avail; from that altitude, I was indistinguishable from a pile of rocks. For the next hour he circled the icecap, scanning its barren contours without success. But the pilot, to his credit, appreciated the gravity of my predicament and didn't give up. Frantic, I tied my sleeping bag to the end of one of the crevasse poles and waved it wildly. When the plane banked sharply and began to fly straight at me, tears of joy welled in my eyes.

The pilot buzzed my tent three times in quick succession, dropping two boxes on each pass, then the airplane disappeared over a ridge and I was alone. As silence again settled over the glacier I felt abandoned, vulnerable and lost. I realized that I was sobbing. Embarrassed, I screamed obscenities until I grew hoarse.

I awoke early on May 11 to clear skies and the relatively warm temperature of 20° F. Startled by the good weather, mentally unprepared to commence the actual climb, I nonetheless packed up a rucksack and began skiing toward the base of the Thumb. Two previous Alaskan expeditions had taught me that, ready or not, you simply can't afford to waste a day of perfect weather if you expect to get up anything.

A small hanging glacier extends out from the lip of the icecap, leading up and across the north face of the Thumb like a catwalk. I planned to follow this to a prominent rock prow in the center of the wall, and thereby execute an end run around the ugly, avalanche-swept lower half of the face.

The catwalk turned out to be a series of fifty-degree ice fields riddled with crevasses and blanketed with knee-deep powder snow that made the going slow and exhausting. By the time I front-pointed up the overhanging wall of the uppermost bergschrund, some three or four hours after leaving camp, I was whipped. And I hadn't even gotten to the "real" climbing yet. That would begin immediately above, where the hanging glacier gave way to vertical rock.

The rock, holdless and coated with six inches of crumbly rime, did not look promising; but just left of the main prow was a shallow, very steep dihedral, glazed with frozen melt-water. This ribbon of ice led straight up two hundred or three hundred feet, and if the ice proved substantial enough to support the picks of my ice tools, the line might go. I hacked out a small platform in the snow slope, the last flat ground I expected to feel underfoot for some time, and stopped to eat a candy bar and collect my thoughts. Fifteen minutes later, I shouldered my pack and inched over to the bottom of the corner. Gingerly, I swung my right axe into the two-inch-thick ice. It was solid—a little thinner than I would have liked, but otherwise perfect. I was on my way.

The climbing was steep and spectacular, so exposed it made my head spin. Beneath my boot soles, the wall fell away three thousand feet to the dirty, avalanche-scarred cirque of the Witches Cauldron Glacier. Above, the prow soared with authority toward the summit ridge, a vertical half-mile above. Each time I planted one of my ice axes, that distance shrank by another twenty inches.

The higher I climbed, the more dialed in I became. All that held me to the mountainside, all that held me to the world, were six thin spikes of chrome-molybdenum stuck half-an-inch into a smear of frozen water; yet I began to feel invincible, weightless, like one of those lizards that live on the ceilings of cheap Mexican hotels. Early on a difficult climb, especially a solo climb, you're hyper-aware of the abyss pulling at your back, constantly feeling its call, its immense hunger. To resist takes tremendous conscious effort; you don't dare let your guard down for an instant. The void puts you on edge, makes your movements tentative and clumsy. But as the climb continues, you grow accustomed to the exposure, you get used to rubbing shoulders with doom, you come to believe in the reliability of your hands and feet and head. You learn to trust your self-control.

In time, your attention becomes so sharply focussed that you no longer notice the raw knuckles, the cramping thighs, the strain of concentration. A trance-like state settles over your efforts, and the climb becomes a clear-eyed dream. Hours slide by like minutes. The clutter of day-to-day existence—the lapses of conscience, the unpaid bills, the bungled opportunities, the festering familial sores, the inescapable prison of your genes—all of this is forgotten, crowded from your thoughts by an overpowering clarity of purpose, and by the seriousness of the task at hand. At such moments, something like happiness stirs in your chest, but it isn't the sort of emotion you want to lean on very hard. In solo climbing, the whole enterprise is held together with little more than moxie, not the most reliable adhesive.

Late in the day on the north face of the Thumb, I felt the glue dissolve with a single swing of an ice axe.

I'd gained nearly seven hundred feet of altitude since stepping off the hanging glacier, all of it on crampon frontpoints and the picks of my axes.

The ribbon of frozen meltwater had ended three hundred feet up, followed by a crumbly armor of frost feathers. Though just sound enough to support body weight, the rime was plastered over the rock to a thickness of two or three feet, so I kept plugging upward. The wall, however, had been growing imperceptibly steeper, the frost feathers becoming thinner. I'd fallen into a slow, hypnotic rhythm—swing, swing; kick, kick; swing, swing; kick, kick—when my left ice axe slammed into a slab of diorite a few inches beneath the rime.

I tried left, then right, but kept striking rock. The frost feathers supporting me were maybe five inches thick, and had the structural integrity of stale cornbread. Below was thirty-seven hundred feet of air, and I was balanced atop a house of cards. Panic rose in my throat and my vision blurred. I began hyperventilating, my calves started to vibrate. Shuffling a few feet right, I hoped to find thicker ice, but managed only to bend an ice axe on the rock.

Awkwardly, stiff with fear, I started working my way back down. The rime gradually thickened, and after descending about eighty feet, I was back on reasonably solid ground. I stopped for a long time to let my nerves settle, then leaned back from my tools and stared up at the face above, searching for a hint of solid ice, for some variation in the underlying rock strata, for anything that would allow passage over the frosted slabs. I looked until my neck ached, but nothing appeared. The climb was over. The only place to go was down.

Heavy snow and incessant winds kept me inside the tent for most of the next three days. The hours dragged. Attempting to hurry them along, I chain-smoked until my cigarettes ran out, and read the few books that had arrived with the airdrop. When I ran out of things to read, I was reduced to studying the ripstop pattern woven into the tent ceiling. This I did for hours on end, flat on my back, while engaging in an extended and very heated self-debate: Should I leave for the coast as soon as the weather broke, or stay put long enough to make another attempt at the mountain. My little escapade on the north face had, in fact, left me badly shaken, and I didn't want to go up on the Thumb again at all. On the other hand, the thought of returning to Boulder in defeat—of parking the Pontiac behind the trailer, buckling on my tool belt, and going back to the same brain-dead drill I'd so triumphantly walked away from just a month before—wasn't very appealing, either. Most of all, I couldn't stomach the thought of having to endure the smug condolences from all the chumps who'd been certain I'd fail from the get-go.

By the third afternoon of the storm, I could no longer stand the lumps of frozen snow poking me in the back, the clammy nylon walls brushing against my face, the incredible smell drifting up from the depths of my sleeping bag. I pawed through the mess at my feet until I located a small green stuff-sack, containing a metal film can with the makings of what I'd hoped would be a victory cigar. I'd intended to save it for my return from the summit, but it wasn't looking like I'd be visiting the top any time soon. I poured most of the can's contents onto a rolling paper, scrolled it into a crooked, sorry-looking joint, and promptly smoked it down to the roach.

The reefer, of course, only made the tent seem even more cramped, more suffocating, more insufferable. It also made me terribly hungry. I decided a little oatmeal would put things right. Making it, however, was a long, ridiculously involved process: a potful of snow had to be gathered outside in the tempest, the stove assembled and lit, the oatmeal and sugar located, the remnants of yesterday's dinner scraped from my bowl. I'd gotten the stove going and was melting the snow when I smelled something burning. A thorough check of the stove and its environs revealed nothing. Mystified, I was ready to chalk it up to my buzz when I heard something crackle directly behind me.

I whirled around in time to see a bag of garbage, into which I'd tossed the match I'd used to light the stove, flare up into a conflagration. Beating on the fire with my hands, I had it out in a few seconds, but not before a large section of the tent's inner wall vaporized before my eyes. The tent's rainfly escaped the flames, so the structure was still more or less weatherproof; now, however, it was approximately thirty degrees cooler inside. My left palm began to sting. Examining it, I noticed the pink welt of a second-degree burn. What troubled me most, though, was that the tent wasn't even mine—I'd borrowed it from my father. An expensive Early Winters OmnipoTent, it had been brand new before my trip—the hang-tags were still attached—and it had been loaned reluctantly. For several minutes I sat dumbstruck, staring at the wreckage of the shelter's once-graceful form amid the acrid scent of singed hair and melted nylon. You had to hand it to me, I thought: I had a real knack for living up to the old man's worst expectations.

The fire sent me into a funk that no drug could have alleviated. By the time I'd finished cooking the oatmeal, my mind was made up: The moment the storm was over, I was breaking camp and booking for Thomas Bay.

Twenty-four hours later, I was huddled inside a bivouac sack under the lip of the bergschrund on the Thumb's north face. The weather was as bad as I'd seen it. It was snowing hard, probably an inch every hour. Spindrift avalanches hissed down from the wall above and washed over me like surf, completely burying the sack every twenty minutes.

The day had begun well enough. When I had emerged from the tent, clouds still clung to the ridgetops, but the wind was down and the icecap was speckled with sunbreaks. A patch of sunlight, almost blinding in its brilliance, slid lazily over the camp. I put down a foam sleeping mat and sprawled on the glacier in my long johns. Wallowing in the heat, I felt the gratitude of a prisoner whose sentence had just been commuted.

As I lay there, a narrow chimney that curved up the east half of the Thumb's north face, well to the left of the route I'd tried before the storm, caught my eye. I twisted a telephoto lens onto my camera, and through it could make out a smear of shiny gray ice—solid, trustworthy, hard-frozen ice—plastered to the back of the cleft. The alignment of the chimney made it impossible to discern if the ice continued in an unbroken line from top to bottom. If it did, the chimney might provide passage over the rime-covered slabs that had foiled my first debacle. Lying there in the sun, I began to think about how much I'd hate myself in a month if I threw in the towel after a single try, if I scrapped the whole expedition on account of a little bad weather. Within the hour I had assembled my gear and was skiing toward the base of the wall.

The ice in the chimney proved continuous, but it was very, very thin—just a gossamer film of verglas. Additionally, the cleft was a natural funnel for any debris that happened to slough off the wall, and as I scratched my way up the chimney I was hosed by a continuous stream of powder snow, ice chips and small stones. One hundred twenty feet up the groove, the last remnants of my composure flaked away like old plaster, and I turned around.

Instead of descending all the way to base camp, I decided to spend the night in the 'schrund beneath the chimney, on the off chance that my head would be more together the next morning. The fair skies that had ushered in the day, however, turned out to be but a momentary lull in a five-day gale. By midafternoon the storm was back in all its fury, and my bivouac site became a less than pleasant place to hang around. The ledge on which I crouched was continually swept by small spindrift avalanches. Five times my bivy sack—a thin nylon envelope, shaped exactly like a Baggies-brand sandwich bag, only bigger—was buried up to the breathing slit. After digging myself out the last time, I'd had enough. I threw all my gear into my pack and broke for base camp.

The descent was terrifying. Between the clouds, the ground-blizzard and the flat, fading light, I couldn't tell snow from sky, nor whether a slope went up or down. I worried, with ample reason, that I might step blindly off the top of a serac and end up at the bottom of the Witches Cauldron, a half-mile below. When I finally arrived on the frozen plain of the icecap, I found that my tracks had long since drifted over. I didn't have a clue as to how I would locate the tent on the featureless glacial plateau. I skied in circles for an hour or so, hoping I'd get lucky and stumble across camp, until I put a foot into a small crevasse and realized I was acting like an idiot, that I should hunker down right where I was and wait out the storm.

I dug a shallow hole, wrapped myself in the bivy bag, and sat on my pack in the swirling snow. Drifts piled up around me. My feet went numb. A damp chill crept down my chest from the base of my neck, where spindrift had gotten inside my parka and soaked my shirt. If only I had a cigarette, I thought, a single cigarette, I could summon the strength of character to put a good face on this fucked-up situation, on the whole fucked-up trip. "If we had some ham, we could have ham and eggs; if we had some eggs..." I remembered my friend Nate uttering in a similar storm, two years before, high on another Alaskan peak, the Moose's Tooth. It had seemed hilarious at the time. Recalling the line now, it no longer seemed funny. I pulled the bivy sack tighter around my shoulders. The wind ripped at my back. Beyond shame, I cradled my head in my arms and embarked on an orgy of self-pity.

I knew that people sometimes died climbing mountains. But at the age of twenty-three personal mortality—the idea of my own death—was still beyond my conceptual grasp, was a notion as abstract as non-Euclidian geometry or marriage. When I decamped from Boulder in April 1977, my head swimming with visions of glory and redemption on the Devil's Thumb, it didn't occur to me that I might be bound by the same cause-and-effect relationships that governed the actions of others. Because I wanted to climb the mountain so badly, because I had thought about the Thumb so intensely for so long, it seemed impossible that some minor obstacle like the weather or crevasses or rime-covered rock might ultimately thwart my wishes.

At sunset the wind died, the ceiling lifted one hundred fifty feet off the glacier, and I found the base camp. I made it back to the tent intact, but it was no longer possible to ignore the fact that I was not going to get up the north wall.

There still existed an opportunity for salvaging the expedition, however. A week earlier I'd skied over to the southeast side of the mountain to take a look at the route Fred Beckey had pioneered in 1946—the route by which I'd intended to descend the peak after climbing the north wall. During that reconnaissance, I'd noticed an obvious unclimbed line to the left of the Beckey route—a patchy network of ice angling across the southeast face—that struck me as a relatively straightforward way to achieve the summit. At the time, I'd considered this route unworthy of my attentions. Now, on the rebound from my calamitous defeat on the nordwand, I was prepared to lower my sights.

On the afternoon of May 15, when the blizzard finally petered out, I returned to the southeast face and climbed to the top of a slender ridge that abutted the upper peak like a flying buttress on a gothic cathedral. I spent the night there, on the airy, knife-edged ridge crest, sixteen hundred feet below the summit. The evening sky was cold and cloudless, and I could see all the way to tidewater and beyond. At dusk I watched, transfixed, as the house lights of Petersburg blinked on in the west. I imagined people watching the Red Sox on the tube, eating fried chicken in brightly lit kitchens, drinking beer, making love. When I lay down to sleep, I never felt so alone. Ever.

That night I had troubled dreams, of cops and vampires and a gangland-style execution. I heard someone whisper, "He's in there. As soon as he comes out, waste him." I sat bolt upright and opened my eyes. The sun was about to rise. The entire sky was scarlet. Still clear, wisps of high cirrus were streaming in from the southwest, and a dark line was visible just above the horizon. I pulled on my boots and hurriedly strapped on my crampons. Five minutes after waking up, I was front-pointing away from the bivouac.

I carried no rope, no tent or bivouac gear, no hardware save my ice axes. I planned to go ultrafast, to hit the summit and make it back down before the weather turned. Pushing myself, continually out of breath, I scurried up and left across small snowfields linked by narrow runnels of verglas and short rock bands. The climbing was almost fun—the rock was covered with large, incut holds, and the ice, though thin, never got steeper than seventy degrees—but I was anxious about the bands of clouds racing in from the Pacific, covering the sky.

In what seemed like no time (I didn't have a watch), I was on the distinctive final ice field. The sky was completely overcast. It looked easier to keep angling to the left, but quicker to go straight for the top. Paranoid about being caught by a storm high on the peak without any kind of shelter, I headed straight up. The ice steepened to seventy-five degrees, then to eighty-five; and as it steepened it grew terribly thin. I swung my left ice axe and struck rock. I aimed for another spot, and once again the axe glanced off unyielding diorite with a dull, sickening clank. And again, and again. Looking between my legs, I stole a glance at the glacier, more than two thousand feet below, and felt my poise slipping away like smoke in the wind.

Forty-five feet above, the wall eased back onto the sloping summit shoulder. Forty-five more feet, half the distance between third base and home plate, and the mountain would be mine. I clung awkwardly to my axes, unmoving, paralyzed with fear and indecision. I looked down at the dizzying drop to the glacier again, then up, then scraped away the film of ice above my head. I hooked the pick of my left axe on a nickel-thin lip of rock, and weighted it. It held. I pulled my right axe from the ice, reached up, and twisted the pick into a crooked half-inch crack until it jammed. Barely breathing now, I moved my feet up, scrabbling my crampon points across the verglas. Reaching as high as I could with my left arm, I swung the axe gently at the shiny, opaque surface, not knowing what I'd hit beneath it. The pick went in with a heartening THUNK! A few minutes later I stood on a broad, rounded ledge. The summit proper, a series of slender fins sprouting a grotesque meringue of atmospheric ice, stood twenty feet directly above.

The insubstantial frost feathers ensured that those last twenty feet were hard, scary, onerous. But then, suddenly, there was no place higher to go. I couldn't believe it. I felt my cracked lips stretch into a huge, painful grin. I was on top of the Devil's Thumb.

Fittingly, the summit was a surreal, malevolent place, an improbably slender fan of rock and rime no wider than a filing cabinet. It did not encourage loitering. As I straddled the highest point, the north face fell away six thousand feet beneath my left boot; beneath my right boot the south face dropped off two thousand five hundred feet. I took some pictures to prove I'd been there, and spent a few minutes trying to straighten a bent pick. Then I stood up, carefully turned around, and headed for home.

Five days later I was camped in the rain beside the sea, marvelling at the sight of moss, willows, mosquitoes. Two days after that, a small skiff motored into Thomas Bay and pulled up on the beach not far from my tent. The man driving the boat introduced himself as Jim Freeman, a lumberjack from Petersburg. He'd taken a day off to show his family the glacier and to look for bears. He asked me if I'd "been huntin', or what?"

"No," I replied. "I just climbed the Devil's Thumb. I've been over here twenty days."

Freeman kept fiddling with a cleat on the boat, and remained silent for a while. Then he looked at me hard and spat, "You wouldn't be givin' me double-talk now, wouldja, friend?" Taken aback, I stammered out a denial. Freeman, it was obvious, didn't believe me. Nor did he seem wild about my snarled, shoulder-length hair or the way I smelled. When I asked if he could give me a lift back to town, however, he offered a grudging, "I don't see why not."

The water was choppy, and the ride across Frederick Sound took two hours. The more we talked, the more Freeman warmed up. He still didn't believe I'd climbed the Thumb, but by the time he steered the skiff into Wrangell Narrows he pretended to. When we got off the boat, he insisted on buying me a cheeseburger. That night, he let me sleep in a derelict step-van parked in his back yard.

I lay down in the rear of the old truck for a while but couldn't sleep, so I got up and walked to a bar called Kito's Kave. The euphoria, the overwhelming sense of relief that had initially accompanied my return to Petersburg had faded, replaced by an unexpected melancholy. The people I chatted with in Kito's didn't seem to doubt that I'd been to the top of the Thumb, they just didn't much care. As the night wore on the place emptied except for me and an Indian at a back table. I drank alone, putting quarters in the jukebox, playing the same five songs over and over, until the barmaid yelled angrily, "Hey! Give it a fucking rest, kid!" I headed for the door, and lurched back to Freeman's step-van. There, surrounded by the sweet scent of old motor oil, I lay down on the floorboards next to a gutted transmission, and passed out.

It is easy, when you are young, to believe that what you desire is no less than what you deserve, to assume that if you want something badly enough it is your God-given right to have it. Less than a month after sitting on the summit of the Thumb I was back in Boulder, nailing siding on the Spruce Street Townhouses. I got a raise, to four dollars an hour, and at the end of the summer moved out of the job-site trailer to a studio apartment on West Pearl, but little else in my life had changed.

Climbing the Devil's Thumb, however, had nudged me a little further away from the innocence of childhood. It taught me something about what mountains can and can't do, about the limits of dreams. I didn't recognize that at the time, of course, but I'm grateful for it now.

from Conquistadors
of the Useless

Lionel Terray

from "Conquistadors of the Uselss" published by Gollancz, 1956

In a few days I shall be forty years old. Twenty years of action on the mountains of the world have left me with more energy and enthusiasm than the majority of my younger companions, yet I am no longer the same person who once rode roughshod over men and the forces of nature to victory on the Walker, the Eiger, Fitzroy, Annapurna, Makalu, Jannu. So many years of trial and danger change a man in spite of himself.

Shortly after my return from Jannu, I was crossing the Fresnay glacier with a client when we were ambushed by an avalanche of seracs. My companion was killed and I was buried under fifteen feet of ice. At that moment, it seemed as though the insolent luck that had hitherto walked by my side had abandoned me at last, but in fact, by one of the most amazing miracles in the history of mountaineering, I emerged without a scratch. Imprisoned under tons of ice at the bottom of a crevasse, I managed by a series of contortions to reach a knife that I had by sheer chance left in my pocket. With its aid, I was able to reach a cavity in the debris which, once again, had formed close to me by the merest luck. With an ice piton and my piton hammer I then carved out a gallery toward the light. Five hours later I reached fresh air. This stay in the antechambers of death, where yet another companion was lost at my side, ripened me more than ten years of successful adventures.

In every adventure, whatever my normal capacity, I have marched with the van. On expeditions or in the Alps, I have accepted every risk and responsibility with a tranquil mind. If I have sometimes led others into danger, I have not hesitated to stand at their side. Today my willpower is no longer quite so intractable, the limits of my courage not so extended. In the assault on the most redoubtable bastion ever invested in a group of mountaineers, will I still be a captain leading his shock troops in the last charge, or will I have changed into a general who waits in fear behind the lines as his men advance into action?

And after Jannu, what? Will there be anything left to satisfy man's hunger for transcendence?

There can be no doubt that others will confront peaks less high, but harder still. When the last summit has been climbed, as happened yesterday in the Alps and only recently in the Andes, it will be the turn of the ridges and the faces. Even in the era of aviation, there is as yet no sign of any limitations of scope for the best climbers of the day.

My own scope must now go back down the scale. My strength and my courage will not cease to diminish. It will not be long before the Alps once again become the terrible mountains of my youth, and if truly no stone, no tower of ice, no crevasse lies somewhere in wait for me, the day will come when, old and tired, I find peace among the animals and flowers. The wheel will have turned full circle: I will be at last the simple peasant that once, as a child, I dreamed of becoming.

But it was not to be for Lionel Terray, a climber's climber who, less than two years after this writing, slipped on a grassy slope above a limestone face in the Alps, and fell to his death.

Terra Incognita
of the Mind

Reinhard Karl

from Ascent, Magazine, winter 1989 Text © 1989 by the
Sierra Club Reprinted with permission by the Sierra Club

Reinhard Karl was one of Germany's foremost mountaineers, yet Yosemite Valley, a land of pure rock climbing, was his favorite area. His preferred routes were on El Capitan, which he ascended four times. The following story, from his book Yosemite, *describes a 1978 ascent accomplished only three months after his successful ascent of Everest. The story, told with a candidness rarely seen in climbing literature, reveals the mental wilderness most wall climbers encounter while slugging up a vertical monolith—but which few are brave or honest enough to ever admit to. Reinhard Karl, as outrageous and generous a human being to ever tie into a rope, was killed in an avalanche on Cho Oyu in 1982.*

In September, I was in Yosemite Valley again, with no firm plan, no set objective. I simply wanted to climb and have fun, to drift in time, to find myself through my travels to the edge of the stratosphere. Naturally, after the expedition, I was in very poor rock climbing shape. Ten kilograms lighter, yes, but I was burned out physically and mentally, and had lost all of my arm and finger strength. Now, I just wanted to climb and to be left alone.

In Sunnyside Camp, I met Richard and Sonny again. Each day we climbed together, and I got back into shape much faster than expected. We made our most difficult climbs, including our first 5.11s. Finally, we wanted to tackle El Capitan.

El Cap is for me the optimal ending of a journey to Yosemite. It always takes me a long time to bring myself to "climb into" a big wall. Because of the dimensions and the steepness of the cliff, and the brutal work, it requires time and commitment to climb such a vertical explosion of granite. One year is the right amount of time to forget the negative and to concentrate on the positive aspects of a wall.

Sonny, Richard, and I decide to climb "Son of Heart," a very difficult route, half difficult free climbing, half complicated aid. "Son of Heart" was first climbed in 1971 by Rick Sylvester and Claude Wreford-Brown in twelve days and had seen four repeats, all by Yosemite specialists. All of them called it "difficult and hard," exactly the right thing for us. The route follows a series of cracks on the southwest face, through a heart-shaped section, over a big roof at the right side of the Heart, then up a crack system below a giant triangular roof about three hundred meters below the summit. From there a thin crack, invisible from the valley, leads to another system of cracks that exits to the top through a completely smooth face. An aesthetic line, "logical," as the climbers say, in spite of the fact that nobody can say what "logical" means in this case.

This is the sea of our climbing dreams, in an ocean of golden granite, in the middle of the southwest face. A mirror-like lake placed in the vertical. However, it is not filled with water, but with smooth granite. Maybe it is a desert you want to ride through, a journey through a world not created for man. From the start, where you leave the level ground, to the end, where you step again onto level ground, gravity rules alone. You stand at the beginning of the climb: The chemical factory in your body starts working, producing a protein compound called adrenaline, which drives up the pulse rate. You feel some pressure on your stomach and swallow more frequently than usual. Your mouth suddenly feels dry and weak. Oh, God, what have we gotten into?

If this will only come to a good end! Is there no other climb besides "Son of Heart?" Each of us is suddenly alone, sees himself fighting high up on this wall, and concludes that there is only one hope: that he will not have to lead the hard pitches, that the other guy will.

"Well, what do we need in terms of hardware? Three ropes, better four; big bongs for the wide cracks; regular angles, knifeblades and lost arrows for the thin stuff near the top—altogether eight pins."

"That's a lot. On top of everything, we need all our chocks and stoppers and vast amounts of water."

"Three liters per person per day makes thirty-six liters for four days—an insane weight! Hammocks, food, haul bags, climbing equipment, sleeping bags, warm clothing. My God, what else do we need to advance one thousand meters?"

It's all lunacy. Playing tennis is a sport for poor people, by comparison. The equipment we need costs more than four thousand dollars. But this isn't the worst of it. It's the work to get to the summit, which is an easy hike from behind. Nobody would be able to pay for this kind of work. A hundred dollars per hour would be too low, and with no extra pay for the risk, or the dirty work and overtime, no severance pay, no Social Security, no health insurance—nothing! Why do we do it, if it is such a shitty job? Let's go swimming and forget everything. Let's look for some pretty girls and drink beer. A big wall is for nuts, for madmen.

We leave our sightseeing spot below the Heart and run down the rocky path to the road. Five minutes to the meadow and into the Merced River. This is fun, to sit in the cold water and look up at the sunny wall, shimmering in the afternoon heat like a field of grain. Only the waves in the wheat, created by the wind, are missing. Everything else is right: the color one week before harvest, the expanse. A crazy world flipped ninety degrees. Of course, we are crazy too, desiring to do such a thing. No matter what normal may be, you cannot be normal if you spend so much money to drag a haul bag weighing almost as much as yourself up a wall, to bivouac in hammocks that squeeze your shoulders, to work like a fiend, only to return, totally wiped out, to the place where you started!

El Cap is not a sickness; it is an obsession, a treasure, and each route through its walls is a precious gem. As soon as you have found one, you want more. El Cap is a quest, a quest for yourself, a quest for happiness.

It's the utopia you're striving for but will never find. You are really glad if you can hold it up for a few seconds before it bursts like a soap bubble.

We start by fixing the first two pitches from the beginning of the Heart Route, then we rappel, leaving the ropes behind. Further progress is delayed, since Richard has been caught by the rangers pilfering in the supermarket. As a penalty, he has to clean toilets for a day in the park. Finally we are ready. In the afternoon, we drag our two haul bags to the beginning of the climb. The five-minute path becomes an hour-long transportation problem; hauling a piano up to the fifth floor of an apartment doesn't compare. Profusely sweating, we arrive at the base. We jumar to the Heart for a bivouac.

By nightfall, we are finished with our furniture transport. Conversation is monotonous; everybody is alone and withdrawn. Everybody chides himself for being a fool. Everybody thinks how glad he would be if it were all over. Unfortunately, there is nothing here like bad weather, the wonderful excuse for cowards in the Alps. Tomorrow will be, with one hundred percent certainty, another beautiful day. A hot day, a hard day. Down in the valley, almost near enough to touch, you see the cars driving by, people looking up, people bathing in the river, loving couples playing in the meadows. And you, idiot, are here on this sidetrack of life! You seem to believe you are doing something extraordinary because of your scrambling around! You are a fool. Why are you doing it? You know what a "big wall" is. Why are you doing it again? You are free. Nobody forces you! You say you want to experience nature? The rock, the palisades of El Cap? Isn't it everything? Then touch it at the bottom—it's the same rock as on top. What can this rock give you? You are hurting your fingers. What is the rock doing for you? Nothing! You say you want to experience yourself, find yourself. Do you really believe you will be able to find yourself in the vertical maze? You will find nothing, nothing whatsoever. You probably cannot die here, but the sun will burn out your brain. And what will you hold in your hands on the summit? I can tell you now: nothing. Leave me alone; I am here now with the other two poor devils, and they are no better off than I. Now it is too late to turn back.

We sit on the wide ledges and stare vacantly into the air. The sun sets California-style, glowing red. It is a particular light here in California, intensely colored, deep red in the sky, and the blue quite dark, almost black. Beneath us everything lies in shadow; we are hit by the last rays of the sun.

"Who's leading tomorrow?"

"Yes, who's leading? No volunteers?"

"Well, I've already led two pitches. I'm not leading tomorrow; so it will be Sonny or Richard."

Richard will lead the two A2 pitches, Sonny the A3 pitch. In the evening, the first A4 pitch will remain for Richard. It is getting darker and my internal life is awakening. The eyes are closed and night begins to work with its boundlessness in my brain. In the dark you are naked: the facade you weave around yourself during the day shatters at night, when you brood over your secrets, secrets you will tell nobody. These thoughts start working like a swarm of ants, eating you up. Actually, you don't want to climb up here at all. Why are you doing it, then? You don't have to; you wanted to get married—now; Eva is in Heidelberg. You have no time to lose. What kind of life is this alone on the rocks, wandering around in the mountains? To be alone is terrible! Can the mountains give you love? You are fleeing into the loneliness of the mountains because you cannot stand the loneliness among people. You need a wife; you know it. You love Eva and you want to marry her. Tomorrow you will rappel, the day after tomorrow you will land in Frankfurt. You will send a telegram that you are coming. Slowly, you are getting as tough as the granite you are always climbing on. You will get emotionally petrified. What is El Cap compared to a woman? Can you remember how it is to spend a night with a woman? Reinhard, you are growing old, you need a wife—Eva. You have spent enough nights on rock and ice. You know that you love Eva. Give up the dead mountains; what can they give you? Imagine, you are with Eva now; lying in her arms, and she kisses you. You are not a little boy any longer. Your other passion cannot give you love any more. You need your wife now—Eva. What kind of freedom is this that lets you travel to the mountains all the time? Alone in the mountains, you will become lonely, an eccentric, a queer character, a tragic figure. When you are married, you can still go to the mountains. Now you have a woman who loves you, and whom you can love, and you, idiot, are hammering around on this stone. The total freedom is not the greatest one. Give up a little of it, and you will get more. Tell the other guys tomorrow that you cannot climb any more, that you must rappel, that you have a premonition of death, or a bellyache—or simply that you don't want to continue. You don't have to! If the others wish to continue, the two of them can do it. I want to rappel tomorrow and marry Eva. What can I do with El Cap when all I want is love? Yes, tomorrow I shall rappel.

It is strange: you fight on the mountain, share everything with your partner—the fear, the exhaustion—and you talk a lot, yet you know nothing about the other guy. Nothing. You know that he climbs well, what he does when he has difficulties or when he falls. There are two figures sitting next to me who want to go climbing with me tomorrow. At this moment, both of them are as strange as robots.

Next morning arrives on time like the German Railway. The three of us sit in our sleeping bags, chewing listlessly on our breakfast. Okay, Reinhard, explain to your buddies that you can't make it. Oh, yes, I'll wait until after breakfast. Richard and Sonny are getting ready.

"Let's go, Reinhard, don't fall asleep again, you have to jumar up and haul the bag!" Oh, God, what a tone of voice, like in a factory. I start working in a rotten mood. No, Reinhard, tell them that you want to rappel; go ahead, you want to marry, what are you doing here? "Reinhard, please stop your stupid brooding; we are waiting for you!" Come on, Reinhard, tell them you don't want to go on. I can't do it; they will laugh at me! "Reinhard, man, if you are so lackadaisical, we'll never make it to the top. Let's go!"

"Okay, I'm coming." Shit, what am I getting into? Why can't I tell them? I'm an ass not to have told them before breakfast; I could already be down by now! My mouth wants to say, "Listen, I have to tell you something," but not a sound comes out of it.

"Look, here's the hauling rope; have you got your jumars?" Automatically I clip the jumars onto the rope and start ascending. Shit, I'm the worst idiot. I'm climbing El Cap against my wish to get married. At the first belay stance we're hanging from three pitons, all tied off, bad pitons, but we could not get anything better. I'm pulling on the rope like a madman. Lord, what a fight when all I want to do is get married. Richard follows on the rope.

"Richard, help me with the sack, it weighs half a ton." Richard stands in his jumars, and we pull with our entire body weight. Suddenly—*ping, rattle.* The pitons have come out! We are flying, falling, Richard, the sack, and I. The shit sack, the shit pins that have failed. Now, Eva will marry somebody else. No time for words. Only amazement at how fast we race toward the abyss. Suddenly—*tsack, rattle*—we hit the rock. Hard. We still dangle from the ropes, Richard below me in his jumars. We cannot utter a sound. Dying can happen so fast. I see Richard's face, twisted with terror, cheese-white, his beard even darker than usual. Last night I had connected the upper and lower fixed ropes. This linkage, and nothing else, had stopped the fall of three elephants like a rubber band.

"Holy shit! We continue this way, I don't see much future for us," says Richard, first to recover his wits. He jumars six meters up to the belay and hammers in new pitons. Sonny, the big mouth, is still struck dumb. Reinhard, be extra careful now. This time the pitons stay in place and the one hundred-kilogram sack is up. Clip the jumars into the fixed rope…move up…rearrange the jumars…haul the sack. The terror has made me forget Eva. The sack is finally up. I tie it off; we have a good belay stance and can even stand. Richard follows. Sonny follows. Critical inspection of the belay anchors. A repeat performance might be the end for us. Richard goes to work, Sonny belays. I call it a day.

The brooding returns, the ants eating at me like a rotten apple. Now you can say it; after the incident, simply say that you are scared to death. Down in the meadow you see the loving couples; you want to marry; yet you're hanging around here. No, it makes no sense; I can't say it. Is it loyalty to my partners? Forget Eva; you have lived unmarried thirty years, more or less lonely. You'll be able to last another four days without Eva. But marriage has become a fixed idea; marry now, right away. Marriage is the flight from El Cap, the possibility to escape the fear. That's correct. What should I do with sexless mountains? What's the matter, Reinhard? You can still get married. There is enough rope to rappel to the Heart. It's your last chance to see Eva within the next three days. If you don't rappel now, you'd better forget Eva.

Look up: wow, that's wild! No, I do not want to be up *there*! What can I do? I can't lose my climbing shoes, and to drop the hammer would do me no good. Both Sonny and Richard have hammers. No reason to give up! What would be a neat solution enabling me to rappel right away?

Richard is struggling with the rock, cursing in a low voice. He hammers piton after piton into the rock. It's not too bad–A2. Sonny belays, dozing away. At the same time my brain works at top speed. Just as an angel appears to me, her face, her hair, I want to tell her something. My love-fantasy dreams are interrupted by a falling piton whistling by. "Shit!" sounds from above.

Now I have an idea! The jumars! Without jumars I cannot go on; without jumars I'd have to rappel. Normally, you cannot lose your jumars; they are attached to the seat harness with locking carabiners. However, if, after hauling, you clip them onto the fixed rope for ascending, you have to disconnect them from everything. Why shouldn't I drop a jumar? This can happen any time, admittedly rarely, because the jumars are really a ticket to the top. Of course, there are also people who lose their tickets sitting in the train. Suddenly the jumar falls out of my hands, and with a fluttering sling it sails in a wide arc down the face.

"My jumar, my jumar, I dropped my jumar; shit, what shall I do?"

"You asshole. It's lying on the ledge where we bivouacked!" yells Richard from above.

Why couldn't the *Scheissjumar* fall all the way? I rappel the two pitches down into the Heart. Above me, I see Richard and Sonny, quite small, in the big granite Heart. There it is, the *Scheissjumar;* it could be broken. I am getting sick of the rappel/marriage story. If the jumar is broken, I rappel; if not, I climb up again. Damn the nervous breakdown story. My hands hold the jumar, this engineering marvel made from aluminum; it is in perfect order. Deep breathing...nothing is broken...everything is functioning...hard to believe!

"I'm coming up again," I yell. I have made a decision.

We have no time to lose. I jumar up. Richard and Sonny have just finished their pitch. I immediately continue jumaring. I don't look down into the Heart. El Cap is standing now between me and the altar; Eva is gone.

Sonny is already occupied with his A3 pitch. We hang like flies on a pig's heart in a butcher ship. "*Herrgottkruziturken!* What kind of shit is this!" The birds might just as well stop singing since their small voices cannot measure up against Sonny's swearing.

"Sonny, you better stop blaring; get up your pitch!" The atmosphere is bad, we are irritated, and the incident this morning has left its marks. Our nerves are fluttering, and "You idiot" is the friendliest term we can use for each other. It's going to be a *Scheisstrip,* I'm thinking to myself. Normally your partner is inviolable. You know he is tense; you speak to him with the gentlest tones; you praise him, build him up, just as you expect to be built up yourself. Everyone needs this praise when he starts doubting himself.

"You're doing this easily; that's child's play for you; you've done it really well." You're still praising, even if the partner does a lousy job, wasting hours, while you are belaying, half asleep, with your legs slowly disappearing into your body. When climbing, you always speak to the other guy in the best tones; the reality of the rock is bad enough for the nerves. If your friend robs you of the last vestiges of your nerves with stupid comments, it can easily turn into a *Scheisstrip*. The mountain is dead as a tombstone. It is awakened to life only by the people you are with. And if the relationships go sour, a climb can turn into a disaster.

Peng, peng, the particular sound when aluminum, steel, and rock clash together. *Rattle—aah—* Sonny flies with a few of his A3 pitons out into space and swings five meters lower on the overhanging face, from the first pin capable of arresting his ninety kilos. Sonny has become quite silent. He is breaking into a sweat; the water is running profusely. I can smell the sweat of fear from fifty meters below.

"Shit, what a shit," are his first words.

"If it's only shit, it can't be bad!" He ascends with his jumars to the highest piton and starts the whole thing over again. This time it goes well. He works quietly, with extreme concentration, literally creeping onto the pitons to check them out. Everybody is quiet while Sonny fights.

I am dozing; it is noon. While Sonny is fighting, Richard belays, half asleep. The heat is maddening. To my left I discover a water strip, a slimy, dirty trace of moisture ending in a tuft of grass. A beautiful combination of colors; the fresh green of the grass and the bronze-colored rock. I aimlessly stare holes into the air, into the rock. My head is empty; I stop thinking. Thinking is impossible with this heat. Suddenly I see the rock moving. A closer look reveals a toad with exactly the same pattern as granite—a living toad here in the dead sun wall. It says, "Quak," and I say, "Quak." The water strip is its territory, its little world; here it is at home saying "Quak."

"Reinhard, come on, the rope's tied off."

I say, "Bye, bye. Nice talking with you," and continue my upward voyage. Sonny's nerves are shot; he can't go on. It is Richard's turn to lead the A4 roof by means of knifeblades hammered into the ceiling. This is hell for the nerves. For the moment he seems to be the best among the three of us. Richard hangs from the rock ensnared by fifty pitons and the same number of carabiners. With the hammer in his right hand, he looks like a construction worker. However, there is no scaffolding on this building: it's outside work without a scaffold. Sonny belays from a hanging stance.

"Slack, watch me! Oh God, the pitons are bad!"

Sonny consoles him: "I *am* watching you. Don't worry, you'll only fall through the air." Talking as a tranquilizer.

At the belay stance, there is no room for me. I stay lower; two six-millimeter expansion bolts are quite adequate for both of us. Richard has climbed the roof without falling, and the rope is fixed. Sonny gets ready and lets the haul bag pendulum, hissing, out into the air, then follows and cleans the pitch. Later, when it is my turn to jumar, I am as distant from the wall as the sack, alone on my jumars, alone on the eleven-millimeter strand, with doubts in the stomach and terror in the sphincter. Richard is at the belay; Sonny is at the belay. I arrive panting from below. For the first time since this morning, the three of us are together. It is six o'clock in the afternoon, and it makes no sense to continue climbing. The belay stance is, thank God, ten centimeters wide and one and a half meters long. You hang from the pins, but you can stand.

Dinner. We have a stove and Richard makes hot water for a real dinner, freeze-dried chicken with rice. What a luxury! Everybody is occupied with his gear, looking in the haul bag for something belonging to him: sweater, sleeping bag, hammock. Then you look for a good piton from which you can suspend your hammock. Taking off shoes...peeing...getting into the sleeping bag without dropping anything. There isn't enough room for three people. We have put in at least ten pitons to prevent the mountain from shaking us off. Richard does the only right thing: he jumars down one of the ropes ten meters until he hangs free in the air, then worms into his hammock and has his peace. The wind moves him slowly back and forth. Sonny and I share the ledge. It is dark by the time each of us hangs in an acceptable position. The night arrives again with the entire soul-circus, but this time I fall asleep immediately. Tomorrow, my nerves must be in good shape; I am supposed to lead. Today I had my day off.

In the no-man's-land between sleep and wakefulness I am suddenly alone on the ocean, surrounded by nothing but water. The waves move up and down. I want to stop swimming because it makes no sense. I am too tired to think of anything. A last deep breath, then I submerge. Water is filling my lungs; my head is bursting. I am finished. I awaken. It is dark. There is bright moonshine, a few bats whisking through the air. A frog croaks. I must piss; I can't help it. I'm looking for the flashlight, trying not to disturb Richard below. In the east, the first light of day brightens the dark blue of the night. Down on the road a car passes by, hurling shreds of music up to us. The stillness of the night is slowly replaced by the light. Everybody is still in his hammock, surrounded by last dreams. It is hard to wish to be a hard man.

Sonny ends the night with a yodel. "What would the gentlemen like to order for breakfast? Coffee, tea, scrambled eggs, hash browns, orange juice?" Unfortunately, the cafeteria opposite Camp IV is closed for us today. Sonny fumbles around with the stove in order to produce some coffee to wake us up. Richard comes up on his jumars, and we hang standing or stand hanging, swallowing listlessly the bone-dry breakfast bars. We stow away the sleeping bags while Richard sorts the hardware. Around my neck he hangs two racks with carabiners and pitons, which squeeze my chest. Today, for the first time, I have the feeling that we are a team. Sonny shits into his paper bag and I hurry upward to get as little possible of his stench. Sonny is in a much better mood than yesterday; his Huckleberry Finn face has replaced the frightened face. "Well then, master Reinhard, don't shit in your pants," are his farewell words.

Above me is a hairline crack, into which I hammer pins. I am making good progress. Piton in the crack—*peng, peng, peng*—clip in carabiner and aid sling, test piton, pull. The piton is okay...step up in the aid sling...next piton. "Slack, tension, watch me." Fifty times until there is no more rope I test the piton, clip in the aid sling; fifty meters of altitude are gained. Set up belay anchor, tie off rope, rearrange jumar, haul up sack. I step with all of my strength onto the jumar; today the sack is far lighter than yesterday. We were drinking a lot because on the first day, you climb in the full heat of the valley. The haul bag moves with a loud, scratching noise over the granite. Below me, Richard removes the pitons. Tie off sack and wait for Richard.

"Nice pitch, well done. What comes next?"

"I think something harder is coming—A4. Give me the knifeblades and the short lost arrows. Are you belaying me?"

"Yes, everything's okay."

"Better watch me carefully, it looks horrible." The only useful pitons are knifeblades and thin, tied-off lost arrows, which are barely good enough to support my weight. "No piton fits anymore. It could go with a number one stopper. Watch me really carefully!"

Step gingerly into the sling, exhale, close the eyes. The slightest breeze could throw me out in a huge arc, but there is no breeze. The stopper holds and I reach the beginning of a good crack. Put the baby angle into the crack, hit it with the hammer, faster and harder than usual, and clip in the carabiner and rope real fast. Exhale—the first good pin in five meters. Ah, this feels good, especially since the next move is a sky hook move. This pitch is a devil. Finally, "Belay off!"

Surely two hours have gone by. In the meantime the sun has come around the corner; I'm completely dried out. Haul the sack; finally the sack is up. First thing a beer! People say the first sip is the one. Not here. Here you first rinse your stinking mouth to get rid of the sawdust taste and the bad odor from unbrushed teeth. Water for brushing teeth is out of the question, and after some time you develop a dead-body odor that scares away even the bats. I let the beer pour into my throat like a waterfall. One becomes another person with fluid in the stomach. The empty can sails in a wide arc down the valley.

For the first time I look at the scenery. I have calmed down. I know that my return to the valley depends only on myself, how I climb. I have accepted the wall standing between me and Eva. I shall do another pitch and one more—it is all routine.

I set up a belay under an overhanging chimney, a flaring chimney. It is already afternoon. "Hey, Richard, what do you think? That's something for you, the crack specialist: a 5.10 chimney." Thank God, Richard says yes. I can call it a day. That's the beauty of a rope of three: you work your share and then you are free. You do not have to belay: you could even read a book. Sonny comes up. "Hey, stinker, what's happening?"

Sonny belays Richard. First, we have to unpack all of our bongs. Three people hang from two bolts at a sling belay and sort bongs. The giant four-inch bongs. The three-inch bongs. All those two-inch bongs and tube cocks, four, five and six inches wide. With everything on his rack, Richard looks like the salesman for an aluminum firm.

"Would you please, Mr. Richard from Kaiser Aluminum, give us a demonstration of how well your products work on rock?"

"With all this gear I am supposed to climb 5.10?"

The chimney above is the worst sort. Overhanging and V-shaped, it is wider on the outside, too narrow to get in, and too wide for jamming. Such *Scheissrisse* are called "offwidths"; by the Americans. The rating 5.10 says nothing. Many 5.11 and 5.12 climbs are simpler, because they have handholds and footholds. But these are exactly what is missing in the crack where Richard now thrashes. We see only his feet; we hear scratching noises from aluminum, rock and bone; we also hear timid hammer blows from attempts to set a bong deep inside the crack, a bong that promises a little safety and eliminates the fear of a fall for at least two or three meters. Richard hammers the six-inch tube into the devil's crack and quickly clips in his aid sling. Richard fights. Blood marks his way. He has torn his ankle to the bone in his fight with the crack.

Evening approaches; Sonny and I begin our preparations for the night. Richard cannot be seen anymore; only his panting and cursing and a few rope commands reach us from above. I'm already in my hammock nibbling on nuts. I am not moved by any particular emotions. This will be the second hammock night, and another will follow. Why should I quarrel with fate? I'm doing all right. I've found peace in my hammock, and I accept it. Next to me, Sonny fiddles with his bedding and belays with one hand.

"You should call it quits for today, Richard; it'll be dark soon. How many meters to the belay stance?"

"Five meters; I can make it."

"How's it going?"

"Shit. I tell you. I'm running out of pitons!" Then quiet, except for some scraping noises. Suddenly the sound of a bat in flight, the rattling of pitons. I'm scared and open my eyes. Richard hangs ten meters above us. A full twenty-meter fall! Sonny has stopped the fall; a lot of pitons must have come out. However, only three or four pulled; the rest Richard had removed himself to save material. This was the explanation for the enormous fall, on top of Sonny's half-asleep belaying and the stretch in the rope. Richard doesn't seem fully aware of the length of his flight through the night. The crack overhangs so severely that he simply flew through the air.

"Richard, it'll be best if you stay where you are; we'll tie you off. You can pull up the necessary things with the haul rope; down here we have room only for two." Nothing can bring Richard out of his quiescence any more. The crack has finished him completely. And everything was in vain. Tomorrow, he has to do it again.

It makes no difference where you hang your hammock; the important point is that it doesn't rub against the rock. Finally, the three of us hang in sleeping position. I say, "Goodbye, everybody." How fast time passes when you climb. Yesterday, we were four pitches lower. And it seems to me as if only a few minutes have passed. A hammock is a fabulous invention. Not more than a piece of fabric! It resolves your sleep and the terror of the night.

Next morning all of us are still tired. The night was long, and nobody slept particularly well — more brooding than sleeping. In a bed, you turn around a couple of times and continue sleeping. In a hammock you lie on your back. Any other sleeping position is impossible. Only old sailors can sleep well on their backs.

"Richard, what does the gentleman wish for breakfast; beer, Coke, 7-Up, or orange juice?" We actually have all of them, a real bar. With such an offer you could open a business over there on the Nose, at the last bivouac, for terminally dehydrated and hallucinating climbers. That would be something! Richard hauls up his breakfast. It is still chilly, uncomfortable.

The higher you get on El Cap, the less you look down at the valley. Below, that's not our world right now, but at least we know that one of these days we shall walk around down there and look up at El Cap. Richard continues his work. Sonny belays. He has crawled out of his hammock and sits in his belay seat, a piece of nylon thirty by fifty centimeters. He has his feet on a tiny ledge, just wide enough for the toes. That's better than vertical, smooth granite, when you stand uncomfortably in slings that cut into the soles of your boots. Sonny does some gymnastics to get lively and warm. Belaying is boring: belaying stinks. Centimeter by centimeter the rope moves out; all of a sudden there's a jerk on the rope. If you do not react immediately because you are half asleep, you will hear your leader yelling, "Slack, you morons; are you sleeping?" The guy above simply needs rope in a hurry to clip into the next pin.

Our belay stance looks like the hardware exhibition at a sporting goods show; I'm organizing our gear; the angles, the small pitons, the big hexcentrics, the small stoppers. We need a sufficient number of free carabiners for climbing. We have a hundred carabiners, not so many for a big wall. A belay stance eats up ten carabiners, then everything has to be tied off, with the result that only fifty or sixty carabiners remain for climbing. As soon as I hear the words "The rope is tied off," I'll start cleaning the pitch. Sonny has to release the haul bag, then he can go on vacation: it's his "hanging day."

I ascend the fixed rope with my jumars, and after three meters I'm at the first bong. I cannot reach it. Above the bong the rope follows the overhanging V-shaped crack, and deep inside sits the four-inch aluminum wonder, pulling the rope and me into the slot. I try all imaginable contortions without success. How great must Richard's fear have been to enable him to press his giant body so deep into this crack. Finally I try throwing the hammer at the thing.

After several attempts I hit it. *Ping*—the bong pops out of the crack. As I fall, the bong hits me right on the upper lip. There is blood; everything is red. I'm half unconscious. Bleeding, I lisp, "Shit! Such a *scheissbong*." I still have all my teeth, but I have a lip like Mohammad Ali, reincarnated as a bat and living in "Son of Heart."

"Reinhard, what's the matter with you?" comes a voice from above.

"Everything's okay; I've donated some blood to the bats," I lisp. I continue, removing tubes and bongs. I reach Richard as an aluminum man. "These were a nice fifty meters," is my greeting.

The crack continues uninterrupted. "Look what's waiting for you. I'm finished for today." I can keep the bongs. Richard hands me the haul rope and I am alone in this crack. It is somewhat wider than at the bottom; I am able to squeeze my body into it. I use all the tricks I know; free climbing, stacked bongs, knifeblades for tiny cracks. When I reach the bolts of the next belay stance, I'm totally wiped out, nerves shot. But I've done it, and I'm proud of it.

"Belay off; the rope's tied off." I haul up the sack and Sonny follows. It is early in the afternoon. Time passes so fast. The crack above me closes to a five-meter roof. Up to the roof the crack goes "clean" with stoppers for aid, without damage to the rock—soft technology. Now I hang underneath the roof and reach for my pitons. A thin crack leads to the right; the pitons must be hammered directly upward. Finally I can see above the roof. Below me is a yawning emptiness. Looking down the yellow-orange wall is similar to looking down from the hundredth floor of the Empire State Building—except the wall is three times as high as that edifice. And I am almost on top. My elevator is not stuck, and no loss of electric power has occurred, but the terrible rope drag all but stops my further progress. I am alone in the vertical. From the left, the climbing rope pulls at me; from below, the haul rope. I look down between my legs; horrible, vertiginous, spacey, as the Americans say. With knifeblades, which barely support my weight, I work my way like a precision mechanic along a tiny crack to the right. Each time, when I tug on the rope, I'm afraid of pulling out the tender iron roots. There is a big hole! I try to drive in a two-inch bong sideways. A shaky guy, but what can I do? I step into it—*ping*—it could not hold. It's only a little pendulum; the tied-off knifeblade holds my weight.

"Hello, you guys below, I need a three-inch and a four-inch bong." The two below tie the desired pitons onto the haul rope, and I can pull up the bongs. A strange feeling, to pull up a rope from the void on which hang the desired presents. The four-inch bong fits perfectly into the hole. Two more knifeblades and a stopper, and I can clip into the bolts at the belay. Such bolts are an island of emotional rescue; six millimeters in diameter and hammered three centimeters deep into the rock, they promise safety. There are four of them on the blank face. I hang in my slings as on the facade of a high-rise building. I am happy.

There are still other islands in our vertical ocean, islands that provide solid ground for the feet of the exhausted space wanderer. Ledges as wide as

El Cap Tower, where you could play table tennis. For two days we have not seen land; we are driftwood in an ocean of granite. And dying of thirst in the desert at the same time. The red and white of a Coca-Cola can appears before me like a mirage. I see the billboard with the ice-cold drink in front of me. And I hear the hissing when the can is opened. My mouth is as dry as sandpaper; I can barely call out the rope commands. Now, haul the sack. Only the thought of a Coke in the sack enables me to do this bestial work. Tie off sack...ah...a Coke! Even lukewarm it makes another person of you. I look at my watch; my God, already five o'clock. The title of our climbing story could be: "Travel Diary of a Snail." Immediately look for the hammock in the sack and begin to get comfortable. I have the leisure time for a long look at the scenery. The meanders of the Merced River have become smaller; they are just curved lines, with the sand on the banks a light brown and the water a greenish brown. The road is a straight line along which the cars move. The giant trees are clusters of dark green dots. The Cathedral Rocks opposite us receive the last sunlight on their somber north faces. We are already higher than the summit of Middle Cathedral, with its beautiful tall trees, the same trees found on the summit slopes of El Cap, trees that announce a new beginning of life, the end of the vertical.

For the first time I think of tomorrow. Tomorrow we may be on top. The last two days were timeless, governed by above and below, by pitons, carabiners, the rope, the hammer that sometimes hits the fingers instead of the piton. Blood flecks on the rock. To judge from my hands, I could have been run over by a streetcar. And to judge from my stench, cold farts, pungent urine, cold sweat, bad breath, cheese feet, I could be a bum. In spite of everything I am content with myself. I feel calm, feel strong, because I have led this pitch.

Slowly, the rock changes from golden brown to orange; later it will become burning red, only for a few moments, because in the east the night has already collected the sky. The last energy of the day appears in the west above the mountains. A sky like in an oil painting, saturated colors, California light. It is strange that normally you are not particularly susceptible to such little things as a sunset. But up here it is different; your perceptions are much stronger. This sunset is the dying of a day you have survived in spite of the terrible nailing, a day that will stay strong forever in your memory.

The third day on "Son of Heart." Fear, as bad as it may be when it is uncontrolled, makes you more receptive, deepens your feelings, makes them more serious, and gives you an intense feeling of being alive. I hear Sonny cursing; following on jumars on vertical rock is most unpleasant, particularly when the pitons are bad. The danger of a diagonal zipper-fall is great. Sonny works in a concentrated manner; fear engenders caution. When Sonny reaches me, it is almost dark. Now Richard is the loneliest person on earth. His only connection with us is a nine-millimeter rope leading diagonally down to him. He clips onto the rope, unclasps the anchor and instantly flies twenty meters to the right across the vertical wall, bathed in the last fiery red light of the day. An astronaut is less lonesome than Richard in those seconds of his flight through the approaching darkness. Fifty meters below us he swings freely in the air. Since there is not enough room for three where we are, we lower Richard his hammock and dinner on the rope. Down in the valley it is already pitch dark. Now and then, headlights plow through the darkness. Up here the light of the stars and the red of the sun, which has long since disappeared below the horizon, maintain a counterbalance.

Once again we are ready for the night, firmly enclosed by the hammocks, anchored to the mountain. Sonny yells something in beer hall Bavarian into the night. Somebody, presumably from the Salathé, yells something back. We are not alone. Somebody is close, reachable only by calling, in effect unreachable.

The first light of California awakens us. If there were a scale of verticality, we would be at the most vertical. In the morning everything looks much more frightening than in the evening. The wall is more than vertical. Because I feel like climbing, and because the crack above us looks so terrible, I offer to lead. Two pitches, interrupted by a short fall, and I am at the end of the difficulties. Sonny has lots of trouble retrieving my panic-driven pitons; his hammer arm is dust. I have had no contact with Richard since yesterday morning; he was always two pitches below me. Three easier pitches—less than vertical and therefore requiring hard work with the haul bag—and the wall is ours.

This is a change that always fascinates. The end of the fear, the end of the tension, the end of the desire. The beginning of living in the horizontal, the beginning of tomorrow, the beginning of going in your own direction. Finally the three of us are on top. Looking around at the scenery has replaced looking down. We shake hands; everybody is glad that it's over. We're not talking a lot.

And I have played my part of the courageous Reinhard to the end. Nobody noticed anything different—what had happened internally; fear, anxiety, damnation. And I appeared as cool, so icy cold in all situations. I played the part so well that I am now being congratulated. If they only knew what a purgatory of weakness had burned inside me! I say calmly, "That was a wild ride!" And it is supposed to sound like, "It's fun to ride a pony." I'm saying this quite casually, still feeling the horror in my guts, the hurricane in my soul. But I'm also proud to be standing here. When I watch the two sorting out their gear. I'm sure they had the same storm in their guts. I know they felt just as alone as I did. And the fear made them as silent as I.

We are the perfect actors! We play the role of the hard mountaineer for the others as well as for ourselves when, barely able to speak with fright, we calmly say: "Watch me, it looks difficult." No, we are neither hard nor foolhardy; we shall never be so. We are miserable, fearful rabbits who overcome our fear, sometimes with a surge of courage if it is really necessary. "Son of Heart" was for me a trip into an unexplored country, the land of my own psyche. I had never thought that I could muster so much faith in myself after so much anxiety and despondency. Even today, the individual experiences of this trip are so engraved in my memory that I can take them like slides out of a box and let them become transparent. On this trip I didn't see much of the scenery; yet surely this enterprise shed some light on the darkness in myself, solving part of the riddle of who I am. Down in the valley each of us will go our own way. These were just four days when three people climbed together. And I shall get married.

Ascent of
Rum Doodle

W. E. Bowman

from Summit Magazine, spring 1990 Introduction © 1991 by Summit Magazine,
"Ascent of Run Doodle" and "The Cruise of the Talking Fish" have recently been
reissued and appear in a single paperback volume which uses the original 1956
illustrations from "Run Doodle." Published by Pimlico: ISBN 0-7126-5479-8

In his highly acclaimed parody of expedition literature, W. E. Bowman chronicled the bumbling ascent of the fictional Rum Doodle peak—at 42,000 $^1/_2$ feet, the world's highest. When The Ascent of Rum Doodle *first appeared in 1956, it was hot on the heels of the first ascent of Everest, and ongoing media hoopla over Himalayan climbing. With the exception of certain members of the Alpine Club of London who perhaps saw a bit too much of themselves in Rum Doodle's heroes, the book was immediately recognized as a comic masterpiece. It pokes such good fun at the details of big expeditions and the books that describe them that every Himalayan chronicler of the last three decades has had to temper his pen accordingly. Bowman's Rum Doodle expedition spoofed everything from a typical expedition's muddled interpersonal dynamics to its troubled dealings with porters and grandiose pretensions. Indeed, Bowman's parody worked so well—especially following its reprintings in 1979 and again in 1983 and 1985—that Rum Doodle proved a hit far outside of mountaineering circles, though most successful in its home country of Great Britain. Rum Doodle has also been published in France, Spain, Denmark, and the United States. It has been read on London radio and reviewed in Britain's largest papers. The* Sunday Times *said that Rum Doodle did for mountaineering what* Three Men in a Boat *did for Thames-going and* Catch 22 *did for the Second World War. In 1957, Mr. Bowman published a sequel,* The Cruise of the Talking Fish, *in which Rum Doodle's narrator, who earned the nickname of Binder, made a journey that parodied Thor Heyerdahl's Kon Tiki expedition. Still, it was* Rum Doodle *that secured Bowman's place in history—and geography: the name "Rum Doodle" now graces a mountain in Antarctica and a restaurant in Kathmandu. The author himself was much more a hill walker than climber, earning his living as a civil engineer and spending his free time painting and writing (unpublished) books on the theory of relativity. Bowman was married and had two children when he died in 1985 at the age of 73. The latest edition of* Rum Doodle *appeared in 1989, published by Arrow Books Limited, London. As we join Bowman's story at chapter 3, "To the Rankling La," we find the expedition leader and narrator aboard ship, sailing for Rum Doodle.*

The voyage was uneventful. My responsibilities as leader prevented me from spending as much time as I should have liked with the others, but I was gratified to see that the *esprit-de-corps* which is so important on expeditions such as ours was uniting our party into a closely knit community. The importance of the team spirit cannot be overestimated. As Totter once said: When you are swinging helplessly at the end of a hundred-foot rope it is important to know that the man at the other end is a friend. It was the spirit, more than any other single factor, which brought success, and I was happy to see it growing during the voyage.

Wish was kept busy with his apparatus. He tested our boiling-point thermometers and was able, by averaging the results of many readings, to fix the ship's height as 153 feet above sea level. Burley said this was nonsense, but Wish pointed out that due to the earth's not being a perfect sphere, but larger at the equator than at the poles, the result was quite in accordance with known facts.

Constant, to his great delight, discovered a Yogistani family on the lower deck, and spent much time with them improving his knowledge of the language. The association came to a sudden end, however, in a rather strange way. One quiet Sunday afternoon, Constant came running up the stairway in a state of terror, closely followed by a small but powerful Oriental person who was waving a knife. After being rescued Constant explained that he had made a trifling error in pronunciation. He had wished to express admiration for the poetry of Yogistan. Unfortunately, the Yogistani word for poetry is identical with the word for wife, except for a sort of gurgle at the end. Being unable, in the enthusiasm of the moment, to produce this gurgle, he had deeply offended his host, with the result we had witnessed. Constant kept to his own deck for the rest of the voyage.

One day a whale was sighted on the starboard quarter. This was naturally an event of great interest to all, but particularly to myself as it enabled me to make up my mind on the very vital matter of grouping of the assault party, to which I had given much thought. Our attack on the mountain was to be made by units of two men, who would climb together on the same rope and occupy the same tent. I considered it important that these partners be brought together as soon as possible, to enable them to rub off those rough corners which become irksome at close quarters. I had, however, been unable to reach a decision. Burley and Wish, I had decided long ago, were the ideal combination to fit into a cramped bivouac tent, one being large and the other small; and their personalities and interests were so different that there was little chance of professional jealousy or monotony arising. Shute and Jungle had each shown a lively and controversial interest in the other's special subject, and I thought it would be a pity to part them. Moreover, Shute was a Cambridge man while Jungle had been to Oxford, which would broaden the horizons of both of them. This left Constant and Prone; and I was not at all happy about these two—both having the professional manner, which might prove somewhat stifling in a small tent. But they disagreed so heartily on so many subjects that I began to be reassured, and the incident of the whale put my mind finally at rest.

While we were leaning over the rail watching the creature blowing, Constant said he wondered whether there was any truth in the Jonah legend. Prone said that he was surprised at such a remark from an educated man, and became so interested in the subsequent discussion that he forgot to be seasick. They argued heatedly for the remainder of the voyage and were quite inseparable, which was a great relief to me.

Just before we reached port I received a radio message: UNFORTUNATELY MISDIRECTED BUENOS AIRES SEND FIFTY MILLION PEONS JUNGLE.

The rail journey was uneventful. Burley was down with heat lassitude and Prone contracted malaria. Constant went into the native portion of the train to improve his knowledge of the language, but soon afterwards a riot broke out and he thought it advisable to retire. Wish spent most of the journey with a stopwatch in his hand timing the telegraph posts in order to calculate the speed of the train. This worked out at 153 miles per hour, but he thought that a certain amount of experimental error should be allowed to cover irregularities in the spacing of the posts. Burley gave him a check and found that the hand of the stopwatch had stuck.

Our arrival at Chaikhosi was a big event, both for ourselves and for the local people. Constant had arranged that the three thousand porters should meet the train, so that no time would be lost. As we pulled in we were surprised and gratified to see that a great crowd, which stretched as far as we could see, had assembled to welcome us. When we put our heads out of the window we were greeted by a deadening cheer. Constant remarked on the friendliness of the natives which, he said, was one of their chief characteristics.

As we stepped off the train we were met by a dignitary whom I assumed to be the local Clang, or headman. Constant engaged him in conversation, putting on his most diplomatic air. They spoke together for several minutes, and a European onlooker might have been forgiven for concluding that they were quarreling violently; but I told myself that this, no doubt, was the local idiom.

Finally, Constant told us that this was not the Clang at all, but the Bang, or foreman porter, and that the multitude before us were the porters he had ordered.

"If you ask me," said Prone, "there are a lot more than three thousand of them."

I was of the same opinion, but Constant said that nobody had asked Prone and he was sure the number was correct.

"Why not ask your friend?" Prone suggested.

Constant engaged the Bang in another lengthy bout, after which he told us that the man spoke an obscure dialect and did not seem fully conversant with standard Yogistani.

"Let's count 'em, then," said Prone. "Line 'em up ten deep."

Constant turned again to the Bang, and after much noise and gesticulation he explained to us that there was no Yogistani phrase for ten deep and, since military training was unknown in the country, the idea of lining up was not easily conveyed to the Yogistani mind.

I told Constant we would leave him to thrash the matter out with the Bang. He said it was a good idea; we were probably making the poor fellow nervous. As we left they went to it again, holding three fingers in the air and scratching on the dusty ground with sticks.

We spent a hungry and uncomfortable night in the station waiting room, for until the dispute with the Bang was settled our equipment could not be unloaded, and in the absence of Constant we dared not risk a night in the local hotel. At daybreak I walked over to the train, to find Constant and the Bang still at it. The former explained to me that the Yogistani word for three was identical with the word for thirty, except for a kind of snort in the middle. It was, of course, impossible to convey this snort by telegram, and the Bang had chosen to interpret the message as order thirty thousand porters. The thirty thousand were making a considerable noise outside, and Constant told me that they were demanding food and a month's pay. He was afraid that if we refused they would loot the train.

There was nothing for it but to meet their demands. The thirty thousand were fed—at considerable trouble and expense—and three days later we were able to set off with the chosen three thousand on our five-hundred mile journey. The 375 boys who completed our force were recruited on the spot. Boys are in plentiful supply in Yogistani; it appears that their mothers are glad to get rid of them.

The journey to the Rum Doodle massif was uneventful. We travelled along a series of river gorges deeply cut between precipitous ridges which rose to heights of thirty thousand feet and more. Sometimes we crossed from one valley to another over passes some twenty thousand feet above sea level, dropping again to river beds elevated a mere 153 feet or so.

The steepness of the valleys was such that the vegetation ranged from tropical to arctic within the distance of a mile, and our botanists were in their element. The lower slopes were gay with Facetia and Persiflage, just then at their best, and the nostrils were continually assailed with the disturbing smell of Rodentia. Nostalgia, which flourishes everywhere but at home, was plentiful, as was the universal Wantonia. Higher up, dark belts of Suspicia and Melancholia gave place to the last grassy slopes below the snow line, where nothing was seen growing but an occasional solitary Excentricular, or old-fashioned Manspride.

The porters were unprepossessing. Mountaineering to them was strictly business. An eight-hour day had been agreed on, for which each received bohees five. Nothing on earth would persuade them to work longer than this, except money. Their performance as porters left nothing to be desired. Although short—few were more than five feet in height—they were almost as broad as they were long, and very sturdy. Each carried a load of one thousand pounds. One cannot praise too highly the work of the porters, without whom the expedition would have been doomed to failure.

We passed through many villages, the inhabitants of which were invariably sullen and unfriendly, except when Constant made overtures, when they became hostile. He explained that they were not typical of the natives, being a degenerate class who, attracted by the soft living to be made below the twenty-thousand-feet line, had become demoralized and lost their original qualities of dignity and cheerfulness.

A month later we stood on the summit of the Rankling La facing the Rum Doodle massif, nature's last citadel against the conquering spirit of man. The great mountain itself, standing majestic against a cloudless sky, struck awe into the hearts of the puny creatures who were soon to set presumptuous foot on those dreadful slopes. What pen could describe our feelings as we viewed the Rum Doodle massif from the summit of the Rankling La?

North Wall: The First Assault

At last, all were considered acclimatized, with the exception of Prone, who had developed blood-pressure; and we set out to assault the North Wall. I sent off the following message by runner: "Moving to attack North Wall, the tremendous precipice which rears above us five thousand feet against the sky. The question on all lips is: 'Will it go?' and every heart whispers a confident: 'Yes, it will!' The spirit of the team is excellent and the porters are beyond praise. All in good health."

The North Wall is a sheer glass-like face of ice broken only by rock, snowfields, ice-pinnacles, crevasses, bergschrunds, ridges, gullies, scree, chimneys, cracks, slabs, gendarmes, Dames Anglaises, needles, strata, gneiss, and gabbro. A formidable obstacle, and one to daunt the hearts of a disunited party supported by mediocre porters.

We had already reconnoitered the lower slopes of the Wall, and two schools of thought had arisen concerning the best method of tackling it. Wish, our cragsman, favored the direct ascent of a precipitous rock face which led to what seemed easy going higher up. Shute, the ice expert, preferred a steep slope of ice which likewise appeared to ease off toward its upper extremity. Since no final decision was possible it had been decided to try both ways simultaneously. Shute and Jungle would tackle the ice, Wish and Burley would attack the rock. Constant and I, after tidying up at base, would follow on to support either part.

Constant and I moved off shortly after midday, and we had not yet left the glacier when my radio buzzed. It was Jungle in a high state of excitement. Shute was stuck halfway up his ice field, having lost his ice axe and being afraid to come down. Jungle's own ice axe was sunk in the ice with the rope belayed to it. He dared not remove it in case Shute should fall. Would we please come and help him?

This was alarming news. I immediately assured Jungle that we would be with him as quickly as possible, and we set off at full speed. But we had gone no more than a few paces when Constant disappeared into a crevasse. The rope tightened between us and I was jerked on to my face. In the excitement I let go of my ice axe and found myself being pulled toward the lip of the crevasse with no means of stopping myself. I was within two yards of the edge when I stopped. The rope had cut into the ice and the increased friction had saved me.

But it was a desperate situation. When I tried to rise, the rope pulled me forward as Constant fell still further. Only by lying spread-eagled could I get sufficient friction to halt his fall. I could do nothing to save Constant; unless help came, there was no hope for us.

Our only chance was the radio. With my heart in my mouth I edged my right hand nearer and nearer, and at last I was able to place the apparatus near my face. I called up Burley and Wish. The former replied, and I asked him to hurry to our help. To my consternation he informed me that they, too, were in difficulties. Wish was stuck halfway up his rock face, being unable to move up or down. Burley was completely exhausted; evidently he had not fully acclimatized. He had himself been on the point of calling for help.

There was only one solution. Jungle must leave Shute, who at least was belayed to Jungle's ice axe, and come to our help. The three of us would then rescue the others. Jungle acknowledged his instructions and told us he was setting off.

I hope I never have to endure such an ordeal again. Every minute was an hour, every hour an eternity. A hasty move on my part might send both Constant and myself crashing into the abyss. My nose itched, but I dared not scratch it; it froze, but I dared not rub it. I was getting colder and colder. Constant, with whom I could converse in shouts, was in a similar predicament. He was unhurt, but as cold and miserable as I was, if not more so.

After a long time the radio buzzed. It was Jungle. He had lost his way. My heart sank, and Burley, who was listening in, gave a groan. It was surely all up with us now. I was suddenly seized with an overwhelming sense of pathos of it all. We, who had set off so confidently, who had worked so hard and come so far; we who were our country's hope and a world's heroes: we were to perish miserably in this stern country, far from home and dear ones.

I told Constant the news and did my best to comfort him. Poor fellow, he took it well, and so did Burley when I spoke to him. If we were to die, at least we would die like gentlemen.

The day wore on.

I was, I think, half unconscious when an idea came to me. The porters! They saved us before; could they save us again? The only way of communicating with them was via Prone. None of the porters would touch the radio; I think they thought it was witchcraft. The question was: Was

Prone within hearing of a radio, was the radio operational, and was he in fit condition to answer it?

"Binder to Ailing. Binder to Ailing. Are you receiving me? Over."

And then came the words that will ring in my ears to my dying day.

"Ailing to Binder. Ailing to Binder. Receiving you loud and clear. Are you receiving me? Over."

I could have wept. I explained the situation to Prone and asked him to get the Bang. He did so, and I began the difficult business of instructing him. Constant translated my messages into Yogistani and I passed them on as accurately as I could to Prone, who gave them third-hand to Bing.

It was hopeless. My stomach and Prone's were quite unused to pronouncing Yogistani. The noises we produced would have been a disgrace in any company; as vehicles of communication they were a total failure. Constant said that the replies which I passed on to him bore no relation at all the problem under consideration. They would, he said, if uttered in the streets of Chaikhosi, result in imprisonment for life, if not worse. He begged me to keep my stomach closed and tell Prone to do the same. If the least suspicion of what he had heard should reach the ears of the Bang, the result might well be massacre; at the very least, the porters would desert, or would be incapacitated for further work.

This was serious. There remained one hope: Was Prone fit to travel?

No, he said; it was out of the question. His legs would not support him.

But he could be carried? Yes; he was fit enough for that. And so it was arranged. Again, we waited, but this time in high hope. Prone, carried by the Bang, gave us a running commentary on his progress. Then they were with us: Bing, short and immensely powerful, with Prone piggy-back; Bung, shorter still but equally sturdy; and a third porter, Bo by name, who was even shorter and sturdier.

In no time Constant was hauled to the surface, chilled but otherwise none the worse. Bing and Bung were dispatched to the rescue of the others, while Constant and I staggered back to Base Camp accompanied by Bo and Prone on his back.

The others returned within the hour. Bing had climbed up to Shute and brought him down under his arm, and later had done the same for Wish. Both were shaken by their ordeal and had to be treated with champagne.

The question now was: Where was Jungle? We called him by radio but failed to make contact. Shute said that we had probably seen the last of him; he said that since Jungle was aiming for Base Camp it was a mathematical certainty he would never reach it; we had better forget about him. I could only conclude that Shute was still suffering from shock.

A search party was clearly the thing. But none of us was fit to go out again. Could the porters help us? Constant put it to the Bang. The latter immediately called out the porters and made them form a straight line with one end at the camp and the other far out on the glacier. With the camp as center they described a circle, and it was not long before Jungle was caught and restored to us, tired but sound. He was quite surprised to find that we had been anxious about him and inclined to take it as a reflection on his competence. I told him that he must allow for our natural overanxiety at the bare possibility of losing him. He saw my point, and seemed satisfied.

Next day, we held council of war. The North Wall was proving a tougher proposition than we had anticipated; our plans would have to be drastically revised. Moreover, Burley said that he would not in any circumstances allow himself to be on a rope again with Wish. He had, he said, promised his fiancée that he would not take any unnecessary risks, and cragsmen who became crag-bound at the very earliest opportunity were clearly an unnecessary risk. Wish retorted that the leading man on the rope had the right to expect help from the second. If Burley had been half a mountaineer, instead of wholly a handicap, yesterday's unfortunate incident would never have occurred. He said that big men were notoriously clumsy on crags, and it would suit him very well indeed if Burley stayed at the bottom of the mountain, where he could do the least amount of damage. Those of us who had fiancées, he said, owed it to them to keep as far away from Burley as possible.

Jungle broke in now, saying that he himself had no fiancée, but if he had he would consider it his elementary duty to keep away from Shute, who, he said, was as little to be trusted with an ice axe as a Red Indian on the warpath. Shute, considerably agitated I thought, said that his fiancée had expressly warned him against companions who let other people do all the work and got lost when their turn came. He said that the sight of Jungle on the other end of one's rope was enough to make the safest iceman drop his axe. He said that nothing would induce him to venture out alone with Jungle again.

All this was somewhat bewildering. It was quite clear, of course, that my companions had not yet recovered from their recent shaking-up. That portion of their remarks which was not friendly plain speaking was doubtless due to nervous reaction from their ordeals; in a day or two they would be their normal hearty selves again. In the meantime I had the responsibility of nursing two friendships, and this did not promise to be easy. My mind was further confused by trying to decide who had a fiancee and who had not.

In the end, all I could think of was to remind them again that Rum Doodle was not Mont Blanc. Shute said that he was glad to be reminded of this, as he had completely forgotten the fact. He asked me if I could recall any of Totter's remarks on the subject which might be of help to him in the future. I quoted to him Totter's famous remark: To climb Mont Blanc is one thing; to climb Rum Doodle is quite another. Shute thanked me and said that Totter's was one of the soundest statements he had ever heard; it would, he said, be a great inspiration to him. He would be quite conscious in future that he was not on Mont Blanc, and would behave accordingly. He said that had he been on Mont Blanc he would have been delighted to have Jungle as his partner; as however, he was not on Mont Blanc, but on Rum Doodle, he insisted on having a third person on the rope—preferably a porter.

This seemed reasonable enough. Yesterday's lesson was that two on a rope were ill-fitted to cope with an emergency. Since the bivouac tents were made to accommodate two, it would have to be four on a rope: Two Europeans and two porters. This arrangement would have the additional advantage that the porters would be able to carry complete equipment for all four, so that each rope would be a self-contained unit capable of looking after itself, if necessary, for several days.

Burley pointed out that this would upset all our planning; but since it would mean that he would no longer have Wish all to himself he was heartily in favor of it. The others were just as enthusiastic, and we decided to adopt the idea. I was greatly pleased by our unanimity, which seemed to me to reflect the spirit of the expedition.

Summertime

Al Avarez

from Mountain Magazine, spring 1979 Reprinted with permission by Al Alvarez

The sun was misty, its light diffused and weak, blurring the long folds of the valley, yellowing its greens and swallowing the distant lake and village in a vague glow. The air was damp and warm and they were tired. It had been a long slog up. Shirtless, sweating, rucksacks bumping damply against their backs, boots heavy. When they reached the cliff above the little tarn, its two great walls were already festooned with climbers. They trudged heavily along the foot of the east buttress, changed into lighter boots, sorted their equipment, and stowed their rucksacks neatly under an overhang. Then they stepped delicately out on to the steep west buttress and climbed across to the wide ledge where their route began. But others were there before them, so they sprawled lazily and in comfort, feeling their sweat dry, grateful for the north face shadow and the cool rock curving above, dropping away below. The party in front was taking its time to cross an abrupt smooth slab, the leader talking, mostly to himself in a light nervous voice, as though to cheer himself up. Occasionally they heard small sounds of other climbers on the two looming buttresses, calling to one another at a distance. Lazy day. Their fatigue was pleasant, lulling. Alan began to doze, wake, doze. John was whistling softly to himself: "Summertime, and the living is easy."

Then for no good reason, Alan was wholly awake. There was a faint noise from the direction of the east buttress and a slight disturbance at the corner of his eyes. Then silence and the humid midday lull.

"Someone's come off," said John.

Alan looked to where he was pointing and could see nothing.

"You sure?" he said.

"I think so."

Nobody moved on the cliff or screes. The disturbance had been no more than a puff of wind. A cool momentary breath and it was gone. Silence. Then someone hurried along the foot of the cliff side. Another man followed him, then another, running awkwardly on the steep path. There were voices calling, a sudden urgency in the air.

"He hasn't moved," said John, and pointed again.

There was a vague shape on the scree. It was crumpled and still. Two men slithered down toward it, loose stones cascading in front of them. They bent over the motionless figure, then straightened and shouted faintly upwards.

"We'd better get off and see if we can help," said John.

"What the hell," said Alan. "It's just some idiot who's slipped and twisted an ankle." He felt irritated at having to turn back from a climb. Another day lost.

"Even so," John apologized, "we'd want someone to do the same for us." Alan made him feel foolish and pompous, like a dull schoolboy.

Alan grunted resentfully and stood up. Carefully and slowly they traversed off the climb. When they reached the rucksacks Alan flopped down and began to unlace his climbing shoes.

"We'd better change boots," he said grudgingly. "Just in case we have to lug some bloody stretcher miles down the mountain." Anything to waste time.

Somewhere on the cliff high above them a man was shouting in a self-important voice about a radio: "Turn it to Emergency. Call Alpine Valley 3. We're Alpine Valley 2. It's in my pack. In my pack. Turn it to Emergency." Even at that distance he sounded as if he were giving orders.

John and Alan ambled slowly back along the path. By the time they reached the foot of the east buttress a small group had gathered on the scree and more were waiting uneasily on the path above, as though frightened to go too close. The body had not moved. A climber, caught in the middle of a route and unable or willing to go down, hung poised on the vertical wall above, peering down on the scene like a stone gargoyle on a church.

"Where's that bloody radio?" A man clambered hurriedly back on to the path.

Alan touched his arm: "Who is it?"

"Dave. Dave Evans. He's not conscious."

"Oh no." Alan felt his stomach turn over once, heavily. The other man's face was greenish.

"His skull's split wide open," he said. He was trembling.

Together John and Alan slithered down the scree. Dave was lying on his side, his back toward them. One hand was behind his knee, puffed up and jaggedly cut. The nails were purple and oozed blood. His legs lay at odd angles, like a doll's, and the hair on the back of his head was matted and bloody. Three men bent uncertainly over him. Alan and John sat down on the opposite side of Dave's body.

"How is he?" asked John in a small voice, as though not wanting to disturb a sick man.

"It's very bad."

They all waited in the sticky air. Alan wanted to go round below the broken body and look at his friend's face. But he hadn't the nerve.

Suddenly, one of the other three said urgently: "I think his heart's stopped. I can't feel his pulse."

"Give him artificial respiration," said another.

They turned Dave on his back. His face was the color of putty, a dead grey, his head a lumpy, gaping mass of blood.

"He's shaved off his beard since I last saw him," thought Alan inconsequentially.

"Push on his ribs as hard as you can," said one of the men. "Don't worry if you break them. They're probably broken already. Just push with everything you've got. Once a second."

Obediently a second man straddled Dave's body, leaned with arms stiff against his chest and began to push, reluctantly at first, then with a gathering, desperate energy. The man who had given instructions pinched Dave's nostrils with the fingers of one hand, and with the other, made a funnel of his lips. He put his mouth to Dave's and blew hard, as if he were inflating a child's balloon. Then he turned his head, sucked in air, and blew again. His lifted mouth was covered with Dave's blood. The third man began counting slowly: "One-and-two-and-three-and-four-and..."

Every so often, the climber giving Dave the kiss of life paused to spit. Once he retched violently and sucked in his breath through clenched teeth like a man screaming. Whenever he lifted his mouth, Dave's lips shuddered with an obscene farting noise.

More people came up. Each couple of minutes, the men giving CPR switched positions. They came and sat heavily on the scree, their lips smeared with blood.

"I don't think we've a hope," one said. "The deep wounds in his head are congealing already."

But they went on just the same, and the terrible, loose farting noise continued.

"I wish they'd leave him alone," said Alan.

"He's got two kids, hasn't he?" said John.

"Three," said Alan.

Another climber, Paul, came and sat down beside them. "He took a...short cut...across the...blocks at the top. I think...something...came away. He went quite...slowly...bounced...on a couple of ledges. Very slowly. I thought he'd...stop himself. Then he just...went on...over the edge...of the main...face. Three hundred feet." He paused, shaking his head. "I thought he'd stop himself," he repeated in an accusing voice.

"Maybe the rock knocked him out when it came away," said John consolingly, as though Paul were somehow to blame.

"He should have been wearing a crash helmet," said Alan.

"Twenty-one-and-twenty-two-and-twenty-three-and..." Again the vibrating farting noise came from the crumpled body.

Then another, busier note began, faintly at first, on the other side of the mountain, but growing swiftly more demanding until the whole amphitheater of rock seemed to shake with the din. A helicopter sidled out of the misty air over the ridge of the valley. It circled once high up, then swooped down over the tarn at the foot of the scree and dropped a smoke flare.

"Idiots," said Alan in his aggrieved voice. "Why are they playing games?"

"That's to see which way the wind is blowing," said John.

The helicopter circled again and then began to nose in like a feeding insect, vivid yellow, its blades whirring. Everybody struggled back up the scree to the path, leaving Dave on his own in the encircling noise.

Three men crouched in the opening of the machine, dressed like spacemen in silver suits and helmets. Two of them were laughing together, as though one had just told an unexpectedly good joke.

The chopper hovered, whirling up dust. One of the spacemen swung suddenly out on a cable, clutching a bulky stretcher. As he descended, he waved his feet in the air like a baby in a high chair. The helicopter circled again fussily. Then another figure was winched down, holding a neat doctor's bag. He hung at the end of the wire, stiff, formal and unmoving. The chopper whirred off once more toward the ridge while the two spacemen busied themselves with the lonely body on the scree. At last one of them stood and waved, and the great hungry insect sidled in like an enormous Christmas parcel. Once again, he and his companion on board smiled brightly to each other as they manipulated their unwieldy load into the belly of the machine. Then the doctor ascended as formally as before, and the helicopter buzzed importantly back down the valley.

The climbers sat, stunned by the silence, as the dust settled.

"They got him out in under an hour," someone said at last.

"Not bad, not bad at all." The men began to stir and stretch.

"Will you tell his wife?" John said to Paul.

"I suppose I've got to." Paul was still staring down the valley into the glowing mist where the helicopter had vanished. It seemed as though he did not yet believe what had happened concerned him.

Alan got up stiffly. "I don't want to climb now," he said. "My stomach feels like knotted old rope."

"No," said John. "Let's go back down." He sounded relieved.

They moved slowly back toward their rucksacks, exhausted, empty, uncertain, like two old men.

High on the cliff above, the single climber was still poised, transfixed on his tiny ledge, watching. From his waist a rope curved across the face and went out of sight round a corner of rock to his waiting invisible companion. The summer air was thick and gold with dust.

The Escapist

David Craig

from Mountain Magazine, winter 1989 Reprinted with permission by David Craig

Colin Banks stood on a ledge high up on the south buttress of Green Pike, gripped by the fact that in fifteen minutes he would have to commit himself and step out onto the sheer wall to his right. Part of him reeled from the insane danger of it. The sheep feeding on the grass slope two hundred feet below, the pair of ravens planing over on the easterly breeze and barking to each other—those were the sane species, living in their element, not forcing themselves to stretch into the impossible. But another part of himself craved the climbing, felt tame and trapped among streets or in the lowlands, and only fired fully into life when the high rocks came into sight and his eyes were drawn upwards along the ramps, faces, and pinnacles that linked the valley floor to the skyline.

"What did you do here?" A call from below, from his partner, Lawrence.

"Have you reached the big crack?"

"I'm just below it."

"Lay away leftwards. Gain a few feet, then pull up on a fist jam and make a high step right to a little sharp flake. Right?"

"Okay. I'm climbing."

Colin leaned back against the rock wall and pulled on the red and yellow ropes which dropped out of his sight below his feet. There was slack to take in: Lawrence was moving slowly up again.

Here on a stance, in the middle of a sheer crag, was now Colin's favorite refuge. He was safe from everything but his own thoughts. Automatically he looked southward toward Branston, fifty miles away across the dales and the bay. Two cooling towers just showed, pale-grey bodies amongst a haze of diffused sunshine. Eight years before it had filled him with happy warmth to know that his home was there, a mile inland from the power station. Mandy wheeling the twins home from the shops, bending down and widening her eyes to make them laugh, racing the last few yards so that the push-chair rattled and jounced on the uneven pavement and the wee boys went into hysterics and swayed from side to side, exaggerating the movement. Where would she be now? Round at her friend Joanne's, bitterly analyzing the deadness of her marriage. And the boys would come home from school to find both their parents out and the house smelling of unwashed dishes and soot from a fireless chimney. But would the boys be any less unhappy if he ended the present purgatory and left home for good?

He pulled on the ropes. There was slack on the red one. He took it till it was firm between himself and Lawrence struggling down below, then braced himself anew on the ledge. As so often happened in these minutes of perfect privacy, his problems—the situations that screened themselves over and over in his head—flowed in on him unstoppably. The stages of his marriage now seemed marked by rows, searing rows in which too much

148

was said—accusations were stabbed home which then fulminated endlessly, like fires underground. The first row in front of the children still shamed and hurt him the worst, though it had been far less violent than later ones. From that time on, he often thought, the feeling of well-being in the family had come to seem a pretense which everyone saw through, and which wasn't worth maintaining.

In the middle of a warm May day they had gone out to attack the mini wilderness at the foot of the garden. "At long last," said Mandy. Colin had long fantasized bold creative improvements in the tangle of nettles, elder scrub and assorted junk, but this had come to be a promise he had failed to keep. Today they had gotten up late. Colin liked to lie naked beside Mandy as the sun shone strongly out of the east and glowed yellow on their bedroom wall. But Mandy was disinclined to make love. Half her mind was on the boys, whose voices were rising shrilly from below. When at last they dressed and went downstairs, the kitchen floor was sprayed with milk and cornflakes.

"Andrew made me," said Ian, pouting his lower lip and starting to breathe fast and jerkily.

"I didn't! You spilled them first. And then you grabbed my plate."

"Didn't. I was trying to reach the packet."

"You grabbed my plate. You're always wanting something of mine."

"Boys! High time you were out in the sunshine. Col—for godsake take them out and get something organized while I clean this lot up."

"You come too. It's too fine for housework."

"How can I? Look at the floor. So long as you keep them happy and stop them fighting..."

Colin was glad to step out of the house, with its litter of toys and soiled clothes. As for his guilt at Mandy's taking on her burden of motherhood yet again, he was used to it. It tainted everything, but he could lose himself in the handiwork, in the atmosphere of turned earth, hedges coming into flower, swifts whistling and arcing across the blue.

"Ian, bring the spade. Andrew, can you manage the barrow?"

They looked comical, like two of the seven dwarfs, staggering along with full-size garden tools. He took the fork, the shears and the sickle and led the way behind the shed and into the rank greenery of the wilderness.

"Now, which things have you to look out for?"

"Those ones." Ian pointed at the nettles.

"That's right. What else, Andrew?"

"Those pricky ones," he said, pointing at a thicket of wild raspberries.

"That's right. Your wellies would have covered your legs better. Let's get cracking. I'll cut down these long stems. Ian, you cut them into bits, okay? You try and pile them in the barrow, Andy."

For a good half hour they worked away amongst the smell of crushed leaves. The sky sparkled between sprays of luminous green. "It's hard," said Ian, shaking a stem between the blades of the shears and trying to break its last tough fibers. He put the shears on the ground and wiped his brow, imitating Colin.

Eyeing his brother, Andrew cautiously picked up the shears, and when Ian said, "*I'm* doing that," Andrew retorted, "It's my turn now."

"Fair enough," said Colin hopefully and felt balmy relief when Ian said, "I'll pile these bits in the barrow." Both boys went busily to work again. For a while Colin crunched into the press of raspberry canes with the sickle. Presently, felled greenery lay scattered everywhere and he took the fork and began lifting the mass aside so that he could see the shape of the ground and what wanted doing next. Pure peace stole through him like soft heat.

Then behind him one of the twins screamed, shrill screams pumping out as though mechanically. Colin turned and crashed through the greenery, which thwarted him like wire. Ian was lying crouched on his side, both hands to his leg. It was streaming blood. Andrew was staring, terrified.

"He took the hook—the hook—and it slipped, and—"

Mandy came running down the path. "Colin? Ian!" She knelt beside the stricken boy, put her arm around him and held him against her, then firmly lifted one of his hands from his leg. A lip of flesh sagged from the little plump calf and blood welled over it. He screamed again, a mindless panic note. "He didn't have the sickle?" Mandy's voice was stark with surprise and she looked up at Colin briefly with eyes that burned hostility into his skin. "Lift him into the house. I'll hold his leg. Andrewcome. Don't cry, love. Come on. We've got to get Dr. Dawson!"

They walked in a huddle up to the house. Ian was made comfortable on the settee with newspaper under his leg; Mandy held the lips of the wound shut and cuddled him into quietness while Colin negotiated fiercely on the phone until the surgery promised to get hold of the doctor "as soon as possible." Andrew was soothed with orange juice and he came through and offered a drink of it to Ian, but Ian only nestled his head deeper into his mother.

Mandy was perfectly calm, expressionless, the skin glossy and tanned on her cheekbones, her blond hair swept behind her ears and gathered in a comb at the back of her head. Colin couldn't get her to exchange signals with him. So it was for the rest of the morning and into the afternoon, while Dr. Dawson came and cleaned the leg, put in stitches with a local anaesthetic, and gave Ian a tetanus shot. The house fell utterly quiet. An alien smell of disinfectant tinged the warm air. Ian was asleep, his cheeks flushed and his thumb in his mouth. Andrew stared drowsily at the Test Match on television with the sound turned off. Mandy sat with her hands in her lap, in a strangely old-fashioned pose of decorum, looking down into the garden. Colin started to mark work he had brought home from school.

"How often is this going to happen?" Mandy said, her voice making a numb statement out of the question. Colin looked round at his wife. She hadn't moved, or looked at him.

"Mandy! One piece of sheer bad luck—"

"Bad luck? You let them do anything."

"I do not. I told them to watch out for stings and thorns."

"Stings and thorns. And you let a four-year-old have a sickle."

"I did not let him have it. He found it."

"Don't quibble. He got his hands on it because you let them do anything. You've said so. 'Let them explore, find out by trial and error.' You're a bloody theorist."

"What do you want for them, Mandy? A tame life—no adventure? Robots, congealed in some office—"

"Theorist. Bloody theorist. Use your common sense. Stuff your ideas. Little vulnerable people want looking after, that's all."

"I do look after them. Not just protecting them. I want them to grow, and get into life for themselves..."

Mandy turned and looked at Colin with clear still blue eyes, as though appraising a stranger.

"It's so familiar, the way you are with them. You let them do anything. You do what you feel like. You're just pig bloody selfish. That time you climbed up outside the fire escape at your father's hotel. Little Ian was scared—he knew it was dangerous—but he sees you doing crazy things, so he imitates you. He'll follow you to his death one day."

"You hate my climbing."

"Keep your voice down. I'm not discussing that again. We'll never agree about that. It's how you are with them. You can't say no. Are you so anxious to be liked?"

"Look—I'm *natural* with them."

"That's right, you do what you feel like. You're like a boy, a greedy boy. A father should be something else. Not just a playmate. And what is all this frenzy down at the end of the garden? Having an eyeful of that new young talent across the road?"

"The what! Mandy, I don't even know who you mean."

"Oh, you're so innocent. Nobody's that innocent. Oh well, look at her as much as you like. Do what you like. Who believes in monogamy any more? Couples locked together..."

"You want to escape." Colin grabbed her by the wrist and she gave a gasp of pain. "You're talking about yourself. You're tired of fucking me—"

"Stop shouting, you bully. Stop telling the boys"

"You're tired of me. I'm too sedentary. And too adventurous. And too self-centered. And too attentive. Nothing's right for you. Nobody would please you. Well, I'm not going to try any more. Why try and please a bitch?"

The ugly word split the air. His voice was amplified by pent-up anger. Ian woke with a violent start, then let out a yowl of distress. The poison in the grown-ups' hissing and then rising voices had gotten to Andrew and he suddenly cried heartily, as though he too had had a physical wound.

Mandy and Colin wrenched themselves out of their deadlock. The hours till the twins' bedtime passed in cooking, shopping, playing, washing up. Colin promised himself to love Mandy into peace again when they had the sitting room to themselves. But the row seemed to have left nothing unsullied. His grievance was like a sour cud in his throat. On an impulse he grabbed his jacket and went down the road to the Freeholders' Arms while Mandy was still reading to the twins upstairs. When he came back two hours later, the car was gone. When Mandy came up to bed around midnight, all she would answer to his resentful questioning was, "Out. You went out so I went out."

They should have tried to settle some of the issues there and then, should have agreed at least on how to behave with the children. But the scope for dispute seemed endless. Colin played and replayed her words in his mind, but flinched from bringing things up with her and she seemed content to avoid him and keep her thoughts for her friends.

This burst of memories had lasted maybe half a minute but Lawrence had gained height and Colin was ashamed to realize he had failed to take in rope. Looking down past his toes, he saw his friend's helmet bobbing like a solid red balloon among the grey slabs and edges of the crag.

"Take in, Col! Take in! This is gripping."

"You wait till you mantleshelf on to this stance. Fly on a wall stuff."

At that moment Colin came to see, with a pang, that he was using the climbing as a drug. The delicious extremity of it left him no awareness to spare for the wear-and-tear of his struggles with Mandy. He had heard of cancer patients pulling out their own hairs one by one to distract themselves from the bad deep pain. But climbing wasn't agony; even the more desperate moments were shortlived and they released a flood of well-being so full it made you feel you could do anything—wing off into midair, float up the rock face immune to gravity. It even felt for some minutes as though you could seize the miseries and impasses of your daily life and pitch them into the abyss. If he could make himself climb beyond his limits, might he not be able to use the same power on the awful intractable grievances that had plagued him and Mandy for years now? It had come to this: There was nothing that wasn't fated to turn out badly and give them fuel for conflict. That luckless party on Midsummer Eve the year before...

Steve and Toni had asked them to their famous annual booze-up, which always, if the weather was fine, spilled out into the garden, into the pockets of turf enclosed by spurs of limestone, or if people got really high, right out onto the Knott beyond. Everyone called it The Orgy. Drink was unlimited, the upstairs bedrooms creaked with excitement. Colin and Mandy were just old enough to take a faintly aloof and amused attitude to these adolescent fevers.

They parked the car beside the pub and walked down the few yards of high street, still warm with heat stored by the stone-walled cottages. "Lucy in the Sky with Diamonds" was singing out from the open windows at Steve and Toni's. They stepped into a cave of shadow, aromatic with martinis, fresh sweat and cigarette smoke, low-lit by table lamps with crimson shades which made even familiar people look indefinite and strange. Armchairs were full of shapes, mostly couples sprawled together. More people seemed to be heaped on the floor. Colin stepped on an arm, apologized, and felt a hand grip his ankle and then slide up his leg.

"Mandy! Colin!" Toni's face hovered towards them from the back of the room. "You're late. Kid trouble?"

"Not really. They're sleeping like lambs."

"Great. Oh! Ouch! I know you, Phil Barnett—keep your hands off. Mandy! Look after this." She tilted a green bottle toward them as one of the shapes pulled her to the floor. Mandy saved the bottle as it started to spill wine onto the nearest bodies. Taking Colin's hand, she led the way through to the back. It was nearly as crammed. They sat on the floor with their legs fitted between various other legs and bottoms and passed the wine to and fro to each other, drinking rather fast to catch up with the atmosphere. Just six feet away from Colin and straight in front of him a small dark girl was sitting with her intense black eyes seemingly fixed on him. She looked like Nana Mouskouri. Music blasted and a drunken hand must suddenly have turned up Sergeant Pepper. As Colin tried to avoid the dark girl's eyes, he heard Mandy whispering fiercely, "Get drunk then! I want to dance."

"Yes, let's," he said at once, but she had already got to her feet and a moment later he saw her stepping over bodies and across the passage to the other half of the house. Everything felt unreal. The dark girl's eyes seemed to press into his, then her head swung loosely leftward. Amongst the hubbub he picked out what she was saying to the man beside her: "Drift away. Like to drift away 'n' lay 'round in the sun with nothing on."

The bottle was empty. Colin eased himself to his feet, telling himself he was going to search for drink, denying to himself that he was keeping tabs on Mandy. His bladder felt unbearably tight and he climbed upstairs between whispering couples. Water was rushing in the bathroom. He looked in and saw an old friend, Bill Britton, sitting in the bath fully clothed, his legs over the edge. The taps gushed, water was rising round his hips, and a girl in a Spanish blouse was pouring drink from a bottle straight into his mouth. He was half choking, laughing, trying to speak: "Netta! Bitch! Mercy! Ohhh." Colin smiled sportingly, sketched a carefree wave of greeting, and went up one more floor. A bedroom door was ajar. He felt suddenly sickened to see a woman with Mandy's hair and Mandy's tanned shoulders squatting over a man beneath her. She was half naked. Her face looked briefly out at Colin from the dressing-table mirror: It wasn't Mandy at all but a girl scarcely twenty. He went back downstairs. Heavy rock had replaced the Beatles and the dancers were making the floorboards shake. Mandy wasn't among them.

Colin recognized nobody—no Steve, no Toni, no familiar faces from the staff room or the cricket club. Suspicion flushed back in. But perhaps she had gone to get some supper? He went through to the kitchen, feeling his head swelling with the wine. Candles were spilling wax onto a long scrubbed table covered with pots of pâté, plates of cheese and pineapple, *baguettes* two feet long. A middle-aged man with a preposterous gut was standing beside the open fridge and tearing a leg from a cold roast chicken. Colin glared at him as though he were an enemy and the man sneered. No sign of Mandy. He stormed through into the garden. The air smelt of night-scented stock. To the north, above the rough black skyline of the Knott, a flawless afterglow of sunset filled the arch of the sky with electric blue, shading into smoky apricot in the northwest.

A yelp of uncontrollable laughter, a woman's laughter, came from the hawthorn bushes beyond the far end of the garden. The party was eddying outwards, propelled by booze and music and the heady air of summer, into the dusky wilderness where mounds of blossoms glimmered like icebergs.

Colin turned back to the house and took another bottle of white wine from a fresh crate under the kitchen table. The remaining clear point in his brain was telling him to drink no more, to hold on to his wits, but this clarity seemed to have become a spectator, who watched his idiotic behavior and let it happen. Time swam in his head like smoke. Hours later, as a blue morning came glowing through the kitchen windows, he found himself on the floor, leaning against the fridge, with a blonde girl on his knees. She had snuggled her frizzy hair close to his chest and was saying in a sleepy, ill-used voice, "Gimme a kiss—go on—gimme a kiss." Colin felt no desire at all, nothing but headache and humiliation.

The back door opened, letting in air cooled with dew, and Mandy was looking at him sardonically. "Tear yourself away, Colin," she said. "We have not been asked to breakfast."

Colin felt utterly wronged. Was she getting at him to cover her own guilt? They picked their way out between empty bottles and a few people slumped on cushions. The moment they were in the street, he broke out angrily.

"I was looking for you—for hours."

"Really? Why didn't you enjoy yourself? Isn't that what we came for?"

"Yes. But together."

"Sitting on the floor getting pissed? With not a word to say to each other?"

"Mandy! Can't we simply be at peace together?"

"We so often are."

"You're picking this quarrel."

"What! It's you who're all uptight."

"And you're perfectly calm?"

"I am. And so is the morning. Everything's calm and blue and lovely."

"So you feel great. It must have been a wonderful walk."

"It was."

"You're telling me you just went for a walk"

"I did. We went up through the woods—the bracken's just uncurling, all green coming through the old coppery stuff—and then through the copse where you found the slow-worm."

"You went to one of our places!"

"Why shouldn't I?"

"We—you said we."

"Oh, the woods were full of people. You know what it's like at these do's."

"I know what it's like all right. Fucking in every corner. I felt out of it, I can tell you."

"Join in, then. You're hopeless at parties. You don't know how to enjoy yourself."

"I enjoy myself with you."

"Do you? It never seems like it any more. Anyway, you stifle me. We are two people, you know. Not some kind of two-headed monster, or Siamese twins or something."

"You lead your life and I'll lead mine? That recipe for disaster? Is that what you're saying?"

"Colin, don't be boring. I'm not in the mood for a row. If parties aren't one of the things we can manage, don't let's go, that's all. I can go dancing by myself."

"You're trying to peel away from me aren't you?"

"You do when you climb. Anyway I simply want to dance."

"But we dance. We have danced!"

"It doesn't work, though. You can't keep time. Oh, don't make me argue. Let there be one uncomplicated thing."

Colin glanced sideways at her. It was true—she was serene, her face smooth, her stride springy. She seemed perfectly free and at ease in this blue morning. He felt sluggish, rasped, his brain heated and tired at the same time. He didn't know what he was feeling. Jealousy, envy, righteous hurt mingled and threatened to choke him, drops of frustrated sexiness were collecting in him like poison. He wanted to caress her and hurt her.

"You're trying to wound me," he said in a growling, brutal voice. "You calculate it like a torture."

"Wound you?" She was wrenching to free her arm. "I can't wound you. You don't care enough. You only care for you."

"Who made me stop caring?" He was driving his fingers into her flesh. "You've goaded and stung me, needled me about every fucking thing—the children, the neighbors, my friends. You're needling me now. Why?" He had her by both arms now, he was shaking her with all his strength and glaring straight into her eyes. He looked mad and distorted.

"You just...want to know..." her words were jerked from her by his shaking... "if I...had a fuck. That's what's...bugging you."

"You did! I know you did! You fucking slut!"

"Your breath stinks. You were too bloody pissed to even give that little doll what she wanted. You are abject. Ohhh!" She screamed as Colin's furious lunges toppled her backwards. Her head bounced on the flags at the roadside. She rolled onto her side, put her hand into her hair, and stared unbelievingly at the wet blood reddening it. She got up, looked around for her handbag, picked it up, and ran off down the street on a wavering line. He caught her up in the car a few moments later and slanted to a stop, half blocking her way. She leaned on the wing, breathing in gasps, and then got in. They drove back home along the dry emptiness of the early morning road, frozen into their own thoughts. They had not been out together since.

Colin leaned forward on the belay. Lawrence's fingers were trying the small flake holds, fixing onto them like separate little animals inching up the rock. His face came into sight, looking quizzical behind his heavy glasses, and he squinted until his pupils disappeared into his nose, then rolled his eyes. "Christ, Colin, how much more? This is like Nelson's Column."

"Just one pitch after this—the best."

"The worst, you mean. You can lead it. I'm at my limit."

"That's what it's all about. Don't hang about, Lawrie. Your fingers will go."

As Lawrence pulled up on ever more slender holds and then set his palms on the ledge beside Colin's feet, ready for the mantleshelf, Colin looked again to his right, for a last appraisal of the coming ordeal. The sheer wall pushed into space, it was undercut below, and the one line across it, on a rising diagonal, led off round a corner. Not even the reassurance of a visible goal. The diagonal consisted of a rock lip sometimes one, sometimes two inches wide, a slender gangway, breached in one place where a section had flaked off and dropped to the scree two hundred feet below. The handholds were mere contact points—nothing to grip. The only way to move along the face was by balancing delicately, center of gravity held close in, feet set sideways, until you reached the gap. Then the stride, bridging across at the full stretch of your legs. It was a step through the air, through the invisible fear barrier and onto a plane of unreal freedom, a place you'd never hoped to reach but which would gradually settle into reality around you.

As Colin had these thoughts, he knew that a lower level in himself was churning with the nausea of fear. This would die down, the fear barrier would part and vanish, the dizzy moves would become simply the next steps that he had to take, the next ten minutes of life that waited to be lived. Lawrence was crowding up onto the ledge beside him. "What a way to spend Easter," he said, holding his arms out sideways and dropping his hands from the wrist. Colin tried to grin and his lips stretched over closed teeth.

"Give us the gear," was all he said, and while he clipped slings and metal nuts back into the harness at his waist, Lawrence tied onto the belays. The sun soaked into them, warmth reflected from the pock-marked grey rock near their faces, and a light breeze made their foreheads feel the cool of sweat evaporating.

The wall pitch now reared before Colin like a test. It had come to him that if he could make it, then, by the same token, he could make it out of the impossible situation at home. He could leave, go off and live in his own way. He was not helpless. The way up that wall loomed frighteningly hard, but it could be done. By his own nerve and cool-headedness and the leathery strength of his own arms. Lawrence was looking at him quizzically, registering his uncharacteristic quietness.

"Well," Colin said, "It'll not get easier by hanging about. And it's closing time at three." He turned his head and shouted, "I'm coming, you bloody rock!"

He unclipped from the belay, turned to face the crag, and stepped away sideways. He grasped the pinnacle that terminated their ledge, felt it solid in the palms of his hands, then let go with his left and pulled sideways on a small rough edge. He set his left foot in a shallow pocket beyond the ledge, put his right foot beside it, gathered himself into balance, and reached with his left foot for the start of the slender gangway. The churning inside him had stilled. His fingers found small roughnesses on the face above head-height and the solidity of the rock passed into him and poised him. The slender gangway rose by a two-foot step onto a flake top and his left leg rose, flexing smoothly at the knee, lifting him in balance, while the abyss behind and below sucked at him. Now the break in the gangway. The transit through emptiness into the plane where he had never been. He began to feel unable. That gap was surely too broadstretching, would unsteady him and peel him off—there were no cracks for a nut runner to protect the move—he wasn't able. But he kept moving. The movement itself would carry him and his qualms and quailings across the void. His left foot squirmed on the far edge of the gangway beyond the break. His left palm curved slightly round a boss of rock, feeling for balance. The fingers of his right hand let go of a tiny edge and hovered helplessly. He started to move his weight leftward across the void and his right leg wavered in midair before pulling after his left.

He was standing on the far side. The gangway led off round the corner, still thin, still sharp, and then he was looking up the final chimney crack. His mind was dimming after the concentration of the last few minutes but his body was unscathed. He pulled up off the gangway, reaching high for broken edges on both sides of the chimney, knowing the drop hollowing beneath his feet and feeling strength pour through his shoulders into his arms in a flow nothing could prevent.

As his mind recovered itself, he came to know how fleeting a thing he had done. It was over, almost before he had taken the measure of it. Forty feet above was the mossy, short-bitten pasture of the hilltop—a zone of pure peace. Other mountains rose and fell around them. The road, the village, and the bay, the cooling towers. The short sharp thing had been done. Now came the long haul into alien terrain where the dangers were all undefined and might last for years.

Leviathan

Geof Childs

from Mountain Magazine, fall 1989 Reprinted with permission by Geof Childes

Kathmandu was cool and lush and muddy from the monsoon. The rail-thin Newar officials at the customs bench passed my bags along with an air of persecuted indifference and returned rapidly to their cold, white tile offices, where they huddled in tight crowds around huge pots of tea on kerosene stoves. The odors of East and West mingled with the crowd in the airport lobby: leek and wool, deodorant and leather. The wind gathered from the fields the scents of jet exhaust and ox dung. I hired a hawk-nosed beggar standing near the gate to help me with my stuff and signaled for a taxi.

The crowded city surged, much the way I remembered Saigon. Instead of soldiers, though, there were Gurkha policemen wearing crisp khaki shorts, holding long, peeled switches and sharing street corners with sniffling Dutch junkies. Instead of Montagnards, Tibetan refugees trotted to market in their red and black rags beneath enormous bundles of willow and alder twigs. Japanese taxis splashed the ooze and shit of open sewers onto sidewalks and sacred cattle. Dogs lay dead and bloated in the streets. And I, Ishmael "Izzy" O'Brien, was once more a pilgrim in someone else's cause. In the thirteen years since my last visit to the Orient, the only thing I'd learned was climbing.

I took a room in the older section of the city at a hotel named the Kathmandu Guest House. There was an enclosed cobblestone parking area out front with a small restaurant off to one side. A yard in the back had white, metal chairs flanked by parallel rows of neat Sussex gardening. The room had four beds and a large balcony overlooking the main entrance. The manager assured me that the beds were clean and that the water in the showers was always hot. A very attractive woman stood beside me speaking to one of the clerks in fluent Nepali as I paid a week's advance on the room. She wore a black leotard with puffy, black silk trousers and Tibetan slippers—probably in her late twenties, possibly European, maybe American. We turned together toward the door.

"It's up there, just left," she told me in a strong Australian accent as we approached the stairs. Then she smiled. "And good luck with the showers."

She walked quickly away, and I hiked my three leaden rucksacks up the steps. I dumped out everything onto the floor of the room and spent an hour separating my own things from the expedition equipment I'd brought with me. The sun came out and the cement steamed. The humidity sat in my lungs like water. I put on a T-shirt and nylon running shorts and stood at the window for a time looking out on the haze of the Himalaya with my mind full of autumnal Colorado.

After a short nap I ate a light supper in the restaurant outside the hotel and walked through the city to Freak Street in the European Bazaar. The evening light was golden and gleaming. A small, wrinkled Hindi in dirty cotton pajamas stopped me as I passed under an enormous lattice of bamboo scaffolds leaning against the side of an ancient temple. He took my arm and pressed a small plug of black hashish into my hand.

"If you like," he grinned, harmless and beatific, "you come back."

I walked through the booths and stalls until dark, then climbed stairs to a second-floor coffee and yogurt shop. The owner was a Frenchwoman with vermillion hair and eyes that hung in her head like broken bulbs. She brought me a bowl of sherbet with a mint leaf. I crushed the hash into powder against the table top and sprinkled it on the sherbet. Names and phrases were carved into the wood table in a Babel of tongues. When I went back outside, I shuffled brainless and awed down side streets where naked twenty-five-watt bulbs backlit alley scenes too strange and alien for Vermeer's brush. I walked aimlessly along labyrinthine passages that reeked of urine and dry rot, buzzing in pot-head amazement at everything. I followed a poor, pumpkin-faced child who seemed rich with omen, but I lost him in a web of side streets. Passing ghostly ruins and a huge, ornately carved stupa, I came to a wide, bustling courtyard filled with night hawkers and coster-mongers. Along the fence stood God's occasional mishaps, laughing and gossiping and swinging deformed arms or legs swollen with elephantiasis to calls of "Baksheesh, Sahib? Baksheesh?" One particularly capitalistic dwarf stepped directly in front of me, poking out his hand and forcing a grin. His head was tilted sharply against his shoulder and the whole of his face and thorax—from skyward ear to his waist— was a single mass of featureless skin. No clavicle, no breast, no separated arm: just melted, homogeneous flesh. An unfinished man. I studied him for some time, then shook the outstretched hand. No, this was not Boulder. I had come a long way on the strength of a voice over the phone and a ticket in the mail.

Two days later, on the eleventh of October, two other expedition members arrived. I met them at the airport and helped them pass through customs. They had met for the first time in Delhi but weren't able to sit together on the crowded flight to Kathmandu. I had no difficulty, however, picking them out from among the other passengers.

Hamish Frazier was robust and heavyset, with a great, ginger-colored beard that flew loose at his temples, the hair thinning atop his rosy, weathered pate. His woollen shirt, tucked carelessly into baggy trousers, barely restrained his huge chest and shoulders. For a climber he had a surprisingly large paunch; for a Scots mountaineer he looked absolutely right. I liked him immediately.

Metikja Martinez was a different sort altogether. A European hard man, he was taller, very dark, broodish, tender, angry and contemplative. His hair hung in a tousled mop; his shoulders were enormously broad, and his hands were almost comically outsized. My hand seemed to disappear in his grasp when we shook. Yet his clothes matched, and he was the only one of the three of us I would have called handsome. Frazier and I loaded most of the gear and ourselves into two taxis while Metikja went off to the Yugoslavian Embassy to straighten out his visa and visit some old acquaintances.

"Fookin' pigsty, this place, eh, Jimmy," Hamish enthused as we sped toward town. "Third time I've been here and I'll be boogered if it smells any better. It's the fookin' cows, ye know, lad? Aye, ye can't have 'em muckin' about the fookin' kitchen without expectin' 'em ta draw flies now, can ye?" Then turning back to me, "Where ye got us puttin' up ta doss, lad? The Kathmandu?"

I nodded, somewhat disappointed.

"Right as fookin' rain, then, Jimmy! I imagine there's the usual clutch of Aussie quim standin' by, right? It's a long good-bye on that, these voyages, in't it, laddie?" He laughed for a moment then and turned to watch Kathmandu arrive. After a time he looked back at me, more serious now. "When's the Major sneakin' inta town?" he asked, as we careened around a corner, scattering shoppers. "I'll bet a pint he dinna tell ye, now, did he? He's a bet queer for surprises, that one."

He thought that over, then started in again. "Fook, I'm hoongry. That wee spot next door still there? Bit dear, I thought, but the woggies cook a potato right. What sort of name did you say Ishmael O'Brien was, anyway, lad?" On and on like that, episodic monologues, almost all of them rhetorical, and less than half, I suspected, meant to be heard.

We hauled the gear upstairs and spent the rest of the afternoon dividing it into two dozen separate piles. "I've a wee taste, O'Brien," Hamish finally concluded. He looked tired from the long flight and the heat. We put on clean shirts and went downstairs to the Star Restaurant. The Nepali owner showed us to a table in the corner beside the woman I had met a few days earlier. "'Ello, Sheila." Hamish muttered in a shammed Australian accent. We took our seats and she never lifted an eye, just kept to her book and tea. Frazier rolled his eyes and ordered six beers.

I had expected him to be more aggressive, louder as a drinker, but mostly we sat in silence. We both drank our first two bottles before he even spoke. He asked if I'd ever met the Major. I said no. In fact, I knew very little about the man. Hamish looked at me doubtfully, almost angrily, then switched his gaze to the room.

"Well, don't you be believin' everything you hear, O'Brien. He's all right. A bit odd, 'boot who isn't comin' on these fookin' crusades, eh? Aye, you get caught up in somethin' like this, spendin' your money, dear as it is, to take a whack at killin' yerself for ten minutes o'standin' in the wind on some nameless mountaintop. Vicar's tits, mon, it'll make ye a bit funny, then won't it?"

He was silent again for a moment, searching for the right words.

"You rich, O'Brien?"

"No."

"Major's rich as fookin' Croesus, I reckon," he said. "Probably crazier than a fookin' Cumbrian goos, too, for all I know about behavin' in public. But I kin tell ye he's a right hard man to have with you on a piss-up, strong and steady as any I've seen touch axe to snow. Aye, game as they come and a straight man with ye, too. The type that'll see ye through a shit storm without a word."

We each ordered another bottle of beer and Hamish got a sandwich. I asked him if he knew much about the mountain or the route. He said no, only that the Major had taken a close look at it the year before during his solo attempt. Some people, he added, were saying the usual thing about its being the hardest thing attempted at that altitude. The Major had spent two-and-a-half weeks on it by himself, he explained. No food at the end, bad weather, and, for a time, not much hope of getting down alive.

"Lost his mind up there, I suppose," Frazier said without lifting his eyes from the remains of his sandwich. "Reckon he thinks he can find it again up on top. We'll bloody well find out about that when he gets there, I guess."

He got up, and threw a few rupee notes on the table. I watched him walk out and ordered some tea and a slice of pie. The food came after a while, and I picked at it, trying to sort through my thoughts. I hardly heard her voice.

"You going with them, then, Yank? Is that it?"

It took a moment before I realized that she had spoken. The atmosphere around her had been so hard I didn't imagine it could be talked through. When I turned, she was facing me, smoking a cigarette wrapped in brown paper. She was impossibly beautiful. I was a little drunk and desperately in love.

"Yeah," I stammered, trying to sound urbane and casual. "We're a mountaineering exped."

"Right," she cut in. "The Kahli Gurkha bunch. I know. The southwest face, I believe?" I nodded and she went on. "The Leviathan—or something like that. Isn't that what you're calling it? Much better name than the Nepali one, I'm sure. Probably bloody hard to go about raising money to climb a mountain with a name the bankers in London can't pronounce. 'The last great problem'," she mused cynically. "Get you laid back home, mate?"

I was shocked. Titillated and overwhelmed.

"Look," she semi-apologized, "I work for the Sherpa cooperative. I get all this shit across my desk, season after season. Every year it's someone off to tame the hardest mountain, the worst route, the steepest face. Christ, our records are like obituaries of who's-been-who in the Himalaya for the last twenty years. The young and the starry-eyed off to get themselves killed for the greater glory of European alpinism and usually taking a few Sherpas with them. Hoo-fucking-rah, mate. I haven't seen a bloody Yank over here with his head on right yet, and you're just the same as the rest of them."

"Thanks," I grinned. I think I grinned. I tried to grin.

"Oh, look. I've offended you; I'm sorry." She smiled and slowed down for a moment. "Listen, I'm a bit off, I guess. I don't mean to come down like your bloody Mum or anything. It's just that I've seen this same act repeated so many times since I've been here I get the feeling that somebody ought to step in and say something, whether it changes anything or not." She caught her rising frustration this time and sat back with it against the bench. She shook her head and smiled. I wondered if she could hear my heart beating.

"'One climbs to know oneself'," she recited, "'and in so doing at last comes to know nothing. The being has been no more than the doing.'" She lit another cigarette, cupping her hand over the flame and letting the significance settle. "Does that mean anything to you at all?"

"Maybe," I shrugged. "I guess it does."

"I knew it wouldn't," she replied after a pause. She smiled again and exhaled a cloud. Westerners seem to glow with spiritual one-upmanship when they have mastered the recitation of some enigmatic Zen parable.

"Do you know what a chod is?" she asked next. I shook my head. "It's a tantric rite whereby the true believer commits himself to encountering his worst fears. A monk, for example, who finds he is frightened of the spirits he believes to inhabit a graveyard, will spend a night meditating in the graveyard. Defeating fear: meeting the dragon and finding out that it is only air, the creation of his own imagination." I nodded my head, anticipating the lesson. "That is why you climb. Because you are afraid to. It is your chod."

"My mother will be crushed," I told her. "Quitting college was one thing, but if I turn into a monk, it's going to kill her." I smiled and she did not.

"The monk cleanses himself," she continued. "He goes expecting nothing and thus is prepared to accept everything. He empties himself of ambition. You, on the other hand, are not going to the mountain—you are going to the summit. Even if you succeed, you fail, because you never left New York or Iowa or wherever you're from. You just brought it all with you. You transpose instead of travel. There will be no understanding because there will be no humility. You do not come to find your God; you come to challenge Him. You long to stand upon the summit, not to be near God, but to slap His face. The mountain is just your method, your tool, and therefore it holds no revelation for you. There will be no truth of success, no conquest for you. The only God you will see will be Masta, the mountain god of horror." She stubbed out her smoke and leaned closer.

"Look, don't be daft, will you. Your Major—I've heard the Sherpas talk about him. None of them will work for him. You know that, don't you? They call him a sennin, a bloody mountain lunatic! That's why he's had to go ahead to Khandbari to find people. No one in Kathmandu will"

"Look, lady," I cut her off. "I appreciate the intro to Zen 101. I'm sure everything you say is absolutely true." She started to speak, but I held up my hand. "Honest to Buddha. I don't know what the hell you're talking about. You've got the wrong guy. I'm just good old, time-flogging Izzy O'Brien, and all I'm doing over here is climbing a mountain. No spiritual mission, no ghosts or anything; just see the sights and do a little climbing. You can read whatever you want into that, I guess, but where I'm concerned, that's all there is to it."

She started to speak again.

"That's it," I almost shouted. "I'm sorry; I'm just not that complex. Christ, I thought chod was a frigging fish or something." She laughed over that one. She let her head fall back, and her spectacular breasts vibrated beneath her leotard. I grinned.

"Look, mate," she said finally, "I'm awfully sorry. Your pie is getting cold." We both laughed until the mood seemed better. "My name is Lucy," she added, sticking out her hand. "Tell me, O'Brien, do you abuse drugs?"

We said good night on the steps below her door. She put her hand on the side of my face, but I made no effort to kiss her. I was beyond arousal, drug-sodden bewildered, strangely mordant. I listened to her door close and went out onto the balcony. It was 3 A.M. and the city sighed. Its potpourri scent and amber lights lolled on breezes that rustled the palm fronds in the garden. Fred Astaire would have danced. I wove awkwardly toward our room and slipped quietly through the door, threading through mounds of gear.

Hamish was in the far bed, snoring and gagging in perfect tranquility. I took off my shirt and trousers, Lucy still cartwheeling through my brain, and slipped under the sheets of my bunk. There was a grunt—distinct, sleepy, and very near—and an unexpected contact with skin. I dived out of bed yelping, "Jesus!" and rolled sideways along the floor. Behind me the entire surface of the bed seemed to rise. I collided heavily with a rucksack and struggled wildly to get the ice axe off it.

"That'd be Metilkja, lad," Hamish explained sleepily. "Bonnie great booger he is. Aye." Then he drifted back into sleep. The Yugoslavian sat smiling as I circled warily to the next bunk, ice axe in hand, trying very hard to seem collected and poised.

"Good day," he said pleasantly.

"Good day."

In the morning we went to work on the gear heaped on the porch, dividing, listing, and crating the food, tents, clothing, climbing equipment and personal belongings into eight-pound loads. We packed the loads into plastic garbage cans and covered them with burlap sacks. For two dollars a day, a porter would carry one of the loads plus his own food and shelter. Lousy union, but they were still known to strike on occasion; so we were giving away sunglasses, tennis shoes, socks and mittens. We also had cheap windshirts, with "Leviathan" emblazoned on the back, packed away for extra commercial leverage later on, should it become necessary. We worked steadily and without much conversation. The sky was clear, and the cement floor reflected the tropical heat at us. It was the first hard work of the trip. Our T-shirts darkened with sweat. Metilkja played dreary Croatian symphonies on his tape recorder. We dragooned a number of gleeful children into fetching pot after pot of tea for us. Hamish referred to the process as the British colonial touch.

By mid-afternoon we had tied off the last package. Twenty-six plastic garbage cans stood in a row, each with "International Kahli Gurkha Expedition" stenciled on the side in red letters. "Don't seem like much when you think about it," Hamish observed, as he clipped an inch off the mainspring of the scale we would carry to weigh out the loads.

"We must be fast on mountain," Metilkja explained, sounding like a Swiss guide with a mouth full of marbles. "Oderwise," he grinned and patted his stomach, "get very thin."

"Right, well, I reckon starvin' is probably goin' to be our least fookin' worry on this whale hunt," Hamish laughed. "Puttin' up the route is goin' to be the hard part."

"Alpine met-tod," Metilkja concluded. "Goot weather, we climb fast." That seemed to be about the beginning and the end of it. Get and go; what else could you say? Not enough food or rope to stick it out for long, anyway. "If you want to last, you got to go fast," was the expression we used in Yosemite. No pain, no gain.

We all took cold showers—the hot water was mythical—got into our best clothes, and went out on the town for supper. The three of us and all our gear were scheduled to be flown out in the morning, and the celebration was dampened only by the question marks surrounding the Major's absence. Behind the laughter was the lingering sense that he was already on the expedition and we were holding him back, slowing him down. I think we all had the feeling of wanting to show him we were as committed and hungry as he was, which was probably just the way he wanted us to feel.

We walked back through the city in the last light. Kerosene stoves burned in the small shops and market stalls; rice and lentils and black tea boiled in tin pots. People were bustling past us on foot and pedalling bicycles. A water buffalo lay on its side in the street, legs bucking spasmodically as its freshly severed head was raised through a haze of flies to a butcher's bench. Rich, crimson blood pumped into the gutter. The same dull lights threw yellow halos around every act of love and antipathy. Turning to take the unpaved alley that led down to the guest house, we passed a beggar lurking in the shadows behind the wreck of a Datsun taxi. He crept out into the dirt behind us, crouched over slightly to one side, thin and tattered, a crude bamboo crutch held under his right arm. He wore the emaciated remains of what had once been a down parka. We had never seen a beggar so close to the guest house, and his appearance caught us by surprise. Hamish took a threatening step towards him, and the beggar cringed back pathetically.

"No, Sahib! Please no, Sahibs," he pleaded, bending even closer to emphasize his terrible harmlessness. "Sahibs go Kahli Gurkha, please?" he asked.

We looked at each other. Hamish answered, "Aye."

"No go, Sahibs. Very bad, you go. Not good mountain. Masta go Kahli Gurkha. Avalokita Ishvara not go that mountain. Cannot see Sahibs. Masta live mountain. Sahibs go back America!" He paused and caught his breath. When he began again, his voice seemed to have changed, to have risen an octave. "Baksheesh, Sahibs? Baksheesh?" His shriveled, cupped hand stuck out at us from his rags.

"G'won, git, ye wee fookin' chough!" Hamish scowled and turned to join us. The beggar dodged off into the darkness and the three of us walked back to the guest house in silence.

We flew east. The valleys dropped away below us to isolated small hamlets on hogback ridges. No roads marred the landscape. I had been told in Kathmandu that atavistic Hindu sects still conducted human sacrifices in villages not forty miles from where commercial jets disgorged loads of camera-toting tourists on "high-adventure" tours of the world's most remote region. To the north, the Himalaya lay in the translucent shrouds of the monsoon season.

We landed on a grass runway with a miniature stucco terminal topped by an unattended bamboo control tower. A complement of police, militiamen, traders and the curious stood watching. Our porters were waiting—thirty of them—under the direction of a rakish, good-looking sirdar named Ang Phu. We shook hands and left him to straighten out the load-carrying while we hiked the six miles into Khandbari, where, we had learned, the Major was awaiting our arrival.

The path was six feet wide, gentle, and well used. At the end of each uphill pitch, benches curled in the shade of walnut trees. Everywhere, small Buddhist prayer walls and tiny stupas were decorated with brightly painted mandalas and symbols. It began to rain after we had walked an hour or so. We unfolded our umbrellas and stopped at a rickety tea shop for chai and cookies. A Nepali child watched us drink. Her mother brought us bananas, for which Metilkja arose and thanked her with a deep bow, sending her giggling uncontrollably back into a corner. Her husband, a withered and tough-skinned old man, brought out his faded ledger. It showed that he had carried for several expeditions going into the Makalu area. We nodded, he smiled and came to attention, saluting. "Ed-mund Hil-lary," he pronounced carefully.

We arrived at the guest house in Khandbari around five. Ang Phu had caught up with us and showed us to a room with five or six straw pallets, where we dropped our light trail sacks. Then we went downstairs to join Major Abrams. He had arranged a side room for dinner and met us at the door.

A tall, lean, dark-haired man in his late forties or early fifties, the Major had sunken cheeks beneath a heavy beard, surprisingly narrow shoulders and awkward, almost feminine dimensions to his posture. Much to my surprise, he walked with a marked limp, one leg noticeably shorter than the other, though he was obviously not crippled. His squinting eyes, framed by deeply weathered crows' feet, threw out the most intense glare I have ever seen. His presence was commanding and authoritative, with a cool, military ferocity that made calling him Major far easier than using his Christian name.

He shook hands with all of us. A solid, reassuring grip. "Ah, Mr. O'Brien! The American," he grinned. "Good, you've got long hair. Something to pluck you out of the crevasses by!" We laughed. As we took our seats around the table, I thanked him for his help and for the photos he had sent me.

"I'm afraid I really haven't been much help at all," he apologized, "but you're welcome, and thank you for the compliment. As you all know, it's been very difficult trying to put this trip together at short notice. Lost paperwork, troubles with permission, the usual Nepal muck-up. Didn't give me much time to help you lads at your end, I regret to say."

We all assured him that things had run very smoothly for us, largely owing to his efforts, and that we all were keen for the climb. As we ate, he asked pointed, knowledgeable questions of each of us. Occasionally, he would jot down a note or pause with his head back, studying a response. He seemed warmer and more accessible than I had imagined. I thought of Lucy's ersatz-Buddhist hyperbole and nearly laughed out loud.

After we were done eating and everyone but me had produced a pipe, the Major ordered chang. It was served hot, in tall bamboo gourds. It smelled richly alcoholic and was the color of milk. Seeds and rice and bits of leaves floated in it innocently. "To Kahli Gurkha," the Major smiled, raising his gourd, "To the Leviathan. To us!"

We raised our chang after him: "To the Leviathan."

In the days that followed we hiked along the single spine of a long, fertile plateau. The Arun River lay to our left, grey and floury with the silt of unseen glaciers. On our right, the terraced fields were black and ripe. We bought potatoes, carrots and radishes, along with an occasional chicken, to supplement our trekking diet of rice and tsampa. The Nepalis we met on the trail were tolerant and friendly, although at night when we set up camp near their villages, the aggressive mobs of curious onlookers made us tense and militant.

Ang Phu had hired an assistant, a bull-shouldered comedian named Bahm, and two cooks, whom we called Sears and Roebuck. Ang Phu explained that he and Bahm owned a trading business and a small hostel together in the Khumbu-Everest area. Both of them had wives and children and were as glad as we were to be away on an expedition. They were intelligent, articulate, sophisticated men out to do a little work and have a little fun. Mornings, we could hear them laughing; always, as the first sun touched the tents, a cup of tea and a warm chapati came through the front flap at the end of a square, brown hand.

None of the rest of us were particularly gregarious men; perhaps the Major and I the least. Hamish could be loud and obscene, and he and Metilkja would walk together from time to time; but by and large we traveled alone on the trail. We carried simple lunches and candy and biscuits in our pockets. Sometime around midday, I would stop at a tea shop, sit at one of the tables, and shout "Namaste!" to the porters as they came by under their huge loads.

The whole experience for me was an ongoing vision of incredible poignancy and beauty, intensified by my solitude. I stood in awe of every hut, every rhododendron, every detail. It was a walk like a dream, a hallucination, a fantastic trot. I watched huge leeches wavering at attention from the ends of trailside leaves, with tropical wildflowers setting off their grotesque dance in a dazzling profusion of colors and shapes. The sun rose out of the high jungle and set in the forbidding aridity of the Kampa Mustang. I took my time and exposed roll after roll of film. I crouched underneath my umbrella during the afternoon showers and wrote long, jovial letters to Lucy and to my family. I wrote about the mountain as if it were the Panama Canal: a place one sailed through, not one where people worked and died. I was very brave in print, of course, incapable of even alluding to the possibility of death. There, in the jungle, far away from the wind and snow, I was immortal.

We dropped down from the last Nepali villages, crossed the Arun on a primitive hemp-and-cable bridge, then hiked uphill for a day to the village of Sedua. For the Khumbu Sherpas, it was a voyage backward through time to what Namche Bazaar must have been like before it became "civilized." We called it Dodge City, guarded our baggage carefully, and moved on as soon as we could.

The days grew colder and clearer. We climbed steadily. At Shipton Col, I caught up with the Major; he was standing alone, above and to the right of the trail, his piercing eyes fixed on the northern horizon. We were at fourteen thousand feet and it was cloudless, perfect. Makalu, the fifth-highest mountain in the world, stood out spectacularly. Just to the east I saw Kahli Gurkha. It seemed small by comparison, but even at this great distance its awesome southwest face—the Leviathan—stood out in startling relief. Illuminated by the southern postmonsoon light, it shone bronze and sepia-colored with a blue-white fin of ice along its spiral summit ridge. As Abrams stepped down from the col, his lips moved silently and his fists clenched so tight the knuckles seemed ready to burst his skin. He strode away from the crest and off toward the Leviathan in brusque, electric silence.

Supper was quiet that night. For the seventh consecutive night we shoved rice and *tsampa* around our plates without much enthusiasm and went to our tents early. Sometime after midnight I got up to urinate and stood for a long time in the moonlight looking down to the Arun Gorge. It was dark down there, as opaque as dirt. I could hear things bumping around: mysterious objects as basic as mud shoving each other about, eternally shifting. The river, a black scratch on a torpid moonscape, gusted its primordial melody. Sighs from the center of the earth hissed and stirred our nylon houses. I listened for a long time. Walking back in the metallic light, I heard the counterpoint: a dreamer in his guttural, midnight torment, the lost soul of mankind, the private horror of fragile limitation in such a hard and unlimited universe that it knew of no words in any language. The dreamer, of course, was Abrams. His photos told us far less about the mountain than his nightmares did now.

Early in the afternoon, two days later, we stood in a gentle snowfall outside the sturdy yak-herders' hut at Kahli La that was to be our base camp. After weighing out their loads, Ang Phu paid off our porters and sent them away with their socks, shoes and Leviathan windshirts. Bahm and the two cooks built a kitchen out of field stones and our huge canvas tarpaulin. We sorted through the loads and heated water for tea. The mountain was veiled in dense clouds and we neither spoke of it nor looked in its direction. It was there; that was enough.

We broke into our best food and had a superb dinner of beef stew with potatoes and barley. The Major produced a can of pears and a large gourd of a Nepali liquor called *rakshi*. For the first time in several days the conversation was animated and crude. The Europeans smoked their pipes and talked about climbing in the Alps. I went outside and dug into the small traveling stash Lucy had given me. I stood beside the river taking long draws and feeling the snow wet on my face.

The snow fell steadily for a week. Avalanches sloughed off the peaks around us and roared unseen above the low-hanging clouds in the valley. We sat inside and waited. We killed time reading, writing letters, playing with our gear. I hung one of the single-anchor bivouac platforms in the branches of a poplar and watched the Europeans struggle with the notion of sleeping suspended in it. They, in turn, grinned at my enthusiasm for the cans of bacon and kippers they included in our climbing rations. We packed it all into our rucksacks along with rock climbing gear, ice screws, pots and stoves, then we lifted, weighed, divided, and revised our loads until the sweat exuded from the soles of our feet. Then we would run and jump naked into the frigid Arun. The Sherpas loved it. They would always gather to watch the spectacle and laugh hysterically.

During the sixth day the snow came down heavily. By noon we were sitting in the hut, listening to the almost constant rumble of the avalanches above us. We warmed our hands on teacups. The Major sat in a corner smoking his pipe and writing in his journal. An unusually loud, baritone roar drew all eyes to the ceiling. "That ought to clean the face," Hamish mumbled. The noise grew nearer and deeper. The ground shimmied. Our eyes came down to meet one another's. Outside we could hear Ang Phu's excited voice and the other Sherpas shouting. Pots and pans began falling.

"Ja-sus fookin' Christ!" Hamish suddenly bellowed. "It's comin' right fer home!"

We leaped simultaneously to our feet and pushed each other through the door, bounding miraculously through the kitchen without knocking over steaming pots, hitting the clearing on the run, and splitting in three separate directions. The ground quaked, and the shock wave blew snow horizontally at our backs, though by the time I had reached the trees at the riverbank the slide had lost its momentum in the talus breaks above the hut. I stood against a tree catching my breath, watching the air clear. The main tongue of the boulders were still rolling on the debris-strewn lower surface of the slide as Hamish approached.

"Christ's eyes, eh, ladies?" he laughed, wiping mud off his sweater. We walked back together. Metilkja and the Sherpas approached from the opposite direction. Metilkja explained with surprising seriousness that he took this to be a sign, that someday one of these was going to catch up with him. For all the noise a few moments earlier, there was an incredible stillness.

The Sherpas set to reconstructing the kitchen and the three of us ducked back into the hut. Abrams was standing outside, some distance away, smoking his pipe. Hands in his pockets, he stared up at the Leviathan as it appeared in glimpses through the swirling clouds. Snow powdered the ground between where he stood and the hut, but I saw no trace of footprints. He had been there when the snow came. He had walked toward the avalanche, not away from it. It had stopped at his very feet.

The next morning dawned spectacularly clear—cloudless and sharp. We quickly put the final touches on our gear and slipped into our windsuits. Ang Phu and Bahm served us a special breakfast of Sherpa horseradish on buffalo sausage with oatmeal and fried potatoes covered with sweet syrup. Hamish honed his crampons and ice axe with a hand file. Metilkja painted his nose and cheeks with zinc oxide. It was going-up day. Abrams wrote a few notes, closed his journal, and placed it in a small plastic satchel hanging near the door. He tapped out his pipe and stuck it in his shirt. His face was set like a rock. This was it, the point of it all, and I couldn't help imagine any human being with whom I would rather have gone up on the mountain. His obsession was like a magnet, a beacon. I was amazed at my own fanaticism. The pointless, the triviality and expense, the whole dramatic absurdity that underlay our climb struck me at that moment as the most important purpose my life could ever have.

The Major stood and stretched. "Well, lads," he said, his quiet voice suggesting neither a question nor command. The three of us rose and he nodded.

"Major-Sahib!" Ang Phu called from the kitchen. "Mens coming Makalu. Four, maybe five, down valley very near now, Sahib!"

We followed Abrams through the door and saw the men emerging from the trailhead at the willow thicket. They looked grim, bent on a mission of importance and solemnity. The snow sparkled in the sunlight and crunched beneath their huge boots. The Leviathan, cut from the cobalt sky, stood massively indifferent to our meeting. Waiting.

We all shook hands. Their leader explained that they were Dutch, part of a team attempting the south face of Makalu. Tears welled up suddenly in his eyes. One of their members, he said, his son, the expedition physician, was missing. He had gone out of one of the tents at high camp two nights earlier and simply disappeared. They wanted our help to search for him. It was two days' travel to their base camp; the search would last no more than a few days, then they would give up. We could be back in a week at the most.

Abrams never blinked. He never paused to search for words. "You are welcome to food and tea here," he said. "You may take our Sherpas to help you if they are willing to go with you. Ang Phu, there, is a fine mountaineer as competent as any European, I assure you. But we did not travel this far to lose hold of our goal because you have lost yours, sir. I shouldn't ask that of you, gentlemen. I'm sorry. That's final. I hope it all comes out well for you. I wish you good luck and Godspeed. Good morning, gentlemen."

He turned and walked to his pack, brought it up onto his shoulders, and started toward the glacier. Less forcefully, the three of us fell in behind him.

"It is you I feel sorry for!" the leader of the Dutch party screamed after us. "I pray that you will find the same charity on your mountain that you have shown us, Abrams!"

The Major did not recoil or turn around upon hearing his name. It was hard to tell if he was even aware of its having been said.

We climbed steadily throughout the day. The going was not technically difficult, and we found the heat more of a problem than the crevasses or icefalls. At noon we stopped and took out the ropes. As the angle increased, the snow became wet and heavy. We sank in to our knees and ran short of breath beneath our monstrous loads. We dug a platform into the side of a crevasse and spent a comfortable night. The incline and mire increased all the next day. We reached a bergschrund where the lower glacier fractured at the base of an eighteen-hundred-foot ice face, and carved out another small platform. We melted snow for tea and tried to make sense of what rose above us. The scale was out of proportion with anything I had ever experienced. The ice face led to a rock head wall, and that to the long, fin-shaped Whale's Tail. Then more snow and the summit. I stacked ropes and whistled with the stoves in joyful ignorance.

The following morning we set off at 3 A.M. to take advantage of the cold. We climbed by headlamps, pushing hard to reach the head wall before the sun touched the face and loosened the afternoon stone barrage. Two teams of too slow-moving dots on a sixty-degree ocean of ice lost and purposeful as gulls. Metilkja and Hamish, on separate ropes, took the leads. The Yugoslav seemed almost to float, one foot flat and the other front-pointing. He was economical and precise, making it all appear effortless. Hamish, on the other hand, brutalized the ice, kicking and hammering his way up, never pausing, never running down. He wore no cap in the dark, subzero cold. The Major and I came along pragmatically at the long ends of our ropes.

By one in the afternoon we stood at the base of the head wall. The mottled and broken skin of the Leviathan reached above us in a turbulent and darkening sky. Hamish and Metilkja dug a cave in the deep powder at the base of the wall while Abrams and I removed the rock gear from our packs.

The Major pointed me to a long, pencil-thin crack that cleaved a narrow buttress and looked to widen to hand size after a hundred feet. I was the Yosemite wizard, the rock jock; that crack was the reason I was there. I reached high, placed a piton, and hammered it home.

Four hours later I was sitting on my foam pad talking about the wall with Hamish. Our cave glowed with the sparkling light of two stoves and a candle. Abrams and Metilkja cooked. The steam from our teacups hung in the warm, moist air, mixing with the smoke from Hamish's pipe. Life was sweet and masculine. We talked about women and home the way sailors do. We ate cookies with yak butter and jam. Metilkja passed around a flask of Croatian *eau de vie*. Three hundred feet of rope was strung out on the rock above. My first contact with the Leviathan had left me ecstatic. It was more spectacular than I could have imagined: El Capitan at altitude, wide and weathered and old as time. Under a muted afternoon sun I had filled its cracks with my hands and feet, twisting and panting, moving quickly, charged by my own elation and energy. The clouds moved in time-lapse and snow began to fall—stellar, soft, collated flakes. My cheeks and hands were moist and hot. I drove a piton when the rope ran out and raised the haul sack before descending, breathless, back down to the cave, whispering "In the morning," to myself.

The snow fell finer but harder the next day. The crack turned incipient and rotten, then disappeared altogether, leaving me swinging from sky hooks with the sweat stinging my eyes. I lost hours drilling holes for loose bolts. Pitons I had hammered barely past their tips creaked and moved under my weight. Just ten more feet, I begged. Scared to death of where I was and too frightened to go back down, my scrotum shrank. I held my breath and swung on a rotten flake lassoed from thirty feet away to reach for a huge, fragmented block. Around more corners, the angle of the face dropped to less than vertical and the cracks were filled with ice. I climbed to a large ledge and secured the ropes. Less than three hundred feet for the day. Abrams prusiked the fixed line to join me and we hauled the sacks. His face was contorted with impatience. He knew he couldn't have done it any faster, but he hated to depend on others, on me; to wait on the expertise and judgements of fools. He did not climb out of love for the climbing. That had passed long ago. He climbed for revenge, out of hate for the mountain, for its superiority, its naked power. And strangely, I admired that in him, wished that I could have his ruthlessness. I was his vehicle, I knew, and he could drive me faster. I would give him his snow ridge.

Early the next morning, our fourth on the mountain, we climbed the ropes to the ledges (the "Hilton"), and pulled up. It seemed like a significant movement; yet it passed without anyone giving it notice. The inclination of the rock continued to ease. I climbed quickly now, rope length after rope length, one boot on rock, one on snow, my mittened hands jammed between dank shelves of granite and rivulets of ice. The snow fell quietly, windlessly. Occasional breaks in the clouds let the sun through, and the rock steamed. We moved steadily up. When I leaned out to study the route, I could see the long, white tongue of snow above us: the Whale's Tail.

The day ended with the four of us suspended from a few shaky pegs without a single ledge in sight. We erected the bivouac platforms and crawled into them head to foot, the Major and Metilkja in one, Frazier and I in the other. The wind picked up during the night and dipped us gently. In the morning we all were eager to fold the platforms and get back to the solidity of climbing. We moved diagonally, gaining less than two hundred feet of altitude in fifteen hours of work. The rock was not steep enough to hang our nylon platforms; so we chipped out whatever small grooves we could from the ice and spent the night there, suspended, with our feet stuffed into our rucksacks. We shivered silently in our individual tribulations, too far apart to pass food or drink. We popped Valium and stared into the storm-basted ribbon of sky that tacked the western horizon.

My feet were cold all night. They ached all day. I led up and left into a system of snow-clogged chimneys that left me, after several hundred feet, studying a conundrum. Above, the main chimney narrowed to a slot three feet wide and blocked by an enormous chockstone. Both sides of the passage were coated with thick rime ice, white and warted. I dumped my pack and bridged out tenuously. My mind wandered intractably, taking me back to Boulder—the corner of Broadway and Pearl, to be exact. Hmmm. Bookstores and French bread, coeds and foreign cars, and—ah, yes—the "wall" at Macky crawling with punks carrying chalk bags, so close to the center of it all, dude, you could touch it. I thought of being warm again, and about dying. I looked down and saw myself tumbling tip over tail forever, the rope streaming like a purple and blue contrail, no longer flirting with space but flying at last, oh yeah.

For lack of anything else to do, I nudged up, shoulders and knees, to beneath the stone at the very back of the depression and thrust my axe up into the snow gathered behind it. Pressure, rest; effort, release. An hour later I was standing above the hole I'd chopped, fixing the ropes to a cluster of ice screws and runners. I shouted down to the others to come up. I thought I heard a voice, two shouts, perhaps more, then silence again. After a while the rope went taut with the weight of a climber. I touched the grey ice and wondered: How long? We were on the Whale's Tail, riding the very back of the beast.

The night was horrid and everlasting. Utterly spent, I passed the evening lapsing in and out of groggy soliloquies about how I had to rest, man, curl up in bed somewhere warm, turn on a tap and get water, rest these weary, cold, cold, arms. We sat huddled in our separate miseries and dreamed our lonely nostrums, hardly speaking, dressed in wool and nylon and feathers. My fingers pulsed, and each throb brought excruciating pains behind fingernails as white and hard as porcelain. We leaned off the edge of our serac and shat hanging from a rope, our turds dropping soundlessly into the impossible abyss.

In the morning, it was still snowing. Gentle waves of spindrift hissed down the face in filmy avalanches. We stayed put and arranged the bivouac platforms. They lacked the gaiety of the cave—they were not so warm or nearly so bright—but they were an improvement on sitting out in the wind and cold with that dark space below and the distance above eating our eyes.

We dined on freeze-dried shrimp creole and drank lukewarm piss-colored tea that tasted like shrimp creole. Food and drink came, and I took it like Communion. Abrams shared my platform, maintaining his complex silence. I heard Metilkja and Hamish talking quietly from time to time, but their words were flat and without joy.

We were in deep. Very, very deep.

The snow grew heavier. The spindrift slides came episodically, great waves of rigid surf breaking over us and surging into the void, tumbling and spinning earthward like paper. We packed without comment in the morning. We left behind the rock climbing gear, a stove, the platforms, and some of the food. The hell with it: There was no going back down that way now, anyhow.

We divided into two teams again: Hamish and the Major, Metilkja and me. Hamish and the Major led off, and soon we were into the old stride, the pace of a thousand different climbs: tool, tool...step, step...rest and gasp for air, then more of the same, the brain as blank as oxygen. The scenery never varied from grey on white. The air temperature was warm, and occasionally, as the day wore on, we would hear the baseball *whoosh* of a stone. We never saw it though, and no one ever got hit. We were too tired to do anything but simply plod and hope. Storm-shrouded silhouettes, we climbed in egocentric removal from one another, companions in nothing more than the movement of the rope. We were shadows caught in random highlight against the whiteout sky. There was no sense of progress, no feeling of getting anywhere. Just the unabating impulse to go on.

In the murk of sunset we gathered on a small, uneven ledge and crouched leg-to-leg as Metilkja passed around sausage and cookies. We dug into our packs after headlamps and sweets. Without shelter it seemed pointless to try to bivouac in the open at such an altitude. So in our independent pools of light, we continued our long crawl, waiting and climbing, waiting and climbing.

The storm, of course, got worse. We were climbing upward into the nastiness of it. The wind came in violent gusts. The temperature dropped. The snow stung our cheeks and walrus snot-cicles hung from our moustaches. I went into long lapses of memory wherein I could not recall if I had been climbing or standing still. I huddled deeper within myself, seeking warmth and coherence, and would increasingly return to reality uncertain of what mountain I was on, or with whom.

I began to hear Abrams.

At first I thought nothing of the voice. I have no idea how long I listened to it before it broke upon me that I was hearing an external sound. It was more the sporadic wail of the storm itself than of a man yelling. It was, I thought, some shrieking in my own mind. And then, clearly, I would hear it again. A shout, a sentence. I could never make out the words, but I became convinced that it was a voice. And in time it occurred to me that the voice was the Major's.

That it did not stop.

That he was crazy. Mad as the moon. A sennin.

And that I was on this mountain with him, being led by him, happy about it. Shit, I was laughing. It got so every time I heard that lunatic howl I'd grin wide as a cat. The chaos of the storm reduced the revelation of our insanity to scale: Who'd have been there but crazy people, anyway? Why go on peg-footing and stiff-lipping as if it all made sense in the first place? I loved it! I too felt like howling, but I couldn't find the air the Major could.

At the base of a sixty-foot runnel of water ice, the angle increased to near vertical. I caught up with Metilkja standing roped into a gathering of ice screws. Above us, Abrams was wailing and shouting, angry and laughing. Two hundred twenty volts of illuminated madness in that wind-bitten gloom. The stoic and dour Croat was grinning, too. We stood there smiling at each other until the screaming stopped and it was Metilkja's turn to climb. I flicked off my headlamp to save batteries and thought of Lucy. She was right, goddammit. The Buddhists were right, too, and hell, so was the beggar in the alley for that matter. Only madmen and tantric Masons up here, embracing their flaky chods, ice men, sennins and their mountain Masta. It was just the right place for them. And for me.

We reached the bottom of the summit ice flutings sometime after midnight. Maybe later. I remember finding Hamish hanging from all kinds of webbing and ice gear and plastered with rime.

"Major's gone up, ladies," he said slowly. "'Fraid me hands 'ave aboot had it. Lost me fookin' mitts down there when we poot on the torches." He was trying to grin. He looked spent and sheepish, letting the rope run through hands jelled into rubbery spoons. He had his parka hood up now, but all the hours without a hat seemed to have had an effect. Metilkja took off his pack and dug into it for some spare socks to cover Hamish's hands. I took over the belay, watching Hamish as I let out the line. He seemed calm, happy, a little guilty, perhaps, but warm and unconcerned. Yet there was a blankness coming into his eyes, an expression that carried the look of wistful martyrdom. When the line pulled tight to his waist, we unclipped him from the anchors and molded his hands around his ice axes. He started singing "The Hair of Her Dicky-Di-Do" and slammed in his tools.

The air suddenly came alive with voices. I could hear Abrams and Hamish, and soon Metilkja shouted and started climbing. We moved faster for a time. The snow stopped and the wind released us. I pulled hard, hand over hand, up the rope and turned a great, pillow-shaped cornice to reach the others clustered on the southwest ridge. The clouds below carpeted the valleys in every direction. The still-dark sky behind us shared its diamond star with the pallid yellow blot of dawn. The Major stood in the saddle, ice axe in his hands, a serpentine black-and-beige rope hanging loose from his rucksack like the severed head of Hydra. His voice was as cracked and scratched as an old recording.

"This is it, boys!" he shouted. "Here you go! She's up there, not five hundred feet, by God, and we're as good as there! Fancy foot you, O'Brien, eh? It's ours, all right, and no wind, no snow to stop us now! Not when we've come halfway around the world to put our footprints up there, I tell you. The hardest wall in the world?" He laughed, pointing the spike of his axe at the heavens. "Don't let me hear that talk again. Not in front of boys like these! Come along then, Frazier! Another few hundred feet and you can spit in the face of the God that froze your hands man, scuff your boots on His horrible face, if you've a mind to, eh?"

His wild hair sprang horizontally as a gust of wind carried off his woolen balaclava. The vapors danced up the wall like steam reaching for the mother-of-pearl clouds obscuring the dreary sky. The Major roared at the enormous, cosmic illusion of futility in which the mountain wished us to believe. Frazier was enraptured, his eyes glazed. Metilkja was harder to read: He went about his business neither awed nor annoyed. Myself, I grinned like a Mousketeer for Abrams. His madness had fueled our upward determination, but getting down was going to take a different frame of mind, and I knew my best chance was with the Yugoslav. Frazier was weakening; Abrams was a whirlwind, vague as chimera. Only Metilkja had the feel of substance.

Metilkja and I lifted Frazier to his feet and the four of us set out. The angle eased, and we used our axes like canes. We hiked heads down into a burgeoning gale and rested on our knees. Again I fell behind the others and had only the comfort of their footprints and the Major's occasional shout until the mists parted and I saw them standing together twenty feet in front of me.

On the summit.

Abrams was hatless and howling. Frazier crouched with his frozen hands cupped in front of him as if he were holding snowballs. Metilkja stood beside him, looking away to the east. We danced, buffeted by the suddenly ferocious wind. After only a few moments Metilkja looked over to me and shouted, "Down! Now!" He gestured with his ice axe in the opposite direction from which we'd come. He spoke as if we were the only one there. Neither Frazier nor the Major paid him the least notice.

"There is no harder wall, no harder ice, no higher point upon this mountain, lads! Tea in hell, I tell you!" the Major shouted.

"Down! Now!" Metilkja screamed and began to stagger off into the full blast of the wind. I gave a sharp tug on the rope connecting us.

"What about them?" I yelled, pointing at Frazier and the Major. Frazier was staring straight up into heaven as the Major babbled his crazy sermon on the mount. Metilkja looked at me, his haggard, black eyes as hard as glass. His glance shifted for a moment to our teammates and then came back to mine. The message was clear and I understood. He turned and worked his way down, and I waited for the rope to run out before following him. I looked at the Major and Frazier as if they were apparitions. I felt nothing for them at all. In fact, I felt nothing about anything until the rope pulled tight and I took my first step down; then all I wanted to do was live. It was all lost now. Nothing was important. I just wanted down and Metilkja was headed that way. He did not need to pull me.

Descending into the storm was worse than climbing up to it. We had fought hard to get up, and now the mountain seemed to want to hold us there. The gale inflated our windsuits and pressed its hands against our chests. The cold was piercing and terrible. My face burned. Inside a thousand dollars worth of high-tech nylon, plastic, leather and rubber, I felt the cold carve through me. I did not turn and look back for the others. I closed them out of my thoughts and concentrated instead on my own wooden steps. There were no voices now: the storm shrieked louder than Abram's feeble hoots. It gave us back the proportion of our real achievement. We hadn't "conquered" the mountain any more than a rat conquers the ocean by hiding in a ship's bilge. We'd skittered across the summit and now crept wretchedly away from any protracted confrontation with the Himalaya's true savagery. We were running away on frozen feet, less victors than survivors.

The hours fused with the snow. We reached a serac and stood in its lee to rest. My knees ached and my legs felt cold to the bone. I kept my mind off my feet. I had no idea whatsoever of where we were or where we were headed. We stood panting, our eyes interlocked. Metilkja looked withered and gaunt, awful. He motioned with his head to something behind me. Abrams came out of the storm, still hatless and striding confidently, crisp as a Yorkshire birder, Frazier staggering along after him.

"We'll be done with this in an hour, lads," the old man cheered. "We head down this ridge till we find the upper valley glacier. I looked this over last year. One man, by God! Happy me, boys, happy me! She'll not hold us off now, will she, eh? We're too close to it now!" he barked, clenching one fist and holding up to the sky. "By Judas, don't anyone talk to me about blasphemy! Why, I'd piss up the winds if I had a mind to. This mountain is mine, I tell you! Send down her storm and snow; I'll shove it up spout and stand this ice while I will!" Then, lowering his arm, his eyes on fire, he seemed to speak directly to me. "Heaven and hell by the short hairs! You'll tell them that for me, won't you? Tell them she was mine!"

Metilkja closed his eyes and for an instant dropped his head. When he looked back up, his face was full of the old sobriety and purpose. He raised his compass and studied it. I touched Hamish's arm and he looked at me. His cheeks were white, his eyes sunken back a thousand synapses from the horrible truths of the tactile world. I smiled and patted his shoulder.

"See you down there," I shouted, and he nodded his head. I walked away, knowing I would never see him again.

The rope drew me down into a well of storm. I thought about dying once more, about falling, about sitting down. I thought about heat and hallucinated a room full of stuffed chairs and couches with a stone fireplace and brandy glasses on a long table spread with a linen cloth and the dirty dishes of a sumptuous meal. Metilkja was standing in the corner of the room in his wretched, wind-torn, rime-sheeted climbing suit. He was wiping away the ice from the headlamp he had been wearing since the night before. I turned on my own light and followed him down through the gloomy penumbra beyond the banquet and into the shelter of a crevasse wall. Just beyond, the ice fell away into an abysmal pit of hurricane updrafts and utter blackness.

Metilkja dropped his pack and pulled out a bandolier of ice screws. Nine in all. I had another six. I groped to fathom our method. The madman had said the ridge would bring us to the glacier and the glacier to the valley. But here? And how far down? And into this storm?

Metilkja suffered none of my neurotic ambivalence. He understood function much better than I. He knew that the doing was the important part and that the outcome would either reward or penalize our boldness. One acted out of strength without hesitation or consorting with hope. One suffered the consequences to the extent he was capable of influencing them. Everything else was either magic or religion.

Metilkja threaded the rope through a carabiner and prepared to back off. The ends of the rope waved above us like tentacles, blown straight up into the night by the surging wind and illuminated by our headlamps. And again, for an instant, our eyes met. Then he was gone.

After several moments I felt the line go slack and then ran it through my breaking device. I tilted backwards and slipped down into the maw of the awful night.

Rappel followed rappel. The cold devoured us, and the wind snapped our sleeves and leggings so hard the material parted. My feet were lost, I knew that. I could feel nothing below my boot tops. I waited out my turns in blank torpor. No thought or feeling aroused me except to clip into the rope and slide down to where Metilkja would be waiting, his eyes always searching. During those silent, piercing, shattering, wind-buffeted meetings, our faces were lit by the dim light of each other's headlamps, like Welsh miners, our silence the only alternative to the storm.

I knew I was barely hanging on, slowing Metilkja down. I tried to meet his glances with a strong gaze, but I knew he must be aware of my growing incapacity to think or move. I held tight to the ropes after he was down to keep him from pulling them through the anchor, stranding me.

And rappel followed rappel.

After so many that I had lost count, I found myself clipped to a set of ice screws, watching the flickering yellow light of Metilkja's headlamp disappear into the murk, when an enormous block of ice grazed the névé just above me and plunged on into the darkness, down the line of ropes. I was so frightened, so dazed, that I simply swung from my runner, cringing, my eyes closed for what seemed like fifteen minutes. The ropes were free when I lifted them; the stance below was empty when I arrived. Metilkja was not there. No screw protruded from the wall. No Croatian eyes. Just the night and the storm, the roaring black. I hung onto the ropes waiting for him. I poked around in the snow at my feet to see if I had missed a ledge. I swung left and right in small pendulums and called for him.

There was nothing but some crampon marks scraped in the ice.

I screamed his name, but my pathetic yap barely reached my own ears.

Perhaps he had begun downclimbing, I thought. Yes! That had to be it! The climbing was easy for him. We were going too slow by rappelling; so he had abandoned me and simply begun downclimbing. He had seen the same shadows in my eyes as I had seen in Frazier's—the confusion, the dependence I had on him.

I screamed until I couldn't breathe. I collapsed against the ropes, gasping and hyperventilating. Live, I told myself, live, you stupid fucker! You *will* do this thing. He's either dead or left you. They're all dead, but I will not die here, hanging on this wall, running away from this mountain. I slapped my arms to make the blood circulate and took an ice screw off my harness. I will do this thing and I will live. "I will live," I shouted, and pulled down on the ropes.

I had only two screws left when I touched the glacier. I huddled in the protection of a small bergschrund and took off my pack. I crawled into my bivouac sack and sleeping bag. I found some sausage and two candy bars, along with an extra pair of mittens in my pack. My headlamp faded to dull orange. In its last light, I found Metilkja's compass lying in the snow beside me.

I awoke at first light. It was overcast and snowing lightly, but the wind had stilled. I felt rested, weak but alert. I packed just the sleeping bag and a few odds and ends, then cut the rope in two and coiled half of it around my shoulders. Everything else I left to the haunting and oppressive silence.

I lost all concept of time. I followed the compass east with no notion of how far I'd come, how many crevasses I'd jumped or circled, no idea of how far I had to go. I found no footprints or discarded gear to suggest that Metilkja was ahead of me. The storm had consumed him as I was now being consumed. Everything was astonishingly white and featureless. I felt like Jonah, floating at peace in the saline bowels of the monster. My mind wandered out in front of me. I watched myself and laughed. I hallucinated fire and food. My body split into Metilkja's half and my half; his side was strong and elegant while mine stumbled pathetically, incompetently. I heard voices—singing, whispers, sighs—but saw nothing. No one. Just the enormous, hopeless white. I was exhausted by midmorning, traveling on slowly evolving sets of rules: walk two hundred paces and rest, two hundred paces and rest again. I lost count and rested. I lied and rested. I quit counting and rested. I came to a huge pressure ridge. Traversing around its south side, I found what looked like the trough a person might make in fresh snow. It was too blown over with spindrift to find bootprints, but I followed its vague, undulating course, squinting to pick out the subtle gradations of white.

I saw the Major from fifty feet away. I felt a remarkable absence of surprise. The color of his clothing against the blank canvas of snow and sky was sensational. He was sitting up against his pack. His skin was translucent. His eyes were open and his hands were tucked underneath the armpits of his open parka as if he had just stopped to warm himself. He was still hatless, his hair moving slightly in the ground-level breeze. The black-and beige rope was crisscrossed over his chest and shoulders in a guide's coil. One end had been cut. I stopped in front of him. I knew he was dead, yet it would not have surprised me if his eyes had moved and his face had turned up. Death had not taken him; he had simply exhausted life, worn it out.

Snow clung to the hairs of his face, and his trousers clapped in the wind. He stared back at the mountain, urging me to turn around, but there was nothing back there for me. Not anymore. There was nothing. I lifted Metilkja's compass and continued my descent.

When it became dark, I used the adze of my axe to dig out a niche between two ice boulders. I emptied what little remained inside my pack onto the snow, crawled into my sleeping bag again, and pulled the pack over my feet and up to my waist. In a small stuff sack I found a tube of Chapstick; I tried to eat it and immediately threw it back up, speckling the snow with blood. After a time I dozed. During the night, the snow changed to rain.

The air was warm and sodden when I awoke. My sleeping bag was drenched, but the rain had also washed away the snow around me, and for the first time I realized that I was no longer on the glacier. I was sitting between stones, not blocks of ice. I was on the moraine. Dirt and earth were below me. I left everything and started walking.

My feet were horrible. I began falling over everything, lying for a long time before I could rise. And then finally, I simply couldn't get any higher than my knees. That was okay. I was prepared for that. It did not come as a shock or even a disappointment, just new rules for the game. I crawled for a while, the toes of my boots dragging in the gravel and leaving twin ruts behind me like those of a tiny ox cart. I struggled through a shallow stream of fast-moving meltwater and reached a large boulder on the opposite side, where I lay back and rested. I tore off bits of my windsuit and used the strips to tie my mittens to my knees.

The rain was lighter, a fine Seattle mist. Through breaks in the clouds I could look up to splashes of green on the south-facing slopes of the valley. I noted this without elation or impatience. I anticipated nothing. I felt no excitement.

I knew that I was off the mountain and that I would live—that, if necessary, I could crawl to the trail between Kahli La and the Dutch camp and from there crawl down to the yak-herder's hut. If the Sherpas had given up on us and left, then I knew, too, that I could keep crawling...over Shipton Col, past Sedua, to Khandbari, to Katmandu, and all the way back to Boulder. It was no folly; I knew I could succeed in this chod.

So I progressed, staggering a few steps on dead feet and then collapsing to elbows and knees, shreds of my blue windsuit clinging to the ends of willow twigs. I left blood on the first grass that I reached. I sat for long periods waiting for the energy to move, clinging always to my talisman, Metilkja's compass. I dragged myself on my stomach through thickets of willow and alder, occasionally stopping to listen for the sound of voices or feet.

It was raining slightly when I arrived at the trail. I crawled down into the rut of it—soggy with black mud and as empty as my memory—and lay there a long time, breathing slowly, letting the rain wash my face, and gazing up at the mountain through elliptical gaps in the clouds. It seemed as pristine and aloof as it had in Abrams's photographs.

Untouched. Unmoved. Unknowable.

Tears ran down my cheeks. I laughed. I laughed and I cried at the same time, gasping and falling over on my side, helium-headed and sick. Just me. Of all the heartbeats and dreams, of all the struggle and obsession, I alone remained, more an abstraction than an alpinist, dumb as the last, great, silent thump at the end of the universe. I was all that was left. I cried and I laughed and I knew nothing. Only the mud and brush and pebbles.

And it was there that the Dutch expedition, returning with our Sherpas from the futile search for their lost son, found me, another soul orphaned by dreams.

Glossary

Abseil: See RAPPEL.

Altitude sickness, mountain sickness: Result of lack of oxygen, usually occurring above 8,000 feet. Symptoms include malaise, loss of appetite, headache, apathy, nausea, dizziness and sleepiness. In extreme cases this can turn into pulmonary edema (the "silent killer"), resulting in excessive fluid in the lungs. Usually occurs above 18,000 feet.

Belay: Procedure of securing a climber by use of the rope.

Bergschrund: A giant crevasse found at the upper limit of a glacier, formed where the moving glacier breaks away from the ice cap.

Bivouac: A temporary camp, usually just for the night, with little or no shelter.

Bolt: An artificial anchor placed in a hole drilled for that purpose.

Bongs: Large angle pitons 2 to 6 inches wide.

Bucket hold: A handhold, large enough to fully latch onto, like the lip of a bucket.

Carabiner: Aluminum snap-links of various shapes used for belaying, rappelling, prusiking, clipping into safety anchors, and so on.

Chimney: A crack big enough to climb in.

Chock: Mechanical device that, by various means, provides secure anchor to the cliff.

Cleaning, cleaning the pitch: Removing the anchoring devices used in climbing a pitch, or ropelength.

Col: A small, high pass.

Couloir: An angled gully, generally ice-filled.

Crampon: Metal devices attached to the bottom of one's boots consisting of 10 to 12 spikes, or points, that allow the climber to find purchase on snow and ice.

Crevasse: A deep crevice or fissure in a glacier.

Dihedral: A point where two walls meet in a right-angled inside corner. AKA, "Open Book."

Direct aid climbing: A technique used to climb exceedingly steep and hold-bereft rock, whereas the gear supports the weight of the climber as he or she ascends.

Downclimb: Procedure of descending a mountain, rock, etc., often dangerous and done without a rope.

Fixed rope: A rope anchored to a route and left in place.

Flute: A fin, usually thin and often insecure, of rock or ice.

Free climbing: To climb using hands and feet. The rope and attending gear are used only to safegard against injury, not for support or upward progress.

Front-point: A crampon-climbing technique using the two forward points (that extend straight out from the front of the boot) and the two vertical points of the crampons. Used exclusively to climb steep to overhanging ice.

Glissade: To slide down on one's feet and/or backside.

Gorp: A mixture of various nuts and dried fruits.

Hooks: Small, metal devices used to grip ledges or small holes. Types include sky hooks and bat hooks.

Hypoxia: Lack of oxygen.

Ice axe: A mountaineering tool 2 to 4 feet long, pointed at the end with a head consisting of a pick and an adze.

Incut: A hold or depression indented in the main wall.

Jam crack: A crack, usually ½ to 4 inches wide, ascended by jamming various combinations of feet and hands into the depths.

Jug hold: Like a jughandle. An excellent hold.

Jumar: A mechanical device used to ascend a rope.

Knifeblades: Long thin pitons used to fit cracks too thin for tiny nuts.

Leading the pitch: Climbing first up a pitch using belayer, rope, and intermediate protection for safety.

Lost Arrows: AKA "horizontals." Thin pitons.

Neve: Old snow.

Pitch: The section of rock between belays. Usually a ropelength (about 150 feet).

Prusik: A type of friction knot that allows a climber to go up or down the climbing rope. A friction knot grips the climbing rope when weight is on but moves freely when weight is off.

Rappel: To descend a rope by means of mechanical brake devices.

Rime: Crustation of snow, like frost, accumulating on the surface of rocks and other objects.

RURP: Realized Ultimate Reality Piton, a postage stamp sized piton used in shallow, incipient cracks. It can usually only support body weight.

Serac: A pinnacle, sharp ridge, or block of ice among the crevasses of a glacier. Often insecure and dangerous. Prone to topple in warm weather.

Spindrift: Blowing snow.

Sticht-plate: A belay device in which a loop of rope is pushed through a slot in a small metal plate and then clipped to a locking carabiner on the climber's harness.

Traverse: Going sideways across a section of terrain instead of up or down.

Tube cocks: Large, tube-shaped nuts which jam into constrictions in a crack.

Verglas: Thin layer of ice.

Zipper-fall: A long fall in which the leader's plummeting mass "zippers" all the pitons out.